Critical Muslim 2

The Idea of Islam

Critical Muslim 2, April–June 2012

Editors: Ziauddin Sardar and Robin Yassin-Kassab
Deputy Editor: Samia Rahman
Publisher: Michael Dwyer
Managing Editor: (Hurst Publishers) Daisy Leitch
Cover Design: Fatima Jamadar

Associate Editors: Abdelwahhab El-Affendi, Muhammad Idrees Ahmad, Iqbal Asaria, Michael Muhammad Knight, Vinay Lal, Hassan Mahamdallie, Ehsan Masood

Contributing Editors: Waqar Ahmad, Merryl Wyn Davies, Farid Esack, Iftikhar Malik, Parvez Manzoor, Usama Hasan

International Advisory Board: Karen Armstrong, William Dalrymple, Anwar Ibrahim, Arif Mohammad Khan, Bruce Lawrence, Ebrahim Moosa, Ashish Nandy

Critical Muslim is published quarterly by C. Hurst & Co (Publishers) Ltd on behalf of and in conjunction with Critical Muslim Ltd and the Muslim Institute, London.
All correspondence to Muslim Institute, CAN Mezzanine, 49–51 East Road, London N1 6AH, United Kingdom
e-mail for editorial: editorial@criticalmuslim.com

C. Hurst & Co (Publishers) Ltd.,
41 Great Russell Street, London WC1B 3PL

ISBN: 978-1-84904-221-5
ISSN: 2048-8475

To subscribe please contact the following to place an order by credit/debit card or cheque (pounds sterling only):
Subscriptions Department
Marston Book Services Ltd
PO Box 269, Abingdon, Oxon
OX14 4YN, UK
Tel: +44 (0)1235 465574
Fax +44 (0)1235 465556
Email: subscriptions@marston.co.uk
Or subscribe online at www.marston.co.uk/encrypted/mbs/Subscription_Renewals_Orders.htm
A one year subscription, inclusive of postage (four issues), costs £50 (UK), £65 (Europe) and £75 (rest of the world).

The right of Ziauddin Sardar, Robin Yassin-Kassab and the Contributors to be identified as the authors of this publication is asserted by them in accordance with the Copyright, Designs and Patents Act, 1988.

A Cataloguing-in-Publication data record for this book is available from the British Library.

Printed in India

THE BRITISH MUSEUM

Discover the Islamic World at the British Museum

From early scientific instruments to contemporary art, explore how Islam has shaped our world through objects for centuries

britishmuseum.org
Great Russell Street
London WC1B 3DG
◉ Holborn, Russell Square

Mosque lamp. Enamelled glass.
Syria, c. AD 1330–1345.

OUR MISSION

Critical Muslim is a quarterly magazine of ideas and issues showcasing ground-breaking thinking on Islam and what it means to be a Muslim in a rapidly changing, increasingly interconnected world.

We will be devoted to examining issues within Islam, and Muslim societies, providing a Muslim perspective on the great debates of contemporary times, and promoting dialogue, cooperation and collaboration between 'Islam' and other cultures, including 'the West'. We aim to be innovative, thought-provoking and forward-looking, a space for debate between Muslims and between Muslims and others, on religious, social, cultural and political issues concerning the Muslim world and Muslims in the world.

What does 'Critical Muslim' mean? We are proud of our strong Muslim identity, but we do not see 'Islam' as a set of pieties and taboos. We aim to challenge traditionalist, modernist, fundamentalist and apologetic versions of Islam, and will attempt to set out new readings of religion and culture with the potential for social, cultural and political transformation of the Muslim world. Our writers may define their Muslim belonging religiously, culturally or civilisationally, and some will not 'belong' to Islam at all. *Critical Muslim* will sometimes invite writers of opposing viewpoints to debate controversial issues.

We aim to appeal to both academic and non-academic readerships; and emphasise intellectual rigour, the challenge of ideas, and original thinking.

In these times of change and peaceful revolutions, we choose not to be a lake or a meandering river. But to be an ocean. We embrace the world with all its diversity and pluralism, complexity and chaos. We aim to explore everything on our interconnected, shrinking planet — from religion and politics, to science, technology and culture, art and literature, philosophy and ethics, and histories and futures — and seek to move forward despite deep uncertainty and contradictions. We stand for open and critical engagement in the best tradition of Muslim intellectual inquiry.

Crescent Films

Crescent Films is an award-winning independent production company with a record of producing high quality, original and entertaining television programmes for, amongst others, the BBC and Channel 4.

Based in London, Crescent films specialises in documentaries on South Asia and the Muslim World. Our recent productions include 'The Life of Muhammad' a three part documentary series for the BBC, 'Seven Wonders of the Muslim World', 'Muslim and looking for Love' and 'Women only Jihad' for Channel 4.

www.crescentfilms.co.uk
crescentfilms@btinternet.com

CM2
April–June 2012

CONTENTS

Istanbul: Model for Muslim Cosmopolitanism?

THE IDEA OF ISLAM

READING THE QUR'AN
ZIAUDDIN SARDAR

'This lucid, scholarly and exciting book could not be more timely; it takes the reader on a spiritual and intellectual journey that is essential for Muslim and non-Muslim alike and addresses some of the most pressing needs of our time.' — Karen Armstrong, author of *A History of God and Muhammad: A Biography of the Prophet*

'If one could pick just one book to connect the Muslim past with its complex present and future potential, *Reading the Qur'an* would be that book. To use a metaphor from the eleventh-century exemplar of rational mysticism, Imam Ghazzali, both Muslims and non-Muslims must "sail into the endless ocean of its meanings", with Ziauddin Sardar the nimble captain on that voyage of hope and discovery.' — Professor Bruce Lawrence, Duke University

'Ziauddin Sardar's *Reading the Qur'an*, is the most exciting book on the Qur'an in recent years; it is a poignant and intimate work on Islam's central text. ... Sardar approaches the Qur'an as both a lay believer, like the majority of Muslims, and an astute scholar of Islam. By providing a personal account of the relationship that he has with the Qur'an, Sardar echoes the cherished position which the Qur'an has for many Muslims. ... This is a wonderfully intelligent reading of a complex text within a contemporary context. ... By providing the Qur'an with a dynamic and empathetic voice on issues such as domestic violence, suicide, evolution, sex and sexuality, art, politics and power, Sardar ensures the Qur'an remains a warm, relevant and vibrant force within contemporary Muslim discourse. — Farid Esack, University of Johannesberg

9781849041072 / June 2011 / £20.00 hardback / 416pp / 225 x 145mm

HURST
PUBLISHERS

41 GREAT RUSSELL ST, LONDON, WC1B 3PL
WWW.HURSTPUB.CO.UK
WWW.FBOOK.ME/HURST
020 7255 2201

WHAT'S THE BIG IDEA?

Ziauddin Sardar

So what is your idea of Islam? To what extent and in what way is there or should there be a choice? Do you agree with Mohammad Sidique Khan or with Tariq Jahan? On the one hand, Khan, leader of the 7 July 2005 London bombers, sought 'martyrdom'. In his suicide video, he told the world that it was legitimate to kill innocent people indiscriminately for 'what we believe'. On the other hand, Jahan lost his youngest son in the Birmingham riots of August 2011. Twenty-year-old Haroon Jahan was killed along with two of his friends when they were deliberately run down by a car driven by youths. Haroon died protecting his community during the month of Ramadan. As far as his father was concerned, he was a *shaheed*, a martyr. In an atmosphere of rising tensions, with the police fearing revenge attacks and killings, Jahan diffused the situation with a few unscripted words of immense dignity: 'Why do we have to kill one another? Why are we doing this? I have lost my son. Step forward if you want to lose your sons. Otherwise, calm down and go home – please'. Revenge, said Jahan, was not part of his faith. But his faith gave him the strength and composure, as Bryan Appleyard noted in *The Sunday Times*, 'to make one of the great speeches of the twenty-first century'. 'I'm a Muslim', Jahan said, 'I believe in divine fate and destiny, and it was his destiny and his fate, and now he's gone'. In less than 500 words, he calmed a convulsed nation and presented an idea of Islam that could not be further removed from that of Sidique Khan.

Perhaps you have imbibed the common Western idea of Islam as all sex and violence, the domain of unfathomable mysteries, cruel and barbaric scenes. This is Islam as the darker side of Europe: depraved and licentious, ignorant and stupid, unclean and inferior, monstrous and ugly, fanatic and hell-bent on revenge. Or, maybe you subscribe to the idea of Jalal al-Din Rumi, the thirteenth-century poet, philosopher and theologian who saw

3

Islam as love and Muslims as a 'community of spirit': 'join it, and feel the delight of walking in the noisy streets, and being the noise', he wrote.

Rumi is undoubtedly one of the foremost mystics of Islam. He founded the Mevlevi Order of the Dancing Dervishes. He explained and explored his idea of Islam as pure love in his lyrical poetry, epigrams and short stories. *The Masnavi*, a compendium of his teachings, is a vast collection of his poetry, fables and meditations in 27,000 couplets. In the poem entitled 'A Community of Spirit', Rumi sees Muslims trapped in 'passion and disgrace': 'Quit acting like a wolf', he tells them, 'and feel the shepherd's love filling you'. 'Close your mouth against food. Taste the lover's mouth in yours'. Muslims, Rumi asserts, are trapped in a prison. But 'why do you stay in a prison when the door is so wide open?' he asks.

The idea of Islam, I suggest, is incarcerated not in one but several prisons. There is the prison of the Shariah, or Islamic law. Almost any injustice on God's bountiful earth can be, and at one time or another is or has been justified in the name of the Shariah: apostasy, blasphemy, misogyny, homophobia, xenophobia. Even paedophilia can be justified as 'God's law', according to Sheikh Salih bin Fawzan, a member of Saudi Arabia's Permanent Committee for Islamic Research and Fataawa, the highest religious body in the Kingdom. In a fatwa that appeared in Saudi newspapers on 13 July, 2011, Fawzan declared that 'uninformed interference with Shariah rulings by the press and journalists is on the increase, posing dire consequences for society, including their interference with the question of marriage to small girls who have not reached maturity, and their demand that a minimum age be set for girls to marry'. There is no minimum age, Fawzan said. The religious scholars – the *ulama* – 'have agreed that it is permissible for fathers to marry off their small daughters, even if they are in the cradle'. As is usual in such edicts, Fawzan quotes from the Qur'an and the traditions of the Prophet to justify his ruling. And he warns: 'It behoves those who call for setting a minimum age for marriage to fear Allah and not contradict his Shariah, or try to legislate things Allah did not permit. For laws are Allah's province; and legislation is his exclusive right, to be shared by none other. And among these are the rules governing marriage'. Allah has also legislated, according to an earlier fatwa by Fawzan, that slavery is an integral part of Islam; and the Sheikh wants it re-introduced in Muslim societies. Rumi would have been horrified by the association of such blatant evil with the idea of Islam – just as we are.

If Shariah is supposed to be Divine, and integral to Islam, then misogyny too is intrinsic to Islam. It is certainly, as Samia Rahman shows, integral to the thinking of traditional scholars – all the way from the celebrated thirteenth century theologian and philosopher al-Ghazali to Maulana Mawdudi, the worshipful founder of Jamat-e-Islami of Pakistan. 'Sure they all say that men and women are equal in the sight of God', writes Rahman, 'but when it came to the crunch women were always dangerous, not to be trusted, not very intelligent, and under no circumstances to be allowed away from the watchful eyes of a male "guardian"'. 'Look at the Muslim world', Rahman says and 'see how badly women are treated. In Saudi Arabia, they have to wear a black (the worst possible colour for that climate) abaya, often stick to the four walls of the home, always have a male "guardian" when they have to go out, and are seldom allowed to be seen in public. Driving is a crime punishable by flogging. In Pakistan, rape victims are often accused of adultery and punished barbarically. In Afghanistan, the Taliban regularly ransack girls' schools. A woman suffering serious illness cannot see a male doctor; and there aren't all that many female doctors as they are not allowed to educate themselves. In India, women can be divorced at almost any excuse simply with the husband uttering "I divorce thee" three times; or he can send a text message if he can't be bothered to utter the words. In the Sudan, women are frequently flogged under Islamic law. In many Muslim societies, women are deemed inferior to men. Their testimony in court is worth half that of a man. Husbands who beat their wives, and there are plenty in our societies, are cheered. The list of horrendous abuse and denial of basic rights to Muslim women seems endless'.

As far as the Shariah is concerned, the believers have to accept its injunctions, and the idea of Islam it supposedly perpetuates, without question. No ifs, ands, or buts – it's all *a priori* given. The believers have nothing to do but obey and follow. No effort is required on the part of the individual, there is absolutely no place for individual conscience or intellectual engagement. 'The way that Islam was presented to me by many Muslims', writes Soha Al-Jurf, 'it seemed that belief didn't come from a personal path of inquiry and revelation, but by accepting what others believed without challenging them — by simply offering one's mind as an empty receptacle for another person's views. It seemed that every time I questioned or expressed doubt towards the views of others on Islam, my views were typically perceived as blasphemous, and they were immediately dismissed. Or, rather, I was immediately dismissed'.

By equating the Shariah, a fallible human construct made in history, with Divine mandate, religious scholars have basically outlawed free will. To be a Muslim, one must submit to the Shariah, or rather the interpretation of well-meaning religious scholars long dead and their cynical, manipulating and power hungry contemporary counterparts – comprised as they are of a spectrum that runs all the way from those educated at prestigious institutions such as Al-Azhar University of Cairo, to the alumni of the fanatical and fundamentalist universities of Riyadh, Medina and Mecca in Saudi Arabia, to the myopic scholars of the Deoband seminary in India, and right down to the semi-literate Mullah in the mosque.

Rumi captures the essence of how free will has been manipulated and appropriated by Shariah-obsessed religious fanatics in a charming story.

A thief climbed a tree in an orchard and started to eat its fruit. He was spotted by the owner.

'Hey, you scoundrel!' shouted the owner. 'Aren't you ashamed before God? Why are you stealing my fruit?'

'If', the thief retorted, 'the servant of God eats from the orchard of God the dates God has given him, why do you blame him? Why do you behave so miserly at the table of so rich a Master?'

The owner asked his servant to bring a rope and a stick. 'I'll give a proper answer to you, my friend'.

He tied the thief with the rope, and set about him with the stick, beating him on the back and legs.

'Have some shame before God!' cried the thief. 'You are beating an innocent person'.

'With the stick of God', the owner replied, 'this servant of God is thrashing the back of another servant of God. The stick is God's, the back and sides are God's. I am the servant and instrument of His command'.

'I repent', the thief cried. 'I'm no longer an advocate of predestination. Free-will it is, free-will, free-will'.

The thieves of free will – the religious scholars – have become a class of their own. Despite the fact that Islam, at least the Sunni version, does not recognise a clergy, its religious scholars now mediate between God and the believers. And in the process they have acquired god-like powers by appropriating both spiritual and political powers into their own hands. Muslims are thus imprisoned in another penitentiary: the 'Islamic state'. In post-revolutionary Iran, the Ayatollah Khomeini developed a system of governance where only those familiar and versed in the Shariah were deemed capable of creating and ruling a Muslim society. On top of an all-seeing and all-knowing Guardian of Jurists sits the infallible Supreme Leader. No one can stand for election, say anything or do anything, without the explicit consent of the Mullahs. In Saudi Arabia, the religious scholars, in cahoots with the royal family, enforce the Shariah with a stick. The obnoxious, semi-autonomous religious police whose formal title is the Committee for the Propagation of Virtue and Prevention of Vice, function as an instrument of state repression. They ensure that believers stick to the narrow, unquestioning Wahhabi idea of Islam.

In these ideal Islamic states, freedom of expression is unknown, justice is arbitrary and politically expedient, and women are treated as dirt. In both Saudi Arabia and Iran, which Shariah-demanding fanatics in countries such as Pakistan, Bangladesh and the Sudan wish to emulate, the prisons are full of dissidents, torture is routine, and criticism of government is seen as blasphemy. The notion of an 'Islamic state', as Parvez Manzoor states so forcefully, is an abomination. It 'conflates norm and history in an eternal now', conceives 'the state as an attribute of faith' and 'seeks a new locus of authority'. The state becomes 'an idealised polity' where politics 'deals not with the existential concerns of the faith-community but with the authoritative interpretation of the foundational text of the Law, albeit through the mediation of the supreme jurist, or a collective corps of self-acclaimed jurists'. The state 'also dons the theocratic mantle, going beyond the acts of governance to the mandate of guidance, identifying itself as the channel of salvation'. What could be more totalitarian?

The religious scholars, 'the jurists' in Manzoor's parlance, are not just the guardians of the prisons of Shariah and the Islamic state, they are also protectors of tradition. And tradition itself is yet another prison. In essence, Muslim tradition is little more than medieval Arab tribal customs that have been enshrined in Islamic law and morality. In his *The Reconstruction of Religious Thought in Islam*, Muhammad Iqbal, the great visionary poet of the Indian subcontinent, called it 'Arabian imperialism of the earlier centuries of Islam'. It is best exemplified in the widely believed dictum that 'religious scholars (the *ulama*) have solved all our problems'. There is nothing more to do. We have to follow not only the interpretations, however absurd or out-of-date, of classical authors, but also their mode of thinking, which they have kindly perfected for future generations for all eternity. In technical language this way of thinking is referred to as *fiqhi* thought, and it requires that all readings of Islam must conform to the understanding and follow the methods of classical jurists, those who initially formulated and canonised the law (Shariah) and jurisprudence (*Fiqh*). For most ordinary believers this dangerously obsolete mode of thought has now become a medieval torture chamber; for the traditionalist it provides ready-made solutions to everything without recourse to the mind, or to unnecessary concerns about justice, equality or even education. And when all else fails, violence can be used to enforce the traditionalist viewpoint.

Consider the actions of traditionalists in Pakistan during just one week in September 2011. A group of masked men from a local madrasa entered a girls' school in Rawalpindi and proceeded to rough house teachers and students. They left after issuing a warning: dress modestly and wear the hijab or we will be back. A panic ensued and schools were closed for several days. Meanwhile, a girl attending school in a remote village was accused of blasphemy for wrongly spelling the name of the Prophet. In Lahore, traditionalists distributed a leaflet calling for the film *Bol* (released in 2011 and exploring the plight of women in Pakistan, the title translates as 'Speak') to be banned and its director and lead actor to be sentenced to death for blasphemy. In the city of Quetta, traditionalist Sunnis stopped buses carrying Shias and executed 40 people in cold blood – simply for being Shia.

There is a reason why traditionalist *fiqhi* thought has degenerated into a morbid pathology. It is totally devoid of ethics or conscience. As Manzoor notes, 'it has evolved into a formalistic system of law that is morally timid but politically expedient, a system that renders Islamic reason indistinguishable from reason of state'. Indeed, Manzoor argues, 'the *fiqhi* tradition, which succeeded in establishing itself as the normative mode par excellence of Muslim civilisation, was actually instrumental in devouring morality and ethics and stifling spirituality'. It 'has become self-authenticating and self-referential'; 'its self-imposed internment estranges us from history and the wider currents of moral reasoning', and it has cut Muslims 'off from the great currents of moral reasoning that have their origins elsewhere but which relate to us in every other way.' 'It is high time', Manzoor asserts, 'for Muslim ethical thought to free itself from this legalistic shell and rediscover its vocation as the delineation of a universal moral vision'.

This is precisely what Rumi was trying to do in his *Masnavi* some seven hundred years ago. In one story he captures the absurdity of religious scholars and their obsession with Arabic, *fiqh* and the rest.

A religious scholar, an expert in Arabic grammar, embarks on a boat. After cross examining the boatman on the dogmas of faith, the rules of Shariah and the intricacies of *fiqh*, he finds him somewhat deficient. 'Have you ever studied Arabic grammar?', he asks the boatman with a self-satisfied air.

'No', replied the boatman.

'Then you have wasted half of your life', said the religious scholar.

The boatman felt very depressed. But he kept quiet.

The wind tossed the boat into a whirlpool.

The boatman shouted to the religious scholar: 'Do you know how to swim?'

'No,' the religious scholar replied, 'my well-spoken handsome fellow'.

'In that case', the boatman remarked, 'the whole of your life has gone to waste, for the boat is sinking in these whirlpools'.

The problem is that traditionalists are hell-bent on drowning all believers in the whirlpools of their fatal fantasies. To question the traditionalist interpretation of Islam, as Carool Kersten notes, is to invite the charge of heresy. The advocates of 'autonomous reflection', from Ibn al-Rawandi, the ninth-century sceptic, to Ibn Hazm, the eleventh-century Andalusian philosopher, all the way to Egyptian Qur'an scholar Nasr Hamid Abu Zayd and Indonesian intellectual Nurcholish Madjid, and countless reformers in between, have been castigated as heretics. But as Kersten argues, it is time for heresy to take centre stage: dissent from orthodoxy, both Sunni and Shia, and independent critical thinking are the only way to break out of the prison of traditionalism.

The vast majority of Muslims, conservative by nature and traditionalist by education, follow the teachings and fatwas of orthodox, conservative scholars blindly. A whole generation has grown up on the literature of the 'Islamic movement' – best exemplified by Maulana Maududi, the founder of the Jamaat-e-Islami of Pakistan, and his disciple Maryam Jameelah, the New Yorker who converted to Islam. As Ehsan Masood shows in his elegant account of growing up reading Jameelah, the seeds of self-destruction in her extremism and xenophobia were always there. 'For Maryam Jameelah no such thing as change or compromise ever existed. And even when she was patently wrong, in her mind she was definitely right', Masood writes. There is no direct connection between reading Jameelah's polemics and extremist behaviour, he concludes. The fact that Jamaat-e-Islami has degenerated into a semi-fascist organisation, defending the Taliban and glorifying the murder of Salman Taseer, the governor of Punjab, suggests that both Maryam and the Maulana have a few questions to answer.

Questioning, of course, is not part of the traditionalist purview. Traditionalist education relies exclusively on rote learning and incessant quoting of the opinions of classical scholars. Reverence is the order of the day in a black and white universe where the emphasis, as al-Jurf notes, is on 'very specific opinions about what Islam is and is not, what it requires of its believers and does not require, and what it exemplifies and does not exemplify'. At the end of the process, Islam is 'reduced to a set of rigid, contradictory concepts that seemed to have nothing to do with anything holy at all'. The flock of the faithful is kept on the straight and narrow by constant reference to hell and damnation. Most of the *ummah* is reduced to the status of Rumi's parrot:

The parrot looking in the mirror sees
Itself, but not its teacher hid behind,
And learns the speech of Man, the while it thinks
A bird of its own sort is talking to it.

An instrument from which traditionalists derive immense power is ritual. It is difficult to walk into a mosque, almost anywhere in the Muslim world, without someone chiding you for not performing the ablution correctly, or praying in the wrong way or not on time, or not having a beard, or not being pious enough. Traditionalists also have a knack of silencing argument or dissent by quoting alleged hadith. Indeed, herds of traditionalists roam the streets checking people's faith (*iman*) and beliefs (*aqidah*), ensuring that they are performing their rituals according to their dictates, and are dressed properly with the correct facial furniture. No wonder Michael Muhammad Knight feels so fed up with people who treat faith as a 'zero sum game'. 'Being Muslim isn't always about what I believe', he declares. Knight has already been labelled a 'heretic'. His essay contains strong language and stronger heresies; and many (regardless of belief) will find some of his statements unpalatable. But it is worth remembering that some of the beliefs that Knight is talking about were firmly held by Malcolm X (El-Hajj Malik El-Shabazz) before he performed the Hajj. The ideas in Knight's essay are held by the 'Five Percenters', who broke away from the Nation of Islam. Indeed they are still in vogue in some circles, particularly the emerging cohort of new Muslims in the US. It is an idea of Islam that the orthodox will have to struggle with. No doubt, it speaks to many young Muslims alienated by the demands of orthodoxy.

Rituals, Knight says, 'bind me to my community'. But more often the cordon of rituals becomes a prison where self-reflection and critical thinking are forbidden. Once again Rumi illustrates the folly of this position with a wonderful story.

A mouse and frog meet every morning on the river bank. They sit and talk at their favourite place. They are the best of friends sharing secrets and telling stories. They laugh at stories they haven't thought of in five years, and the telling might take five years. Then one day the mouse complains. 'There are times when I want your company', he says to the frog, 'and you are out in water, jumping around where you can't hear me. We meet at appointed times, but the text says, Lovers pray constantly. Five times a day, once on Friday is not enough. Fish like us constantly need the ocean around us. Do camel bells say, Let's meet back here Tuesday night? Ridiculous. They jingle together continuously, talking while the camel walks'. 'Do you', adds Rumi, 'pay regular visits to yourself?' Ritual, the great sage seems to be saying, has become a barrier that prevents traditionalists from visiting themselves, and a mechanism that is used to keep Muslims from self-reflection.

Self-reflection demands that Muslims ask certain key questions about their faith. Does God speak to twenty-first-century people? Does He address them directly or through classical scholars and their contemporary disciples? What is revelation? Should hadith be a source of Islamic law? What did the Prophet really want? Are Muslims doomed to follow the *tabiun*, the generation born after the death of the Prophet Muhammad, forever? What exactly is this thing called Islam: a static, monolithic presentation or a dynamic vision? Such questions are often excluded from critical examination and constitute what the late Mohammed Arkoun, the Algerian French scholar, called 'the Unthought' of Islam. In his *Rethinking Islam*, Arkoun raises a series of similar questions; and unless we critically engage with such questions Islam can be nothing more than a fundamentalist fantasy.

Many of these questions concern the fundamental sources of Islam. Regarding the Qur'an, for example, we need to ask: is every injunction in the Sacred Text universal? What in the Qur'an is contextual and thus merely historical? Is it a text to be consumed or interrogated? What are we to do with the 'difficult' verses – the one, for example, that allegedly allows men to beat their wives? Does all morality and knowledge converge towards the Qur'an or diverge from it? Is classical exegesis, which knew nothing of modern linguistic, interpretative theory and hermeneutics, eternal? Why can't we undertake a philosophical critique of the Qur'an, which has been applied to the Bible and the Old Testament without affecting their integrity? And what's wrong with ordinary Muslims interpreting the Qur'an for themselves?

When it comes to hadith, questions multiply rapidly. If hadith are the actual words of the Prophet, why do Sunnis, Shias and the Khariji use three different sets of compilations, which are frequently contradictory? Does that not suggest that hadith served as a political instrument? Was the methodology of hadith collection (involving scrutiny of the chain of narrators, their character and circumstances) really so perfect that it cannot be questioned? The compilers of hadith did indeed perform a Herculean task, and we are told numerous stories about how meticulous they were in their work. There is the story of Imam Bukhari, for example, who travelled for miles to collect a hadith from a man. When he arrived at his house, he saw that the man was enticing his donkey with a bundle of hay. He returned without talking to the man, saying that a man who tricks his donkey is not a reliable witness. Correct. But what if he had arrived a few minutes earlier, or a few minutes later? It is said that he collected over 600,000 hadith, talking to over a thousand men, but only included 7,275 in his collection of authentic hadith, *al-Jami as-Sahih*. What happened to the rest? Did they remain in circulation? And what can one say of the men who fed him all those inauthentic hadith? Given the fact that hadith compilation was a human effort, was it not susceptible to human error?

Moreover, if *Sahih Bukhari* does indeed contain 'authentic' hadith – that is words actually spoken by the Prophet himself – then what are we to make of a string of dubious hadith and their contradictions. For example: 'The sun rises between the two antlers of Satan' (Bukhari 2:134); 'Seeing a black woman in a dream is the sign of an oncoming epidemic' (Kitabul Ta'abir); and 'Do you ever see an animal born with deformed organs?' (Bukhari 1:525). Could the beloved Prophet have uttered such words? And what is this obsession with sex that we find in Bukhari? 'The (Exalted) Messenger used to visit all nine of his wives every night.' (Book of Nikah 3:52). How could any man, no matter how close to the Prophet, have known this? And how could any man, particularly when we are told elsewhere in the same collection that he used to pray all night, so much so that his feet swelled, do this? And would Aisha, his youngest wife, utter these words: 'Aisha relates, the Prophet used to have intercourse with us and kissed us while he was fasting. Then she shied away smiling' (Bukhari 2:691); and 'Aisha said to the Prophet, "Ah! My head is bursting". He said, I wish it would. Aisha responded: "You want me to die so that you can spend the next night with another wife"' (Book of Medicine, vol. 3).

Clearly, these hadith reflect the obsessions, concerns and misogyny of the time. The question arises: if the meticulous methodology of hadith compilation could allow hadith of such dubious nature (and there are many even worse), what can we say about the authenticity of others? Are Bukhari's and other similar collections really *sahih*? And should we be using hadith as a source of Islamic law – allegedly Divine and eternal? And how much of the Shariah, from punishments for apostasy and adultery right down to dietary rules, is based on the Bible?

There is an urgent need for Muslims to interrogate their basic sources and tackle such questions. Now we have intellectual resources that our ancestors lacked. We have nothing to fear from such critical engagements.

But if we fail, we will have to agree with Rumi: there are no Muslims in the world; and if there are, these Muslims are really non-existent.

Fortunately, there are critical Muslims; and critical Islam open to change. Arkoun himself, as well as a host of scholars mentioned by Kersten, confirm that alternative ideas of Islam are not just 'out there' but are gaining momentum. Reform is not only possible, it is being implemented. Take the new Islamic personal law in Morocco, known as the Moudawana. It treats the Shariah not as Divine but as a human construction, and introduces some revolutionary transformations with the explicit aim of establishing true gender equality. It throws out the centuries-old notion that the husband is the head of the family and the wife a mere underling in need of guidance and protection. Rather it suggests that the Qur'anic notion of equality means that women are equal partners in marriage and family life. Moreover, the Moudawana regards women as independent, thinking beings and allows them to contract a marriage without the legal approval of a guardian. It also raises the minimum age for women's marriage from 15 to 18, the same as for men. It consigns 'triple *talaq*' – where a man can divorce his wife by simply saying 'I divorce you' three times – to the dustbin of history. Outlawing verbal divorce, the Moudawana requires men to have prior authorisation from a court, and gives women equal rights to divorce – no questions asked. Moreover, under the Moudawana women can claim alimony and can be granted custody of their children even if they remarry. Husbands and wives must share property acquired during the marriage. The old custom of favouring male heirs in the sharing of inherited land has also been dropped, making it possible for grandchildren on the daughter's side to inherit from their grandfather, just like grandchildren on the son's side. While it apparently permits polygamy, in reality it all but abolishes it. The ambiguity here is a reflection of the ambiguity of the Qur'anic verse which gives permission to marry 'two, three or four' but 'if you fear that you cannot be equitable to them, then marry only one' (4:3). The Moudawana allows a man to take a second wife only with the full consent of the first wife and only if he can prove, in a court of law, that he can treat them both with absolute justice – an impossible condition. All these reforms, introduced in February 2004, are justified with verses from the Qur'an and examples from traditions of the Prophet Muhammad. And every change required and obtained the consent of the religious scholars who, it must be noted, also included women. It is not surprising that even Islamist political organisations welcomed the change.

The notion of politics in Islam, attacked so vigorously by Parvez Manzoor, is also being reformed. Listen to Rached Ghannouchi, the leader of the An Nahda Party of Tunisia. After winning the election of October 2011, he declared: 'we will continue the revolution to realise its aim of a Tunisia that is free, independent, developing and prosperous, in which the rights of God, the Prophet, women, men, the religious and the non-religious are assured because Tunisia is for everyone'. The sentiment could not be further from the notion of an exclusivist, misogynist 'Islamic state', ruled by the Shariah, and led by obscurantist clerics.

Ghannouchi received some valuable advice, in a personal letter, from Ebrahim Yazdi, former Iranian Minister of Foreign Affairs. Yazdi, leader of the banned Freedom Movement of Iran, played a major part in the 1979 revolution and before that served in the interim government of Mehdi Bazargan, but resigned in November 1979 in protest at the Iranian hostage crisis. He had seen revolutionary fanatics devour his comrades who fought so bravely against the Shah. Yazdi pointed out to Ghannouchi that, in his experience, overthrowing dictators was not the same thing as overthrowing dictatorship. 'Despotism is not just a political structure. It has its corresponding social and cultural dimensions which enable it to persist and which become ingrained in individuals and lead to whole societies being afflicted by despotism for a long time. The result is that we Muslims overthrow despots only to see a new despot take the place of the old one. This is what has indeed befallen us in Iran. We deposed the Shah, but neglected to address the "shah" personality within our own selves. Thus the vicious circle continues'.

To break the cycle, Yazdi argued, Muslims need to relearn and embrace three basic concepts central to Islam. 'The first concept is the recognition and celebration of the diversity of human society and pluralism'. The Qur'an reminds us of this repeatedly and commands us to tolerate each other. Far from judging each other, and measuring the faith and beliefs of others, Muslims should acknowledge that it is for God to judge us all. However, where there is immense diversity and all variety of contradictory opinions, there is always a danger of 'confrontation and the re-emergence of tyranny'. As such, we need a second concept: tolerance, which has to be established as a social institution. But tolerance itself is not enough, says Yazdi. We also need a third concept: compromise. 'Tunisia's social and economic development will require the compromise and cooperation of all of your citizens, regardless of their ideological, racial and religious affiliations. Compromise does not imply neglect of one's beliefs and agenda. Rather, it is the recognition that cooperating with each other is essential for the cause of national salvation'.

No doubt, Ghannouchi also learned a great deal from Indonesia. It was there, writes Carool Kersten, that thanks to the efforts of reformers such as Nurcholish Madjid and Harun Nasution, who, as rector of Jakarta's Islamic State University, 'was able to push through a radically progressive, inclusivist and open-minded curriculum that encouraged students to think critically', the whole idea of 'Islamic politics' was redefined during the 1990s. Delinking it from the notion of the 'Islamic state', the Indonesian intellectuals argued that politics in Islam was all about creating a civic society, holding politicians to account, promoting ethics and responsible behaviour and encouraging the citizenry to participate in decision making. The open, pluralistic and democratic nature of Indonesia owes a great deal to this idea of Islam.

However, it is to Turkey that most reformists are now looking. Like the An Nahda Party of Tunisia, Turkey's ruling Justice and Development (AK) Party has roots in the Islamist movement. But Turkey has totally redefined what it means to be a Muslim in the twenty-first century. As Bruce Lawrence notes, it is now 'the model for progressive, modern and – yes – cosmopolitan Islam'. On first sight, 'cosmopolitan' and 'Islam' seem like antonyms. But the glories of Islam are intrinsically linked with the cosmopolitan idea of Islam. Think of Umayyad Damascus, Abbasid Baghdad, Mughal Delhi, the Cairo of Salahuddin Ayyubi ('Saladin') and Samarkand and Bukhara and Timbuktu. Istanbul is fast emerging as a modern counterpart. What distinguishes Istanbul 'as an emerging model for Muslim cosmopolitanism', Lawrence asserts, are its 'multiple public moments to celebrate, a calendar of performances or events that monopolise the everyday gaze and suggest the huge importance of this one city as a perpetual resource of social capital. Celebration is also linked to restoration: buildings must be maintained but also renewed, just as heroes must be recalled, their memories expanded, in the public domain'. Its urbane and progressive urban elite are 'adroit at both recuperating the past and reinforcing its present value'. They have skilfully mobilised heroes and icons from the past and the present, religious and secular, as signposts towards a pluralistic, open, democratic and viable horizon. Lawrence sees something similar happening in Bukhara. Muslim cosmopolitanism, Lawrence asserts, has its 'competitors, detractors, dead ends, and detours, as well as no-win options' but it is the best option for Islam and Muslims to 'advance towards a global future'. It is an idea whose time has come, or come back. 'The conclusion remains indisputable: cosmopolitanism not fundamentalism and puritanism inflects the brightest Muslim future for the perilous twenty-first century'.

Muslim cosmopolitanism requires us to go forward with the pluralism and tolerance that Muslims have demonstrated in history, particularly in Andalusia. The historical Islamic *conviviencia*, as Ben Gidley hints, 'might be a model for pluralism today'; particularly 'if Israel could re-connect with its Middle Eastern self it could have different relations with its neigh-bours'. But we must not look at the *convivencia*, living together, in Moorish Spain in a 'roseate light'. *Convivencia* too has its problems. It 'collapses together 1400 years of Muslim history into a monolithic story'. The nar-rative 'only works if it edits out the times and places when Muslim rulers were less than tolerant of their Jewish subjects; as with all historical nar-ratives, it requires a systematic forgetting of some things in order to remember others, even if in this case the forgetting is benign and forgiv-ing'. Here, as in dealing with other aspects of Islamic sources and history, we need honesty and integrity. We 'need to develop a better sense of the complexity and contradictions involved in our evolving story, to acknowl-edge both the shadows and the light', says Gidley. Ameen to that!

So finally back to Rumi. A camel, an ox and a ram were walking along together when they came upon a bunch of grass lying on the road in front of them. 'If we divide this up', the ram said, 'it is certain that not one of us will get his fill of it. But whichever of us has lived the longest has the best right to this fodder; let him eat it. Muhammad has set an example for all to follow, to give priority to one's elders. Comrades, since such a piece of luck has come our way, let each of us declare his age. The oldest has the best right; the rest keep silent'. After a pause, the Ram said, 'as for myself,

I shared the same posture in those long ago times with the ram that Abraham sacrificed for Ishmael'.

'I am the most ancient in years', said the ox. 'I was paired with the ox with which Adam yoked. I am the yoke-fellow of the very ox with which Adam, the father of all humanity, ploughed the earth in the season of sowing'.

The camel listened to the ox and the ram in amazement. He lifted his head, seized the grass, and raised the bunch of green barley in the air. 'I don't need to rely on age', he grunted. 'Not with such a body and such a high neck'.

It is time to leave the prisons of Shariah, stop worshipping at the shrines of our ancestors, break free from traditionalist thought and bury the notion of the 'Islamic state' – surely by now we should have the capability to seize the grass.

MUSLIM COSMOPOLITANISM

Bruce Lawrence

Muslim cosmopolitanism seemed to me the most natural of dinner table topics. But my family and friends around the dinner table had other ideas. Many had never heard of Muslim cosmopolitanism, and so when I asked for initial responses to what it might mean, I received some unexpected responses.

My daughter thought it sounded like an oxymoron. Isn't 'cosmopolitan' the opposite of religious identity? No one talks about Christian or Jewish cosmopolitans. How can there be Muslim cosmopolitans? My brother-in-law exclaimed, 'I think it's too elitist. After all, cosmopolitans are jet setters. Perhaps some wealthy Gulf Arabs might qualify. But the Arab spring is moving towards summer: no folks from Cairo or Tunis or Tripoli are eager to be called cosmopolitan, and so the term is meaningless for them, and for most Muslims.' My nephew, a high school junior who is studying Arabic, gave his perspective: 'Kids in my school aren't too keen even about the Arab spring. They think it's just another part of Muslim violence. Muslim terrorism, they reckon, is here to stay; none of my friends anticipates a cosmopolitan future that includes Muslims.' My other daughter and her husband, both college professors, were equally sceptical: 'How can you use the term Muslim cosmopolitanism when Muslims themselves don't think that they are cosmopolitan? Aren't you imposing categories on others? Wouldn't it be better to talk about networks or citizenship? After all, aren't Muslim cosmopolitans just Muslims who want to be global citizens? Doesn't it make more sense to talk about Muslim world citizens instead of Muslim cosmopolitans?' Finally, my niece, a junior high school student, took the serious edge off the discussion. 'Whatever it is,' she said with her characteristic humour, 'it has to rhyme, and Muslim cosmopolitanism is just too long and clunky. What about Muslim cosmo – nifty combo?' How could I justify the category Muslim cosmopolitanism faced with this barrage of criticism?

It was three years ago that I first began to think of conjoining 'Muslim' with 'cosmopolitan'. Since then I have defended the term's value to aca-

demic audiences in a number of seminars and conferences. But here I want
to answer some of the queries raised by my relatives around the dinner
table. The objections that they voiced were: 1) no religion can infringe on
the 'secular' nature of cosmopolitan identity; 2) every cosmopolitanism is
class based and socially restricted; 3) the media has defined Islam as 'terror', and so the decoupling of Islam from terror and relinking it with a
perspective at once normative and even 'cosmopolitan' challenges members of Generation Y; 4) Muslims themselves do not universally embrace
cosmopolitanism as their preferred identity but 5) even if they did, and
also saw it as the basis for future social capital, one would have to find a
more catchy way to describe it, perhaps linking it to motifs, moments and
heroes of the Islamic past.

To address these questions, we need to move from the contemporary
bias, one reinforced by the pervasive omnipresence of global media, and
look beyond to structural elements of Islamic civilisation that can be recu-
perated for a vision of Muslim cosmopolitanism. I do have my own bias, of
course. It is historical and urban. I believe that cities are crucial to the past
glories but also to the present spectrum of Muslim norms, values and
options. Cities provide the critical nodes for tracing, then analysing the
larger frame of Islamic civilisation. In linking cities and civilisation to Muslim cosmopolitanism, I will ask: how does the historical background of
Islamic civilisation inform strategies for implementing Muslim cosmopolitanism in twenty-first-century metacities? While I argue that any notion of
cosmopolitanism requires specific cities, I will focus on Istanbul as one
such city, above all because it demonstrates what is observable everywhere:
cosmopolitanism is more process than product, and to the extent that
Islamic culture is radically cosmopolitan, its development must be traced
in the ceaselessly changing nature of metacities. To be clear, the focus on
metacities in general and Istanbul in particular does not deny or disclaim
the importance of rural, regional and transnational forces, yet I contend
that it is only in major cities or metacities that one finds the physical urban
locus that provides both context and catalyst for the metaphysical, urbane
reflex of Muslim cosmopolitanism. Always an ideal, Muslim cosmopolitanism has to be at once urban, Islamic and inclusive: it is nothing less than the
urban, trans-cultural arc of an Islam inspired engagement with the inclusive, generous and creative imagining of our common humanity.

The Larger Frame

Yet to talk about Muslims and cosmopolitanism in concrete cases one must go beyond standard nomenclature. Though culture is not religion, they are interactive and often inseparable. The best neologism to make sense of their elision for Muslims is 'Islamicate culture'. It was the visionary world historian Marshall Hodgson who invented this word to help him explore what he termed 'The Venture of Islam'. While 'Islam' or 'Islamic' refers to religion, 'Islamicate' expands the reference to include aesthetic or literary elements shared between Muslims and non-Muslims living under Muslim rule. It is especially evident on the edges of empire, as in Muslim Spain or Mughal India. Andalusian arches in Santa Barbara, California, and Hindu poets composing Persian verse – are but two instances of Islamicate culture at work in America and South Asia. Persianate is often linked to Islamicate since Persian as much as Arabic became part of the cultural self-expression of Muslim empires.

Hodgson's vision needs to be invoked but also amplified. Islam is radically cosmopolitan in its origins. It goes back to Arabia but quickly expands beyond it. Islam, born in an Arabian niche, became a cultural and trade entrepot linking the Mediterranean world to the Indian Ocean via the Red Sea. As Islam spread in all directions, it brought a cosmopolitan sensibility to the cultures with which it interacted, even as early Muslims retained strong spiritual, aesthetic and cultural ties to the desert environment out of which they emerged. Centuries after the founding of Islam, Mecca and Medina remained deeply tribal desert cities, filled with foreigners, but they were also connected with new centres of cosmopolitan activity under Muslim rule – Cairo, Damascus, Baghdad, Cordoba, Delhi, and Bukhara.

Nile-to-Oxus, as Hodgson announced, then demonstrated, is the core region that defined, and was itself redefined by Islam. The Muslim presence became established through trade, cultural exchange and political experiments. There were no Muslim empires, but rather a commonwealth of networks marked by caliphates, sultanates and kingdoms, each reflecting an ethos of internal reciprocity as much as external competition with regional rivals. There was no equality – itself an Enlightenment concept – but there was parity: a longstanding feature of Islamicate norms, ethics, and practices.

Foreigners, far from being excluded, were welcomed to the major cities of Muslim empires. They provided alternate worldviews and a spectrum of skills. Some were Muslim, some were not, but all shared in a world marked by cosmopolitan structures, activities and values. Patronage was channeled into and through the major Muslim courts. Greek thought into Arabic science, but also Indian numerals, with Chinese designs – all evolved under the crescent of Islam. The astrolabe, for instance, though not invented by Muslims, became an instrument of shared scientific interest. As the eleventh-century Persianate scholar Ahmad Al-Biruni noted, it did not matter if the Byzantines had first used the astrolabe; it became Muslim when five daily prayer times were superimposed on the Byzantine calendar. And to those purists who objected to his recycled use of a 'Christian' instrument, claiming that it showed imitation (*tashabbuh*) of unbelievers, Al-Biruni rejoined: 'The Byzantines also eat food. Then do not imitate them in this!'

Al-Biruni was sarcastic yet he made a point worth stressing: what makes science or culture or political structures specifically Muslim is not their origin but their dedicated use. The crucial question about all objects or practices is the same today as it was a millennium ago: how do public choices begin to reflect a worldview that is Islamicate, encompassing both Muslims and non-Muslims and thus projecting a new ethos suffused with the spirit of Islam?

The Muslim Accent

Muslim cosmopolitanism is, above all, Muslim because it focuses on public choices transmitted and reinforced through tribal/urban networks.

It is the scope of activity defined by Islam and Muslim rulers that gave force to Muslim cosmopolitanism. The major elements of Muslim cosmopolitanism had become evident from Spain to China by 1402, when Ibn Khaldun met Tamerlane in Damascus. Culture was inseparable from patronage, and both were channelled through civilisation: Ibn Khaldun's *Muqaddimah* introduces the benchmark for reflecting on all human history. It is the inhabited world, the oikumene, mapped by the Nile-to-Oxus, but also including the Mediterranean and Indian Oceans. Of course, there was cosmopolitanism before Islam, but what made Muslim cosmopolitanism distinctive was its location on the bridge of the Afro-Eurasian oikumene, at the heart of what became the first cosmopolitan world system.

While cities are the crucial index of a Muslim difference, one cannot and should not forget the relationship of urban to rural or tribal norms and values, structures and options. In reviewing Ibn Khaldun's *Muqaddimah* and Hodgson's *The Venture of Islam*, especially Volume Two, one finds a recurrent accent on both tribalism and urbanism. They are intertwined in a synergistic coil – not just as geographic markers but also as ethos or value systems, each having benefits that exceed their limits.

What is needed in 2012 is not an escape from history but a bold effort to revisit its shadows as well as its bright lights. Beyond the end of empires and the rise of the modern West, we must rethink comparative world systems through an Islamicate lens. Tribalism, for instance, is not just a fixed moment in history now surpassed by modern-day cities. Tribalism can be an urban as well as a rural ethos. The key term *'asabiya*, translated from Ibn Khaldun, means connectedness or boundedness. It projects tribalism as a metaphor that applies to all elites who are internally bound together by blood ties (or their functional equivalents), whether the Medicis in the sixteenth century, the oil/steel/railroad barons in late nineteenth century America, or the Arab Gulf emirs in the twenty-first century. Small urban polities patronise and sustain a myriad of cosmopolitan projects – musical and literary as well as aesthetic and architectural. While religion may not be their main theme, it is an inescapable index of their belonging to one space and time, matched with their longing to be part of a transterritorial and trans-temporal ethos. Islam, like other religions, is also always and everywhere part and parcel of networked connections.

The major distinctiveness of Muslim cosmopolitanism is the expansive arc of cities that serve as nodes of cosmopolitan networks throughout the Islamicate world. Tracing the influence for Muslim cosmopolitans requires attention to metacities that have been eclipsed as well as those just beginning to come into prominence: from Aden to Doha, from Bukhara to Kuala Lumpur, from Harar to Dakar. Other major urban locations that qualify as long-standing Muslim cosmopolitan metacities include: Aceh, Baghdad, Beirut, Cairo, Dacca, Damascus, Delhi, Herat, Isfahan, Jerusalem, Khartoum, Lagos, Lahore, Marrakesh, Muscat, Penang, Sarajevo, Xian, and, of course, Istanbul.

Istanbul

In 2010 Istanbul was feted as the European Capital of Culture. It was a new high mark in the upward trajectory of that city's symbolic prestige within and beyond Turkey. The current article asks a related but more difficult question: Is Istanbul also the capital city of Muslim cosmopolitanism? To answer that question, one must address the prior question: Is Istanbul genuinely cosmopolitan?

Istanbul is the jewel of the East. It straddles Asia and Europe. It looks north to Russia, south to Greece. It borders three expanses of water: the Bosphorus Straits that run to the Black Sea, the Sea of Marmara, extending to the Aegean Sea, and in between them the Golden Horn, along with nine islands that dot its several horizons. From the shores of Africa to the isles of Indonesia, there are many maritime ports that have also become major metropolitan centres, but none combines the topographic complexity or scenic beauty, matched by strategic advantage and historical longevity, of Istanbul.

But is Istanbul cosmopolitan? If the stream of tourists who visit the city every year could vote, the answer would be a resounding YES, and they could use as confirmation of their choice the tagline from one of the many Lonely Planet promotions on Turkey: 'Istanbul is the cosmopolitan heart of Turkey,' writes Lonely Planet author Virginia Maxwell, and she goes on to provide 'her insider tips on the city she fell in love with – from kooky cab drivers and awe-inspiring mosques to one of the world's most dangerous liquors: raki!'

The sights and sounds, from music festivals to upscale museums to outdoor theatres to rides on the Bosphorus – all contribute to the notion that Istanbul is not just the best that Turkey can offer but also the best that pluralist pleasure seekers could hope to find, to explore, and to enjoy in the twenty-first century. In the parade of European cultural capitals, *Istanbul 2010* was marked by an explosion of entries in local, national and international presses, including Facebook, which began with the upbeat glowing announcement from the Turkish government:

ISTANBUL: A Tale of Two Cities

It's a city of contrasts, brought together by east and west, Islam and Christianity. The people of Istanbul are tolerant by nature, which explains why the mostly

Muslim city harbours a significant Jewish presence as well as Greek Orthodoxy. It's a crossroads between north and south, east and west.

The accent on Istanbul as a model of social, geographic, and religious integration continues till the end of the entry, where we are told not only that synagogues flourish but that also:

Istanbul remains a place where such antiquated symbols of Judaism can survive alongside the twentieth-century mosques, where an ever-increasing influx of peasants can bring a time-honoured tradition to the most progressive of Muslim cities.

Whether or not this amounts to confirmation of a cosmopolitan identity or mere hype for commercial gain by Turkish and Euro-American holiday vendors is another question. Istanbul's identity has been thoughtfully explored, with a teeming set of entries on keywords, in a 2008 multi-authored publication, *Becoming Istanbul – An Encyclopaedia*. The book finds that there is no fixed something called Istanbul. The city is always in process, ever changing and becoming something else and so to address the question of Istanbul as a cosmopolis, one faces the daunting entanglement of motives, agendas, and outcomes that shape and reshape the city. They are exposed by several contributors under diverse entries that include 'Cinema', 'Cleaning', and 'Cultural Transformation', and then extend down the alphabet to encompass 'Museum', 'Ottoman Neighbourhood', and 'Scaffolding'. What one discovers is a repeated, detailed, and blistering critique of the consumerist practices that mark and too often mar the cosmopolitan image of early twenty-first-century Istanbul. From a ground up view of Istanbul, it seems, one must exercise restraint about large-scale generalisations. Instead, one is compelled to conclude that the verdict about the cosmopolitan status of Istanbul is at best mixed, the outlook for future upward adjustment opaquely contingent.

One cannot ignore, but one should not overemphasise, the blatant economic motives that inform some advocates for membership in the EU, as well as global arts promoters and commercial agents for heritage branding. Behind the crush of capitalist and consumerist motives, agendas and outcomes, is there sufficient surplus value to warrant framing an everyday or vernacular cosmopolitan vision of Istanbul?

Perhaps the most thorough effort to recuperate contemporary Istanbul as cosmopolitan is provided by the Turkish anthropologist, Öykü Potuoğlu-

Cook. In her broadly gauged 2006 article, 'Beyond the Glitter: Belly Dance and Neoliberal Gentrification in Istanbul', she moves beyond categorical judgements. Challenging both an abstract notion of cosmopolitanism and the holistic claims of cultural tourism, she looks at performance in general and belly dancing in particular. She highlights 'the aesthetics of performance codes, venues, and processes that consequently restructure public intimacies and the broader cultural logic of neoliberalism.' Among her everyday Muslim subjects is Zeynep, a veiled prospective university student and clerk, who belongs at once to the *ummah*, the global Muslim community, and to the Turkish nation. Zeynep struggles with both daily class limitations and strict secular regulations against public Islam. Her lifestyle choices, from belly dance to veiling, generate and reflect 'the embodied possibilities and constraints along the national-cosmopolitan spectrum, a spectrum defined by commodified Ottoman nostalgia'.

By bracketing together belly dancing and veiling, the global *ummah* and Turkish nationalism, European aspirations with Ottoman nostalgia, Potuoğlu-Cook raises the question central to this essay: can Istanbul be considered a Muslim cosmopolitan city, and if so, what does that mean both for the status of Istanbul and the content of Muslim cosmopolitanism? Rather than discard a cosmopolitan label, she redefines what it means to be poor and marginal as well as Muslim and cosmopolitan in contemporary Istanbul.

A parallel, equally interesting question is: can Istanbul also be considered a Jewish cosmopolitan city? What does it mean to relate Istanbul or any city to a religiously coded projection of cosmopolitan longing, whether Muslim or Jewish? Until recently, the answer to the query regarding Istanbul as a site of Jewish cosmopolitanism would have been both Yes and No. Yes, because during its earliest period as a Muslim capital city (for the Ottoman Empire, from 1453-1924) it did provide refuge, opportunity and quasi-citizenship for Jewish refugees from autocratic, discriminatory regimes, especially Spain after the Reconquista of 1492. And no, because after the formation of the Republic of Turkey (1923), with its emphasis on Turkish ethnic over Ottoman pan-ethnic identity, life became increasingly difficult for Turkish Jews in general, and Stambouli Jews in particular.

That assessment now has to be revisited, and revised. An American anthropologist, Marcy Brink-Danan, has argued that representational codes as much as diachronic narratives and constitutional norms shape the

Sultan Ahmet: 'Blue Mosque'

status of minorities. She examines how Stambouli Jews deal with the issue of representation, and how this kind of knowledge is interpreted and mediated by different actors and audiences as well as through the prism of what these various participants think is expected of them. What they exhibit is not an ethical showcase of universal, timeless norms but instead, 'lived cosmopolitanism: an awareness of multiple audiences, some of whom might be antipathetic ones'. Indeed, 'cosmopolitanism among Turkish Jews involves a much more private, practical, and protectionist way of managing difference. Rethinking cosmopolitanism along these lines suggests not just a shift at the level of theorising the phenomenon but also a shift in method, towards studying cosmopolitanism as knowledge per formed, focusing on the dissonance between rhetorical cosmopolitanisms and lived ones rooted in local contexts.' It is a shift away from choice andethics, the presumptive Kantian approach, and towards a complicated knowledge of difference, the approach etched by Walter Mignolo and other border-thinking theorists. In tone it echoes and compliments thesame particularist, contextualised approach to Muslim cosmopolitanism etched by Potuoğlu-Cook. What both authors make possible is the use of cosmopolitan logic to depict minorities – ethnic minorities such as the

Grand Bazaar

Gypsies or religious minorities such as the Jews – and not just the dominant group.

Icons

The issue of whether or not Istanbul – however varied and disputed its
historical/contemporary profile – can be viewed as an emerging model for
Muslim cosmopolitanism depends on local actors, but it also draws on a
set of contradictory indices that need to be marked, and then explored.
Part of what distinguishes a mega-city from its parallel urban neighbours

is its sense of celebration. There are always multiple public moments to celebrate, a calendar of performances or events that monopolise the everyday gaze and suggest the hinge importance of this one city as a perpetual resource of social capital. Celebration is also linked to restoration: buildings must be maintained but also renewed, just as heroes must be recalled, their memories expanded, in the public domain.

And so urban elites – whether governmental or private – must be adroit at both recuperating the past and reinforcing its present value. This process always involves linking individuals to major institutions, putting a public face on heroes who embody the narrative, the memory and the virtues projected as local and global, at once national and cosmopolitan. This process of symbolic archaeology can be charted throughout Istanbul's millennial history but especially since the 1990s, the city's advocates have proven themselves skilful in asserting their ownership of four individuals crucial for all Turks. These local/national/cosmopolitan heroes can be sorted into two sets. The first defines the public, political role of Islam. They are: 1) Mehmet II, known as Fatih (the Conqueror) Sultan Mehmet, said to be the guiding figure in the initial Islamisation of Istanbul; and 2) Atatürk, or Mustafa Kemal, Mehmet II's opposite and yet also his complement, the guiding figure for the secularisation of post-World War I Turkey. These two military heroes embody not only contradictory ideologies but also competing roles as emblems from the Ottoman past and at the same time signposts for republican Turkey as it approaches its centenary in 2023.

Equally important is the other set of heroes, at once exemplars and icons. They are explicitly religious pioneers who mark milestones from the Turkish past while also prefiguring some of the contours for its future. Though there are several candidates, two stand out in Turkey as a whole and Istanbul in particular: 1) Mevlana Jalal al-Din Rumi, whose mausoleum is in Konya but some of whose important dervish lodges or tekkes are in Istanbul; and 2) Fethullah Gulen, the spiritual force of the Gulen movement that pervades not only Turkish education, society and politics but also many of the neighbouring Turkic republics of Central Asia.

Political Icons

Among the many ironies that link Mehmet II and Mustafa Kemal are their names. Both have names that can be traced to the Prophet Muhammad.

Mehmet is a Turkish abbreviation of Muhammad, while Mustafa is one of the alternate titles he enjoyed. Mustafa means 'the chosen' (one), and while it referred to Muhammad as the one sent by God in 610 to be the last prophet in an Abrahamic lineage stretching back to Adam, for Atatürk it was an accidental choice. He was given the name by his father, yet it signalled his 'divine' role, as the one chosen or destined to be the Turkish leader of a war against European and local enemies securing the Republic of Turkey as a new nation-state with defendable borders in 1922. Despite the span of 1300 years separating the Prophet of Islam from the Father of Turkey, the name Mustafa binds them together symbolically, albeit at the most superficial level.

The overlaps between Mehmet II and Mustafa Kemal extend further. Each is marked by a set of four traits: 1) military skill, including maritime prowess, to secure battlefield victories, often against great odds; 2) expansionary zeal, to not only conquer but to incorporate other domains within their own empire/state; 3) administrative/bureaucratic finesse; and 4) the indefinable yet critical trait of charisma. While none of these traits is cosmopolitan, their combination projects individuals whose life stories redirect society and shift the historical trajectory toward inclusive futures unimaginable without them.

Mehmet II inherited a powerful Turkic warrior state that had claimed much of Anatolia and extended into southern Europe. But it had been denied the greatest urban prize, the capital city of the Byzantine Empire that had rebuffed all efforts at Muslim conquest and had only been breached once, by fellow Christians, in the Crusader invasion/occupation from 1204-1261. When Mehmet II went against the advice of senior officers and resolved to capture Constantinople, he had to make extraordinary preparations for a combined sea-land assault.

No less brave was Atatürk's decision to fight against the British-Australian soldiers who were determined to capture Istanbul from the then Ottoman Empire in 1915. The impact of Gallipoli is emblazoned in numerous guidebooks and histories. In Turkey the battle became part of a durable repertoire of stories concerning the nation's revered founder, Mustafa Kemal. The Turkish victory did more than any other event or person to create the myth of Atatürk the fearless, indefatigable and undefeatable leader. Like Mehmet II, he went against the advice of his commanders, and also overcame huge enemy forces with an order to his troops that every Turkish school child can still repeat: 'I am not ordering you to attack; I am ordering you to die. In the time it takes us to die, other troops and commanders will arrive to take our places.' His regiment was wiped out, and later he himself was hit in the chest by a piece of shrapnel, but, as the story goes, his pocket watch prevented fatal injury. Despite the loss of more than half the Ottoman forces, he went on to become not only the hero of Gallipoli but also the general who carried Turkish fortunes beyond the war.

Following their initial successes, both leaders, Mehmet II and Atatürk had other military engagements, many of which they won, some of which they lost, but all of which expanded their domains, across Europe for the Ottoman Empire in the late fifteenth century, and across Anatolia in post-World War I Turkey.

Also important for Mehmet II was the myth of completion, to wit, that his conquest of Constantinople marked a centuries-old ambition of previous Muslim warriors, dating back to the era of the Prophet Muhammad. It is for that reason that the huge flux of pilgrims to Eyub Sultan's grave and mosque projects the image of Mehmet II as the devout ghazi or warrior to present day Stambouli Muslims. No less relevant, though much less noted, is Mehmet II's connection to another popular saint's tomb, located not on the Golden Horn but on the Bosphorus. Well beyond the urban centre of Istanbul lies the modest mountainside tomb of Telli Baba, who is said to have watched over the Bosphorous and safeguarded the movements of Mehmet II in his bold assault on the Byzantine capital. Located near Saruyer district, the Telli Baba Turbe has become the frequent destination of Muslim pilgrims seeking to have prayers answered, whether for prosperity, safety or marital success.

An element of charisma pervades the recollection of Mehmet II and even more Mustafa Kemal. There is the impressive Diorama 1453 which opened in 2009 in the Topkapi district of Istanbul. Bus drivers can, and do, download from its website onto their Blackberries films of Fatih Sultan Mehmet's conquest, while Atatürk's picture is everywhere, even in the form of tattoos on women's arms. Especially notable is the Atatürk museum in Istanbul and, of course, his monumental tomb, with the museum attached to it, in Ankara. Beyond all the impressive display of military memorabilia, are two items that tell more about the man than his destroyed watch fob (which actually travelled to Berlin, then disappeared, after World War I). There is the rowing machine that he used to maintain a daily regimen of physical fitness, and then his extraordinary library – at once huge, diverse in topics and multilingual in the books that it contained. We now know from recent scholarship that he even concerned himself with Turkish vernacular translations of the Qur'an.

Though this might seem like a slim connection to Turkey's religious past, it is not lost on devout Turks that even the 'secular' Atatürk did concern himself with religious meaning as well as religious laws, structures and institutions. To make the Republic of Turkey succeed the core of Islamic faith had to be accessible to modern Turks. Unlike Bourgiba in modern Tunisia, Atatürk did not try to modify one of the pillars of Islam, but instead to convey its scriptural anchor, the Holy Qur'an, in a language that was at once authentic and modern. Yet his efforts came at a cost: the systematic attempt through the Turkish Language Association, founded in 1932, to cleanse Turkish of all Arabic and Persian terms, which was so intense that some outspoken readers of Osmanli (Ottoman) script were imprisoned.

Religious Exemplars

Neither Mehmet II nor Mustafa Kemal was identified with Sufism yet Sufism is enormously pivotal in Turkish national identity. The Mevlevi order is the one Sufi institutional network most firmly linked to Turkey. It was founded in 1273 by followers of Jalal al-Din Rumi. It was his successor, Husamuddin Celebi, who decided to build a mausoleum for the Mevlana in Konya, a major trading centre of Anatolia. Though the central focus of the order remains Konya, Mevlevi influence radiates throughout Turkey and beyond. Its link to the Ottoman Empire was confirmed when one of Rumi's descendants, Devlet Hatun, married Sultan Bayezid I, and their son Mehmet I became the next sultan (1413-1421). Known as Celebi Sultan Mehmet I, to distinguish him from his grandson, the future Fatih (The Conqueror) Sultan Mehmet II (1444-1481), who conquered Constantinople, Mehmet I endowed the order with many land grants. Several members of the order later served in various official positions during the heyday of the Ottoman Empire. Among the several Mevlevi lodges in Istanbul, the Galata Mevlevihane was the first to be established, in 1491 during the reign of Sultan Bayezid II (1481-1512). Two other major melevihanes were added subsequently in the Uskudar and Topkapi districts of Istanbul.

In stressing the quest for union between the Beloved and the lover, the Divine and the human, God and the seeker, the Mevlevi order placed central emphasis on music and dance. It is said to have been the first Sufi order to make music a central part of its religious practice. The *ney*, *kudum* and later the *tambur* were used in Mevlevi ceremonies. At gatherings the Mevlana, Jalal al-Din Rumi, first recited poetry set to music before he engaged in the whirling dance (*sema*) for which the order is now renowned. Following his father's death, Sultan Veled laid down specific principles for the performance of dance, with musical accompaniment, and these principles are said to have been honoured by Mevlevis ever since.

In 1925, however, the Mevlevi order, together with all other Sufi networks, was publicly outlawed in Atatürk's new Turkish Republic. The Galata and other Stambouli dervish lodges were closed down on the grounds that they were sources of reactionary movements against the programme of modernisation launched two years earlier. The dervish lodge in Istanbul, Galata Mevlevihanesi, eventually became the Mevlana Museum, as did the father lodge, where the Mevlana was buried, in Konya.

Yet after 1925, Rumi's descendants still practised their unique form of meditative dancing in private. In 1954 the Mevlevis were given partial rights to perform the *sema* in public, and though banned as a Sufi order, Rumi's descendants and adherents accepted their reclassification as a non-political organisation, subject to the laws of the Republic of Turkey. Till today contemporary urban Turks, along with visiting tourists, admire and enjoy the Mevlevis. They remain twenty-first-century custodians of both the Ottoman past and its cosmopolitan legacy.

No account of Istanbul as a potential showcase of Muslim cosmopolitanism would be complete, however, without examining the impact of another Sufi-like movement. It is linked to the controversial Fethullah Gulen. Like his precursor, Bediuzzaman Said Nursi, Fethullah Gulen is a devout Muslim activist with strong ties to institutional Sufism, banned under Atatürk's radically laicist view of public religion. Though Gulen's views have altered over time, they inform both the movement named after him and many public figures in the AKP (Justice and Development Party), including the Prime Minister and President first elected in November 2002. While the scope and influence of the Gulen movement have been publicly debated with often contradictory assessments, the overriding need is to move beyond the dichotomous categories that frame a battle between two separate, oppositional and irreconcilable groups: Muslim advocates for a religious public order, and their opponents, secularists who (re)claim Turkey in general and Istanbul in particular as the site of Kemalist reforms that outlaw religious preference, from dress codes to dietary rules to prayer observance.

It is the context of Gulen's movement as much as the man himself or his ideas that make him a force in Turkey generally as also in Istanbul. He was shaped by the powerful teachings of Nursi, a Kurdish mystic forced into exile in the 1920s. Nursi wrote and wrote, producing a voluminous legacy known as *Risale-i Nur*; its 6,000 pages of expanded Qur'anic commentary continue to be cited and propagated by his numerous followers in Nurcu organisations. After Nursi's death in 1960, Gulen became even more popular as a preacher, attracting disciples throughout Anatolia. By the late 1970s he had established himself separate from other Nurcu groups. Beginning in the 1980s, he developed a nationwide following that focused on education as well as media. An Istanbul daily newspaper, *Zaman*, began publication in 1986, and was followed by its English counterpart, *Today's Zaman*, and then a decade later a prominent new university was opened in Istanbul, Fatih University. Gulen himself moved to self-imposed exile in Pennsylvania in 1999, but he continues to project his image, and to exercise influence, in a broad segment of Turkish society as well as in several of the formerly Soviet Central Asian republics which form a larger Turkic cultural sphere bridging European and Asian audiences.

The Gulenist movement strives to project its influence across ethnic, religious and even national boundaries. What the case of the veiled belly dancer Zeynep cited above illustrates, is replicated again and again in the actual lives of men and women who participate in the Gulen movement today: secular and religious Turks are more alike than they are divided. Beyond the tension, conflict and contestations that mark the public exchange of Gulenists and Kemalists is convergence over key values: the primacy of Turkish nationalism, loyalty to the memory of Atatürk, and, above all, advocacy of education, commerce and dialogue as the keys to a brighter future not just for Turks but for all Turkic peoples.

The embrace of a Turkic past is crucial. It comes through the Gulen movement's outreach to several neighbouring countries of Central Asia, including Kazakhstan. There Gulenists promote engagement not debate or contestation with both secular and religious opponents. They advocate cultural diversity under the rubric of political pluralism, and remain committed to secular values, dress codes, and privileges in the public space. If Atatürk represented authoritarian modernisation and a laicist republic that excluded religious actors, his successors have accommodated new links between the state and Islam, which permit options not previously imagined for ethnic minorities, especially Kurds, but also for the religious majority, that is, whether nominal or observant Muslims. Instead of a polarised society and a military-cowed government, Turkey has tried to have regular, open elections. Although some remain dissatisfied with the role of the army or with the religious agenda of the ruling AKP party, those leaders elected since the mid-1990s have begun to forge the elements of a Muslim democracy. While it is far too early to offer a definitive judgment about its likely success, many observers within and beyond the Middle East continue to tout Turkey as the model for progressive, modern and – yes – cosmopolitan Islam.

But there are limits to the Turkish experiment. It rests on a delicate, shifting consensus, the sense of engagement not only with internal others but also with immediate neighbours, such as Syria, a former ally and now a potential enemy, and Iran, always an unpredictable player, whether friend or foe. The economy must also continue to grow, and the generals must be content with military, not political, ambitions. At the same time, Turks abroad must continue to relate enthusiastically and supportively to their homeland, as most now do.

Despite such demurrals, can we deduce that Istanbul will thrive as a cosmopolitan centre blazing the path for other Muslim megacities of the twenty-first century? The answer is again both yes and no. Yes, all can and should be drawn to understand both the continuities and transformations of Istanbul during the recent past, but at the same time, there is no Turkish template for Muslim cosmopolitanism. If there is a culturally specific, Turkish Islam, as some have claimed, then it is, in its best light, an Islam marked by cosmopolitan traits: liberal, tolerant, pluralist and democratic. But every light has its shadow, and these variables have been, and continue to be, contested even within Turkey. Moreover, to the extent that they derive from Turkish history, society, culture and religion, they are not easily transferable. They have shaped – and one hopes, that they will continue to shape – the distinctive trajectory of Istanbul in the post-Soviet and now the post-9/11 world. To the extent that other cities, other regions, and other networks find their path to a cosmopolitan future, it will parallel rather than emulate the Turkish, Stambouli model.

Signposts

What derives from looking, even cursorily, at the question of Muslim cosmopolitanism with an Istanbul-centred focus is the need to imagine Muslim cosmopolitanism as a permeable category, one with multiple local variants and contingent criteria that are never asserted without also being simultaneously contested. Just as Zeynap, the devout Muslim belly dancer, projects a paradox, so do contemporary Turks: they embrace both the ghazi hero Fatih Sultan as the emblem of their faith and the anti-Caliphate nationalist Atatürk as their exemplar patriot.

A Jewish or Christian – or Hindu or Buddhist – cosmopolitanism is as viable and as contingent as is its Muslim counterpart. Whether minority or majority, Asian or European, all cosmopolitan projects stretch the canopy of time and meaning across a spectrum of the cosmos that is also marked as polis or city state. All have common interests as well as competing agendas.

Counter-cosmopolitan forces also exist in major parts of Muslim majority and minority pockets of the Afro-Eurasian oikumene. One cannot eradicate the forces of counter-cosmopolitanism, those who advocate tribalism or terrorism or tyranny or a mixture of all three. At the same time, however, by projecting the persistent longing and belonging of multiple groups who embody and perform cosmopolitan traits, Stamboulis, the current residents of a great city and citizens of an evolved republic, demonstrate that true cosmopolitanism is always possible as long as it is denoted, that is, specified and complicated in multiple local contexts, usually bearing religious markings.

The major traits that mark Stambouli Muslim cosmopolitans are place specific. First, there can be no cosmopolitanism apart from cities, yet cities differ from one another even when they share common values. Those cities which dot the maritime expanse of the Mediterranean Sea and the Indian Ocean, moreover, share certain characteristics that include an accent on religious identity most often defined as Muslim. While Beirut or Alexandria or even Smyrna (pre-World War I) could be counted among the major Mediterranean maritime ports with a large or majority Muslim population, Istanbul remains exceptional, both in its long history and in its recent experience.

Istanbul provides a signpost not a template for Muslim cosmopolitanism. Part of what makes Istanbul remarkable is its intense diversity, especially in welcoming, then managing refugees from less hospitable neighbours. One cannot understand Muslim cosmopolitanism in Istanbul without reference to antecedents and parallels, especially Jewish cosmopolitanism, but at the same time one must account for the complex admixture of social traits, defining moments, and symbolic heroes, all of which define the Muslim variant of global/Mediterranean cosmopolitanism distinctive to Istanbul.

The most significant, overriding conclusion concerns the greyness or piebald quality of all calculations that have as their subject cosmopolitanism. No cosmopolitan effervescence can be attributed either to a secular or to a religious identity, but rather to their admixture. Equally crucial is a Turkish Muslim majority which welcomes, rather than restrains or denies, other minorities both non-Muslim (Christian/Jewish) and non-Turkish (Armenian/Kurdish). Dissent and debate, i.e., engagement in the public square, is essential to all evolved forms of cosmopolitanism. And some could complain that Turkey has not reached the take-off stage due to the difficulties it has experienced with its minorities. In retrospect, it could be deduced that Atatürk was not just a national leader but a hyper-nationalist who promoted the ethnic cleansing of Greeks and Armenians from Anatolia, Arabs from Hatay province, and unmitigated suppression of Kurds throughout the republic.

While the legacy of Atatürk will continue to be debated, what makes cosmopolitanism both possible and visible in twenty-first-century Istanbul is precisely debate, that is, a series of very public skirmishes between groups labelled as conservative or progressive, Islamist or secular, all of whom contend for the same mantle: to project Turkey as a majority Muslim, non-religious state that dominates Eastern Mediterranean-Central Asian networks of commerce, communication, cultural and social

exchange, with ambitions that exceed the region, even if they have so far
not been acknowledged as globally pioneering by those outside the region.
That goal is an advance for Muslims, for Turks, and for all cosmopolitans.

But for Muslim cosmopolitanism to work as a global project there must
be many other such focused studies on Muslim cities. It is a daunting but
dazzling project. One could approach the task synchronically, looking not
just at 21st century candidates but at major metropolitan centres from a
medieval timeline. A snapshot from 1200, for instance, would include
Cordoba and Seville, Marrakech and Fez, along with Jerusalem, Damascus,
Baghdad, Herat, Delhi, and Lahore. Variant timelines would encompass a
distinct constellation of Muslim metacities, including several urban nodes
from Sub-Saharan Africa, South-East Asia, and Central Asia.

Among the major cities of Central Asia, one city looms large: Bukhara.
Already it is attracting the attention of scholars: a recent European Society
for Central Asian Studies conference at Cambridge University (September
2011), convened 'The Bukhara Project – Cosmopolitanism and the City'.
Like Istanbul, Bukhara boasts a past of both ethnic and religious diversity.
Also, like Istanbul, Bukhara has a multi-layered, centuries-old history as a
major urban entrepot for trade, commerce, and civil exchange. Today, its
majority Muslim inhabitants strive to project themselves as harmoniously
interactive with fellow citizens who are similar to, yet separate from, them.

The Cambridge conference addressed the central question: how does
twenty-first-century Bukhara provide for all its citizens a platform that
encompasses processes at various levels, for different ethnic/religious
groups as also between individuals within these groups? Participants at the
conference explored how the nature of cosmopolitanism is constructed in
part through inter-ethnic and inter-religious mixing, but even more,
through trade, education, community and cultural institutions. The outcome of these deliberations, it is hoped, will clarify the dynamic underlying spaces for interaction where Bukharans have achieved something more:
a way to celebrate differences and to coexist peacefully.

Similar to Istanbul, Bukhara can claim a Jewish minority, but it is a
reverse example of tolerance. Till recently Bukhara was home to a small
community of Muslim Jews, Chala, or Jews who converted to Islam. The
Chala tag often had a derogatory tone, yet under Soviet rule these Chala
were revalued as ideal Soviet citizens and celebrated as role models bring-

ing both tolerance and civilisation to Bukhara and, by extension, to the Uzbek Republic. It was a parody of tolerance, and the subsequent history of Bukharan Jews has been bleak. Starting in 1972, one of the largest ever Bukharan Jewish emigrations occurred, as Jews from both Tajikistan and Uzbekistan emigrated either to Israel or to the United States. Worse was to come. After the fall of the Berlin Wall and the end of the Soviet Union, almost all of the remaining Bukharan Jews left Central Asia for new homes abroad, some choosing Australia rather than Israel, the United States or Western Europe as their destiny.

And so a central problem for all academic reflections on Muslim cosmopolitanism is to balance the narratives of those who remained – whether in Istanbul or Bukhara – with the competing narratives of those who left. How do the contingencies of history and the hopes of cosmopolitan advocates commingle in 2012 Bukhara? At the Cambridge conference the participants supported their judgement that the rich historical experience of Bukhara would continue to shape its present, helping to articulate a practical example of cosmopolitanism at work beyond Western Europe and the Middle East. Broad-gauged professionals, they are pragmatists who remain optimists.

Will the Bukharan legacy of cosmopolitanism have a dimmed, if still discernible, future? No prediction is certain, yet across the Afro-Eurasian oikumene, from Western Europe to South-East Asia, a Muslim cosmopolitan option is coming increasingly to the fore. Though it has competitors, detractors, dead ends, and detours, as well as no win options, it remains the best advance towards a global future marked by binary striving (different but together) rather than by dyadic defeatism ('my way or the highway'). It is an idea whose time may have come, or come back, depending on your view of history. One conclusion remains indisputable: cosmopolitanism, not fundamentalism and puritanism, inflects the brightest Muslim future for the perilous twenty-first century.

JIHAD, ANYONE?

S Parvez Manzoor

Is Islam an imperial idea, forever beholden to the perpetuation of a historical order to which 'conquering the world' is intrinsic? For all the absurdity of this claim, it remains indisputable that a number of non-Muslim critics and some of our own 'rightly misguided' zealots subscribe to this fantasy, albeit for different reasons. I intend to provide a rebuttal to this calumny. The ultimate stake in this bid to refute the charge of 'Islamic imperialism' is not merely the ideology of 'Islamism' and its anti-politics of nihilistic and suicidal jihad but the very notion of 'Islamic' rule. Perhaps I should make it clear that I am not questioning the necessity of 'Muslim power', the Muslims' right to act politically in the historical world, nor the legitimacy of their just struggle (jihad) for self-preservation, the right of the Community (*ummah*) to ensure its survival. What are being rejected are the reified conceptions of 'Islam' as 'state', its faith as coercive order, its universalist spirit as imperial body-politic, its search for a human community as the subjugation of the other, its utopian dream as perpetual hegemony!

Before we turn to the conundrums of norm and history, faith and existence, transcendence and textuality, that are all integral to any act of Muslim reflection and self-criticism, we are obliged to respond to the duplicity of the current political discourse within which the myth of Islam's irredeemably imperialist nature is routinely sermonised. It is this medieval, atavistic passion that makes it impossible to see Islam in historical, existential terms. Islam now looms as a phantom without a human face. It defines the West as 'non-Islam', sets limits to the expansion of the European project, provides libertarians with compelling reasons for self-acclaim, solves the problem of identity-crisis for many nation-states of Europe, supplies humanists with ingenious arguments for betraying their ideals and routinely transmutes xenophobia and racism into patriotic fervour. Indeed, 'Islam' even gives licence to academics to propose the most undisciplined and baroque meta-theory – with no pretence to historical veracity. Alas, Muslim extremists have adopted this racial caricature, this barbaric monster, this spectre of doom as their own hero! The scorn of the powerful has become the pride of the powerless!

Little wonder that when it comes to the dead-ends of Muslim thought, there is no obligation on the part of the 'critical' thinker to dwell on the reciprocity of universalism and imperialism that is mandatory in all intra-western discussions and which is invariably conceded as a given of 'the human condition'. Islam, it appears, is always the exception that cannot be subordinated to any universally valid human paradigm. The insight, that every aspiration to unite mankind on a single platform ineluctably entails some project of creating a trans-national imperial order, produces no ambiguity and discomfort when the judgment is about Islam. Christianity in this self-glorifying narrative, is all mission and no empire; the modern West is all about human rights and freedom of conscience and not a whit about murderous wars and predatory capitalism. 'Islam', whether of yesterday, today or tomorrow, however, is all imperial ruse and no faith!

Starting from the reality of Muslim existence, as it confronts us in our own times, it is plain to see that any claim about the imperial aspirations of the Muslims is pathetic and disingenuous. Ever since the launching of modern imperialism, Islam has been on the receiving end of civilisational strife and racist polemics, and remains so to this day. Given the unabashed display of genocidal passions against Muslims and the brazen deceit and lies of the current Islamophobic discourse, it would therefore be obscene to lend support to this slander by adding another, Muslim, voice to the inquisitional choir. The real victims in the global market of smear and vilification are, without doubt, Muslims.

To reject the charge of 'Islam's' imperialist deceit in the name of faith is not to deny that prior to modern times, the political structures that Muslims created and ruled over, were imperial in nature. It needs emphasising however that the preeminent form of political organisation before the birth of the modern state, whether in the house of Islam or elsewhere, was the empire. (We must however be cautious against conceiving the relationship of the pre-modern empire and the modern nation-state in paradigmatic, evolutionary terms.) In fact, for pre-modern times, there hardly exist any phenomenological criteria for distinguishing Muslim rule from that of the others. In terms of form, structure, organisation and the puta-tively transcendent moorings of the body-politic, they all shared the same imperial worldview. Thus, in as much as Muslims exercised 'sovereignty' and ruled over a multitude of peoples, nations and tribes that were both Muslim and non-Muslim, they too wallowed in imperialist glory and indulged in imperialist fantasies. As political beings Muslims too could not help creating empires and power structures, not because of the dictates of their faith but in spite of them. It was the tribal instinct and lust for the riches of the world that provided the principal rationale for the dynamics of past Muslim rule – not unlike the story of European nation-states-cum-empires that ushered us into modernity.

Thus, to claim that the Muslim political landscape 'in the age of empires' was distinctive and singular, that it was a unique gift of the Islamic faith, is plain nonsense. Imperialism is no more intrinsic to Islam than it is to Christianity, Buddhism, Communism or Liberalism. Or, paradoxically, the reverse: it is an indispensable constituent of all universal projects, be these religions or 'merely' secular ideologies. The human quest for order that is premised on the construction of a symbolic reality and the exercise of political power commissioned by it knows no boundaries of faith or ideol-ogy. With regard to imperial rule, or the quest for 'sovereignty', there is no Islamic exception.

Power however brings its own nemesis and every imperialist is sooner or later forced to recognise that we inhabit an unconquerable world. And so it was in the case of the Muslims. The imperial adventures of the Umayyad 'jihad state' came to an abrupt end in the reign of Hisham bin 'Abd al-Malik (740). Not only did it spell the end for Muslim unity in a single state, the putative link between *din* and *dawla* (mission and empire) was sundered once and for all, forcing the Muslims to turn inwards, towards the meaning of faith for spiritual and societal wellbeing. This of course is the academic historian's verdict. The traditional narratives of the birth of the Muslim community are even more insistent on the claim of a definite break between the pristine order of faith and the imperial expan-sion of the Arab state. According to the traditional Sunni view, the legiti-mate Islamic order lasted only till the reign of the Righteous Caliphs (around thirty years, from 632 to 631); whereas the Shiites regard all post-Prophetic regimes as illegitimate. Either way, imperial rule is separated from the Caliphate of the Rightly Guided, and the legitimacy of the former is unanimously denied. The worldly triumph of the Umayyad dynasty does not make their regime 'Islamic', nor is their territorial expansion ever regarded as part of the jihad narrative. In short, to affirm one's belonging to the redeeming community always entails an affirmation of the values of faith and a rejection of the politics of Empire. So, from both the historical and the normative perspectives, faith and empire are not coterminous. The fundamentalist's dogma of the identity of faith and state is a modern heresy; inspired by the Orientalist's phantom Islam — a Platonic idea with no history.

Islamic State as Oxymoron

All political order, we'd do well to remember, is founded on power and is sustained by the ideology that legitimises it. Of course, power is not synonymous with military power alone; economic, scientific, ideological and cultural factors are intrinsic to any conception of power. Muslims were no exception to this rule; their share of the fortunes and misfortunes of 'sovereignty' (*dawla*) in the historical world was commensurate with the power they possessed or lacked. And yet, Muslims do possess norms that are transhistorical, norms that pass judgement on history and which require a constant affirmation of the ultimately transcendent order of being.

Were it not so, Islam would be indistinguishable from any secular ideology and would not proclaim itself to be a revealed faith. It would be coterminous with the Muslim historical project and Islamic conscience would be a contradiction in terms. Norm and history would be synonymous and the postulation of a transcendent order of being quite superfluous for the Muslim's faith, indeed for his/her self-definition as well. Islamic thought would not have to exhaust itself by constantly searching for the criteria of the legitimate Islamic order, nor would its unending reflection and debate on the significance of the formative history of the community have any purpose or meaning. The very existence of the term 'Islam', with its inexpugnably transcendent semantic content/connotations, is a living testimony to its normative nature, and a telling refutation against its reification as a phenomenon of history. As W C Smith, the Canadian scholar and professor of comparative religion, has tellingly brought to our attention, prior to modern times the term 'Islam' denoted, originally and for most of its history, a verbal noun, the self-commitment of an individual Muslim to submit to God. The denotation of an empirical reality, or a Platonic ideal, as 'Islam', as it is the case in the modern usage, is a recent phenomenon, and a tell-tale sign of the depletion of transcendent consciousness in modernity. The least one may demand of the Muslims today is not to confuse the transcendent order of faith (Islamic) with the mundane reality of the historical order (Muslim), and consequently, not identify the coercive order of the state with the voluntary act of submitting to the Divine will. The semantic distinction is not a matter of terminological niceties but reaches to the heart of Islam as personal faith. The Muslim collective enterprise in history is not and cannot be the be-all and end-all of Islam. Certainly, Muslims have not renounced power, nor dismissed history as an illusion. But the Muslim rationale for not dispensing with worldly power is not power or history or glory, or even the existential imperative to survive, but their commitment to the transcendent truth. Their calling is to give testimony to their faith in history and not let history be the ultimate arbiter of their faith. The fundamentalist obsession with success in history, accordingly, is not an Islamic value, let alone an imperative of faith.

While we may conceptualise the formative phase of the establishment of the Muslim social contract, the historical regime of the Prophet, as body-Islamic, to proceed from this fact to the claim that the body-Islamic was a body-politic, a theo-political unity of religion and state which constitutes the timeless norm of Islamic politics, is to betray the canons of logic as well as the testimony of history. True, later jurists constructed a constitutional theory which did include the stipulation of Islamic rule, but it was not a model of practical politics or a pillar of statecraft. Indeed, Muslims universally accepted the separation of the religious and the political, and did in fact produce their own theory of the two powers of statehood. There was no pretence that statecraft must follow the jurist's writ, or that it must constitute itself as the rule of the religious scholar, as is the case with modern ideologues. Even as perceptive a thinker as Ibn Khaldun who defined *khilafa* as the best possible regime for mankind was not averse to conceding the merits of secular kingship (rational regime) for the advancement of the common good.

The modern reversal of the classical theory of government, a literalist and fundamentalist misreading of the jurists' text, bestows Muslim reason and conscience with a number of intractable problems. Apart from the fact that the notions of state and politics, even body-politic, are contingent upon the acceptance of the secular conception of historical order, and may be filled with any kind of content, including the transcendence-denying semantic mass of modernity, it is unmindful of the fact that the theocratic regime comes to an end with the Prophet, and the unity of faith and politics, which was a necessary corollary of the revelatory process, is no longer possible under any other system of rule. The modern theory of the Islamic state, of which medieval jurists had no inkling, conflates norm and history in an eternal now and produces a radically unprecedented reading of the Muslim faith as secular and temporal transcendence, is indeed heretical. Or, an alternative reading of the theory would maintain that it fortifies a longing for the continuation of the Prophecy, or for bringing the shia notion of *imama* back to history, and hence re-opens the problem of *khilafa*, the search for the succession of the Prophetic regime and its meaning. Either way, it ends up prescribing a secular faith and a sacred state and renders the notion of Islamic rule an oxymoron.

Far more disturbing than the logical inconsistency of the modern heresy is the hidden premise of its ostensibly political theory: by conceiving the state as an attribute of faith, it initiates the quest for a new sovereign, and thereby seeks a new locus of authority. The state in this scheme of things becomes an idealised polity whose routinised authority displaces the tenet of the historical uniqueness and finality of the Prophetic regime. Or, conversely, by conceptualising the state as a legal automaton, a political robot as it were, the modern theory not only divests the state of legislative functions, but also severely circumscribes the political community's options for dealing with history. Politics, accordingly, deals not with the existential concerns of a faith community but with the authoritative interpretation of the foundational text of the Law, albeit through the mediation of the supreme jurist, or a collective corps of self-acclaimed jurists as is the case with the majority community. The putative 'Islamic state' also dons the theocratic mantle, going beyond the acts of governance to the mandate of guidance, identifying itself as the channel of salvation. From the canons of traditional Islam, again, it advances a heretical claim.

By contrast, in the traditional civilisation of Islam governance was never made part of the Islamic commitment, it was deemed a *fard kifaya*, a collective enterprise and a lesser obligation which could be dispensed with when circumstances allowed. It was certainly not at par with the unconditionally obligatory acts of worship and piety, *fard 'ain*, for which the individual alone was responsible. Or, in modern parlance, establishing Muslim government is not 'an article of faith', not even in the jurist's system. For all its pretence to authenticity and the rhetoric of going back to roots, the Islamist model of government is a refutation of the jurists' ethos and a travesty of their conception of governance.

Finally, we cannot ignore the havoc that the whirlwinds of history have wrought upon the edifice of the jurist's constitutional theory and its institutional foundations. It should be immediately apparent to anyone that there is no state, no church, no pope, no caliph, no court of law, no parliament, etc that represents Islam. Islam cannot be reduced to the workings and sayings of any human institution. No one, indeed nothing, incarnates it. Islam is a faith without any structure, whether political or ecclesiastical. For all the objections that may be raised against this characterisation of Islam, the simple answer is that it is true at least for the present. In other words, to speak of Islam as a historical agent is meaningless. Far from incarnating the unity of faith and state, 'Islam' cannot be located in any historical edifice. Or, if the metaphor is not too distressing, contemporary Islam may be likened to a soup without a bowl, all faith and no empire, all spirit and no body, all ideology and no body-politic. Some sobering thought for the prosecutors and defendants of 'Islamic imperialism'!

The idea of Islamic rule is thus an oxymoron and the concept of the Islamic state a heresy. Nevertheless, the rejection of the concept of 'Islamic imperialism' must not be equated with the renunciation of Muslims' right to political power. No one is suggesting that Muslims are not part of the historical world where power-politics is the norm and the ultimate price for survival; or that they alone should renounce power *qua* Muslims, or that the only true Islam is the spiritual, apolitical Islam. On the contrary, on both historical and normative grounds we are justified in claiming that Muslim politics as the practice of self-rule and as a bid for power and sovereignty in the world of history is a proper and legitimate vocation for Muslim communities. It is also indispensably linked to the Muslim striving to contribute to the wellbeing of humanity, the heart and soul of the Islamic commitment.

Anti-Politics as the Politics of Exception

Contemporary political theory, it is no exaggeration to claim, moves in the footsteps of Carl Schmitt, the notorious German thinker with Nazi sympathies who propounded radical, anti-liberal insights on the nature of sovereignty and the political. The neoliberal War on Terror is but a translation of Carl Schmitt's vision into the practical politics of Empire. Schmitt conceptualised 'the political' in terms of the primordial and seminal antithesis between 'friend' and 'enemy'. For him, the political is primordial; it comes before the State and transcends its mundane and routine policies. It reveals itself, historically, at the foundational moment of the polity, and conceptually, in the unwritten metaphysics of the constitution. Indeed, the political in the specifically Schmittian sense incarnates existential totality and determines a choice between being and nothingness. It also follows that the state, which is forever threatened with conflict and annihilation, requires a sovereign who, given the uncertainties of political existence, must incarnate an authority that is superior to that of the law. Hence, the thundering opening of Schmitt's treatise: 'the sovereign is he who decides on the exception'.

Schmitt seems to argue that it is not law but the sovereign, not the legal text but the political will, which is the supreme authority in a state. States are not legal entities but historical communities; nations rather than constitution that are engaged in a constant battle for survival. Any moment of the state's existence may constitute an exception; it may engender a political crisis that cannot be remedied by the application of the law. Further, the problem of the exception, for the constitutional jurist Schmitt, can only be resolved within the framework of a decision (an actual historical event) and not within that of a norm (an ahistoric and transcendent idea).

That Schmitt's existential theory of politics exercises such fascination over contemporary political scientists and thinkers is not merely fortuitous. After the demise of communism, the secular model of international relations, proper to the ideological politics of the cold war, has been abandoned for a kind of neomedievalism that relies on the idiom of 'Just War' for the pursuit of imperial ambitions. For progressive thinkers, however, the reappearance of the medieval term in the political language of our times represents a clear instance of moral regression. For Bruce Holsinger, this 'post-9/11 medievalism functions as a means of reducing a host of very complex geopolitical forces to a simple historical equation, freeing its users from the demands of subtlety, nuance, and a rigorous historical understanding of the nature of inter- and supra-national conflict in an era of globalisation'. In their famous work, *Empire*, Michel Hardt and Antonio Negri lament that 'there is something troubling in this renewed focus on the concept of bellum justum, which modernity, or rather modern secularism, had worked so hard to expunge from the medieval tradition. The traditional concept of just war involves the banalisation of war and the celebration of it as an ethical instrument, both of which were ideas that modern political thought and the international community of nation-states had resolutely refused.' Certainly, critical Muslim thinkers have their own reasons to bemoan this development. The transformation of political theory into political theology in the modern discourse is the doing of Carl Schmitt, for which nobody except the die-hard fanatics need to feel grateful!

The number of studies dealing with Schmitt's oeuvre is a legion and is growing by the day. The latest addition is Paul W. Kahn's *Political Theory*. Kahn is relevant to our inquiry for making explicit what was merely implicit in Schmitt's thought, namely that the concepts of redemptive violence and holy war are part of the Biblical legacy. Thus, Kahn produces a biblically inspired reading of Schmitt that, if anything, leads to the further mystification of the concept of 'the political', and convinces even a Muslim thinker as to why the sacralisation of war ethics, whether in the tradition of Holy War, Just War or Jihad, needs to be totally abandoned. Let these terms be purged of all the martial and militant connotations and remain confined to the semantic fields of moral, non-violent struggle.

Political theology according to Kahn's interpretation 'rests on an experience beyond discourse. It rests on faith not argument, and on sacrifice, not contract'. The danger with political theory is that 'it will reduce politics to justice.' The origins of the political community, or the state, lie steeped in violence, incorporating the exceptional and the revolutionary moments of history. 'The experience of revolutionary foundations', Kahn continues, 'is captured neither by a model of discourse nor by one of violent coercion. Standing apart from both is an idea of sacrifice. This is the image of Abraham... Politics, on this view, begins with an act of willing self-destruction that rests on faith not reason.' Little wonder that Kahn returns to the Jewish Bible and its Holy War logic to make a point about the survival of the political community: 'There can be no nation of Israel as a community sustaining itself through history until families are willing to sacrifice their children for the sake of the existence of the state'. Sacrifice, for him, is the appearance of the sacred as a historical phenomenon. 'Its domain is silent faith, not reasoned discourse. ... This is the faith that connects the transcendent experience of revolution to ...... the judicial decision, and both to the state of exception in the defence of the nation.'

Kahn's exposition of Schmitt unfolds even further: 'Sovereignty is constituted in the imagining of the sacrificial act: the willingness to kill and be killed establishes the temporal and geographical boundaries of the state.' Consequently, 'the sovereign people may speak with the voice of God, but this is an enlightened God who reads his script from political theory. It brings forth not the content of a divine covenant but the content of an Enlightenment understanding of justice. An idea of justice alone, however, has no power to create a political order. No one sacrifices for a universal ideal, which has no locus in space and time.' The problem with liberal political theories, then, is that they pay all attention on the idea of justice and none on the revolutionary tradition of authenticity. Just as for Schmitt, the sovereign is the one who decides on exception, suspending the rule of law, for Kahn, 'the paradigmatic political moment' is the one at which 'the sovereign conscripts the citizen. Exactly here, one confronts the sovereign claim on life'.

Given the reduction and destitution of the political to the existential, it is just a short step to canvassing for War on Terror. The Jewish, also quintessentially American, version of 'political theology' which is generally associated with the Christian Right, reads, in the words of Kahn: 'We are radically mistaken if we think this manner of conscription is behind us. The contemporary war on terror represents the point at which conscription become truly universal, escaping even the purely formal structures of juridification. Conscription can now occur to anyone at any moment: It is just a matter of finding oneself on the wrong aeroplane at the wrong time. At that moment, there is no further discussion, there is only act. We exist then in the Schmittian exception.' The exceptional moment, when speech comes to an end, requires decision, action and sacrifice. 'As long as we can imagine such a moment, we remain within the political imaginary.' The

genuinely political, in this vision, is existential; it is located at the border-
line between existence and extinction, the moment of sacrifice. And, as
sacrifice denotes an act of faith, and the act is beyond the law, it need not
offer any justification for itself. In sum, a politics of exception is one that
relies on revelation and faith rather than on argument and reason.

The most striking claim here is not the theory of exception, but the
normalcy of this kind of thinking in our nihilistic age. Much of what
Schmitt/Kahn articulates here could have come straight out of a training
manual of Al-Qaeda, or from the sermons of Al-Zawahiri, its current leader.
Contrary to the calumny of Islamic exceptionalism, it appears that the ethos
of jihad is enshrined right in the heart of the political and is indistinguishable
from the existential politics of Empire. In fact, the roots of jihad as Holy
War may be traced to biblical politics and may, of course, remain sub-
merged in prehistory or the political subconscious of mankind.

The political, which in Kahn's reading of Schmitt is sacrificial, may also
be regarded as primordial and pre-noetic. For other mortals like us, it follows that for the creation of any kind of historical order, whether faith-
based or secular, the political must be harnessed by the yoke of law. Just as
Al-Qaeda's terror is a travesty of the juristic conception of jihad (rule of law
even at the moment of sacrifice), existential politics (exception dispensing
with the law) is a refutation of the entire Western tradition of moral and
political philosophy, of the Christian ethics of Just War as much as that of
post-Enlightenment humanism. We must reject all notions of politics, or of
the political that seek, no matter how provisional and short-lived, the abolition of the law without which there's no state and no governance, indeed
no political existence worth the name. The modern concept of sovereignty,
which degenerates easily into antinomian and nihilistic ideologies must
therefore be rigorously questioned, indeed it must be arraigned before the
tribunal of moral reason and not merely judged on purely political grounds.
While we wait for a definitive refutation of the spurious and fraudulent
ideology of Al-Qaeda that justifies itself in the name of jihad from our
jurists, it is gratifying that the task of totally abandoning the philosophical
moorings of Schmitt's political theology is already under way.

In his recent work, *The Power of Religion in the Public Sphere*, the distinguished German philosopher and political thinker Jürgen Habermas makes
a very cogent and deftly argued plea for abandoning Carl Schmitt's legacy

in political science. Indeed, he is convinced that Schmitt's radical conception of the political needs to be thrown in the dustbin of history. Though Habermas never squanders an opportunity when it comes to debunking Carl Schmitt's retrogressive thought which is antithetical to his own Kantian project of visualising a universal legal order, in this essay Habermas seeks to completely sever all connections that contemporary political theory has with the Schmittian concept of the political. The simple, and highly disarming, reason adoption of this stance is that Habermas despairs whether philosophers and political scientists can ever 'give a rational meaning to the ambivalent concept of the political.' His counter-argument, however, is normative as well as empirical, not averse to treating the political as a genealogical query, indeed as an archaeological relic.

From an empirical point of view, Habermas asserts, 'the political' at best 'designates that symbolic field in which the early civilisations first formed an image of themselves.' His historicising argument is framed within an evolutionist paradigm according to which the political structures and legitimating claims of the modern nation-state are not only non-negotiable normatively, they are also irreversible historically. They have the self-referential authority of the transcendent as it were. The political, according to Habermas, represents the image of society as a unity, the unity of the sacred and the secular, the unity of state and society. But now the society has become differentiated from the state, and religion is no longer the ideology that legitimates it. The state today is secular, and society can no longer be understood as a totality 'precisely because its self-representations are now plural, contested and contestable.' These historical developments have thus rendered the concept of the political not only obsolete but also regressive.

History and Juristic Discourse

If the constitutive act of state formation is always a violent act, if the birth of a polity is always steeped in war, it is equally true that every theory of state also incarnates a doctrine of legitimate violence. It is the function of the law to delineate a boundary between illicit violence and legitimate force. The law is the foremost agent of the coercive order within which the state proclaims and exercises its monopoly on violence. State, law and violence are indissolubly linked to each other in any theory of politics as well as in the historical existence of any political community. In the case of modern Islam, the theory of the Islamic state has also spawned its own ideology of legitimate, sacred, violence. However, like the political doctrine, the fundamentalist conceptions of jihad turn the classical theory upon its head. We are sadly brought face to face with the insight that every sublime and transcendent idea also carries with it seeds of its own caricature, parody and debasement. Never was this truth more in need of an affirmation than at this time of the wanton and nihilistic violence, glorified by Al-Qaeda and its allies, that goes under the name of jihad, but which is a travesty of it.

Al-Qaeda's cultic violence and terror need not be subsumed under the rubric of jihad (no Muslim scholar of repute has, to my knowledge, come out in support of this nihilistic ideology), but the ultimate stake in the re-examination of the nexus of violence, rule and law in the Muslim tradition is not the legitimacy of violence itself but of its conditionality, not of the morality of just war but the ethics of its conduct. True enough, the juristic discourse, or *fiqh*, preoccupies itself with these concerns and its texts are far less hawkish and jingoistic than its critics give them credit for. There is no doubt that juridical reflection on jihad advanced the cause of ethical thinking in the Muslim civilisation. Nevertheless, the march of history has rendered a great number of these texts out of date and irrelevant for our moral sensitivities. A fresh interpretation of the juridical doctrine of jihad from the vantage-point of moral and political philosophy is therefore urgently needed. No matter how this challenge is to be faced, by the resources of *fiqh* as well as that of the Islamic ethics and moral consciousness, some of the historical developments that have taken place since the formulation of the 'classical' theory of jihad cannot be ignored.

To start with, the historical argument with which Habermas dismisses Schmitt's political theology is even more appropriate in our case. History has as much claim on our tradition as it has on the Western one. That Muslim radicals have been seduced by the European nihilism of the nineteenth century and that their fascination for revolutionary violence has modern, not Islamic, roots cannot provide any solace in these times of endless, sectarian and intra-Muslim carnage. Their ideology, whatever its putative Islamic trappings, has to be rejected and banished from the realm of Islamic discourse forever. Just as in the case of the modern heresy of 'the

Islamic state', a re-examination of its cognate doctrine of legitimate violence leads us to some alarming insights about the entire paradigm of
Islamist politics.

The most obvious difference is its perception of the ideal faith community as a single body-politic and the perils of constructing any strategic
theory from this premise. The cruel irony is that the fundamentalist's quest
for authenticity and return to the ways of the pristine (*salafi*) community
results in a form of politics that merely unleashes sectarian passions and
sanctifies bloodshed. The outcome is not greater unity but increased sectarianism. The starting-point for any Muslim bid to make sense of history,
on the other hand, ought to be the realisation that the *ummah* (the united
international brotherhood of Muslims) of the juridical discourse is a thing
of the past. Not only has it lost all vestiges of political unity, it is no longer
an agent in history.

Paradoxically, the *ummah* may be the victim of its own success. It does
not face any viable threats that can endanger its physical survival. What was
a real possibility at the seventh century battles of Badr and Uhud, the
actual extinction of the community, is no longer a credible scenario. Muslim communities certainly face a number of grave challenges, including the
spectre of ethnic cleansing in some areas, but a world without Muslims is
inconceivable. It is also undeniable that the gravest challenges to Muslim
existence are not external and military but internal and ideological. What
is at stake is not the physical survival of the Muslims, but the relevance of
their commitment, not the tranquillity of their way of life but the rationale
for maintaining it. Meeting the intellectual, spiritual and moral challenges
of history requires far greater effort than fending off the immediate strategic threats. Obviously, the monumental ontological transformation of
the *ummah*, from a rivulet to an ocean as it were, demands a sea change in
our understanding of the modalities of its historical existence, of which
politics is just a sub-category.

Jihad as a 'pan-Islamic' response to the encroachment of 'Muslim identity' has become anachronistic, frequently leading to immoral acts, and
almost always suicidal. In a word, a pan-Islamic jihad today is nothing but
a nihilistic orgy, a revolutionary anarchy, indeed a Trotskyite hallucination.
Again, the conceptual and terminological apparatus bequeathed to us by
tradition is far more helpful in dispelling the haze of moral ambiguity than

the relativising discourses of modern philosophy. The distinction between *fard 'ain* and *fard kifaya*, between obligatory and dispensible acts of piety, is of capital import in any theory of jihad. By the application of this distinction, the military and the peaceful, the strategic and the moral, ends of the just struggle can be duly identified and pursued. The strategic fight is a defensive act, a collective enterprise that must uphold the rule of law and submit to the *fiqh's* instrumental reasoning and its ethics of common good (*maslaha*). It seeks a pragmatic outcome of the conflict, follows a compromising course and exercises rational choices. There's nothing of the fanatic's passion for martyrdom and sacrifice in the *fiqhi* reason. It seeks victory not self-annihilation. Jihad as *fard 'ain*, on the contrary, is an individual act of piety and penance, without strategic goals and beyond the calculus of victory and defeat. It is a pre-eminent paradigm of moral struggle. In sum, the ethos of jihad is self-preservation and survival, and not seeking glory and the riches of the world. To assert this, however, is not to claim that its moral mission cannot be perverted and distorted. The defensive rationale of self-preservation may be thwarted by the cunning of reason, by construing the moral struggle as pre-emptive, even aggressive, warfare. This, however, relates to the problem of human nature that all moral doctrines have to struggle against and not a specificity of the jihad theory.

The moral order of traditional Islam, always under the aegis of juristic discourse, is under attack by the forces of radical fundamentalism. The secular consciousness of modernity, of which Islamism is a brainchild, pursues politics of immediate return. However, by so doing, it not only thwarts transcendent goals and legal injunctions, but also breaks all moral taboos. Little wonder that the ultimate causality of this unholy crusade is the humanity and universality of the Muslim's faith. The modern stratagem of treating acts of personal violence as *fard 'ain* makes it indistinguishable from the secular state's granting of 'licence to kill' to its agents. It denotes a total denial of God's sovereignty and an ultimate affront to the moral man. The fundamentalist revolt against the juristic tradition has given us nothing but nihilistic anti-politics, moral paralysis and estrangement from history. And yet, Muslim conscience is not at ease with the legacy of the *fiqh* either.

Despite the solace of the jurist's pragmatic conception of politics, it cannot be denied that its quietist ethos and path of least resistance have not all been salubrious for our historical mission. Nor can it be denied that the *fiqhi* discourse fails to satisfy the ethical demands of Islamic conscience. For whatever reasons, it has evolved into a formalistic system of law that is morally timid but politically expedient, a system that renders Islamic reason indistinguishable from reason of state. Indeed, it has been claimed, not without reason in our view, that the *fiqhi* tradition, which succeeded in establishing itself as the normative mode par excellence of the Muslim civilisation, was actually instrumental in devouring morality and ethics and stifling spirituality. Like every other system of law, *fiqhi* reasoning does not always advance the cause of 'justice' but reinstates its own circular claims. More than that, the *fiqhi* tradition, which has the claim of deciphering God's law, has become self-authenticating and self-referential. Indeed, even more lamentably, its self-imposed internment estranges us from history and the wider currents of moral reasoning. One fatal consequence of the *fiqh's* claim to self-sufficiency is that the Muslim civilisation has been cut off from the great currents of moral reasoning that have their origins elsewhere but which relate to us in every other way. It is high time that Muslim ethical thought free itself from the legalistic shell and rediscover its vocation as the delineation of a universal moral vision.

To return to our query: all rhetorical questions ultimately rest on ontological postulates whose truth-claims are both hidden and in plain sight. Any rejoinder to questions which solicit disregard of historical diversity in a transcendent faith is fraught with epistemological horrors. The theologian may conjure a normative answer, but it will collapse before the testimony of history, while the historian's method may initiate inquisitional proceedings but it will fail to deliver a verdict. Neither does the fact that we are able to find an answer to our query guarantees that it will be acceptable to the majority. The theory of Islamic rule belongs not to the world of history and politics but to that of myth and transcendence. As such it will always remain, like other normative queries say about the nature of democracy, contentious.

However, even if a definitive, normative or historical answer cannot be given to this question, it must not be dismissed as a futile exercise in wishful thinking. For us, it leads to the paradoxical realisation that any articulation of a normative Muslim vision, any prescription of a desirable Muslim future, must stand within the stream of history; it must drink from the font of common human knowledge, if it is to have any 'Islamic' credentials. What is required of the critical Muslim thinker is not the declaration of a political charter that establishes Islam's compatibility with the current world order but a moral vision that imparts meaning and significance to humanity's own narrative of suffering, struggle and ultimate emancipation. It cannot be a purely historical account, un-redeeming and meaningless, where one civilisation supplants another, one victory and triumph begets another clash and retribution. For that would be the secular, imperial fallacy. If all politics, including the Muslim, need be local, territorial and this worldly, there is still a need for cultivating a reflexive, ethical and visionary discourse that may be conceived as Islamic politics. In keeping with the distinction between the transcendent and the historical, between the faith of Islam and the history of the Muslims, Islamic politics may not be a quest for earthly glory but heavenly peace, for we need a moral and trans-political meditation on the nature and meaning of God's trustees on earth, of the mandate of humanity to create a just and equitable order on the planet. Only such a vision of a politics of humanity will transcend the nightmare of clashing civilisations and warring empires.

The imperative for peace and moral order that supersedes the regime of war and strife is beautifully impressed upon our conscience in the following story that must bring a closure to our inquiry:

> The Prophet upon whom be prayer and peace, was returning from one of the battles, when he said, 'You have made the finest of returns; you have returned from the lesser jihad to the greater jihad.'
>
> They said, 'And what is the greater jihad?'
>
> He answered, 'The jihad of the heart.'

'THE RACE OF WOMEN'

Samia Rahman

As an array of condoms burst out of her handbag, a skimpily dressed Samantha flails about on her knees scrambling to retrieve her ribbed, strawberry-flavoured and extra-sensitive assortment of paraphernalia. The farcical turn of events betrays an air of menace as a baying crowd of robed and bearded men gather, lauding over her. Berating her immoral and obscene conduct the men are wild-eyed and intimidating. But our formidable heroine is not to be cowed. A personification of sexually liberated and emancipated Western feminism, she gathers together her belongings, gyrates suggestively and screams at the misogynists: 'Yes, I have sex'.

Perhaps you have not recognised the scene. It is from the appalling but commercially successful *Sex and the City 2* (SATC2). I admit it: I have seen it. SATC2 was ostentatious in its cultural clichés and blundering social observations. An unashamed Orientalist fantasy, it was contemptuous in its portrayal of Muslim men as misogynist while depicting Islamic society - through the oh-so-representative prism of Abu Dhabi - as repressed and oppressive. Defenders of the film point out that the plot also comments on challenges women in US society face, but this is bland when compared with the Muslim stereotypes bludgeoned on the screen. Even more disturbing is that the film came out in 2010, so its portrayal of Muslims cannot be excused as a caricature consigned to the history books. As SATC's main character, Carrie, would no doubt muse at this point, 'I got to thinking about gender relations and Islam: a whole lot of misogyny or just misunderstood?'

This was far from the first time I had cringed at assumptions about gender roles in Islam. Since developing a youngster's innocent and awe-struck awareness of what it means to be a Muslim, I have been quick to counter accusations that Islam is a misogynist religion. My childhood and upbringing were so removed from the stories of oppression and inequality that many people have come to associate with Islam, and that are played out so brazenly in SATC2. It just did not occur to me that the two could be linked. In fact it was some time before I began to suspect that this may have been because my experience of being a Muslim female was not particularly run-of-the-mill.

I was born in Bradford to parents from Karachi. The influence of south Asian culture on their method of child-rearing proved different when I compared it with my peers. For many other second-generation Pakistanis I knew, being a Muslim girl meant wearing traditional dress and being well-versed in cooking and domestic chores. At primary school I was the only Muslim pupil who went on any school trips and invited friends over to play regardless of their religion, ethnic background or gender. My parents have always been religious but did not equate faith with rigid gender roles or denying their daughter the right to enjoy the same freedoms they would grant a son. On the contrary they were anxious that we studied hard and developed enquiring and creative minds. Housework and toiling in the kitchen can come later – life was also about having rich and diverse experiences, a concept they felt was not at all opposed to being a Muslim.

My parents moved our family out of Bradford when I was still at primary school. They felt that it had become a place where being a Muslim was too narrowly defined. Dad worked as a teacher, and was all too aware of the double lives some Pakistani-origin Muslim adolescents would lead as they choked under repressive cultural mores, grappling with their sense of identity and belonging in the midst of conformity and otherness. Moving to suburban Surrey brought with it its own set of challenges but my sense of self thrived. I appreciated what it meant to be 'other' without expectations from fellow 'others' of how we 'others' must represent ourselves.

There was never any question that I could not live away from home to attend university. This seemed to be an issue for other Muslim girls I knew. My parents encouraged me to see my leaving home to study as a great adventure, albeit one that should remain within Islamic parameters. I absolutely couldn't wait! They stretched themselves financially and emotionally to support my siblings and me through higher education and they trusted us to work out life as a student for ourselves, having laid the foundations. And that is what I did. I prayed, kept my fasts during Ramadan diligently, dressed modestly but in harmony with a teenager's desire to be cool, and never lost sight of my 'Muslimness'. My wonderful friends, who I cherish to this day for their respectful curiosity and enthusiasm to be educated on all things Muslim, were so accepting and unflustered. I remember to this day the two trifles my university friends Esther and Laura made when we piled over to their house for dinner. One sherry trifle for all and a non-alcoholic trifle for me. I went backpacking around South Asia with a school friend at a time when the tick-box 'Gap Yah' excursion for middle-class youth was far from compulsory. And, of course, I was free to choose who I married. And I married someone I liked.

Free to chase my dreams and take charge of my own destiny, I could never reconcile Islam and misogyny. But Muslim misogyny kept rearing its ugly head as I grew older. I became more conscious of what had always been there but what my romanticised view of the world refused to compute. I received a jolt one evening in Bradford. I met a group of young women for coffee and conversation on a Friday night in a trendy shisha cafe in Bradford, one that is popular with Muslim bright young things. A cursory glance around the café revealed that fuchsia and turquoise were very much in vogue. Confident voices emanated from faces in meticulous make-up as groups of young women laughed together, tossing back dedicatedly straightened hair. These were stylish young women, some wearing hijab, which would always be co-ordinated to match their outfits and handbags. Others not. They were the *Sex and the City* girls of Bradford, with perhaps no actual sex, enjoying a night out after a week spent working or studying. What's more, this vibrant scene was not confined to women. There were many young Muslim men enjoying the, I'm guessing, halal and, from what I could gather, mostly respectful company of the opposite sex. They were empowered and assured young Muslim women and men. At ease, casual and utterly remarkable in their unremarkableness.

Asma was smoking shisha and drinking red bull. She'd had a 'right mare' getting away from work that evening and regaled me with stories of her job as a social worker. 'Noooo'would be her friend Fatima's frequent interjection at appropriate moments during the tales of hilarity. Northern accents with that subtle Pakistani inflection unique to the area boomed. They were open and warm and fun. I liked them. I steered the conversation to try to build a picture of their lives. 'Aw, I just wanna meet someone' Fatima revealed, 'I really want to get married, I really want that.' Fair enough, that's a pretty unexceptional aspiration among twenty-somethings

(I later found out they were both 26). It turned out that Asma had divorced three years earlier and Fatima's divorce was being finalised although she had been separated for at least two years. They had both been married to cousins in Pakistan at the age of 17 and their marriages had broken down. They told me how they tried really hard to make it work, gave their marriages their best shot but for different reasons (domestic violence in Asma's case) they couldn't work out their differences. What struck me as they related their personal tragedies was that their priority was the effect their marital status had on others: 'It broke my mum's heart when I got divorced and I want to get married again so badly to make her happy'. This was accompanied by a misunderstanding of their Islamic duties and obligations, 'I would proper wind him up and he was from Pakistan and he didn't get what I was like because I'm from here. But he took it that far. My mum said to do everything you can to please your husband and you'll get rewarded for it. I'll remember that next time.'

Both Asma and Fatima seemed feisty and self-assured, not a million miles removed from the SATC girls, sharing the same preoccupations. Yet their lives had been determined for them. They both matter-of-factly stated they had had no say in how or when they married or to whom, and were resigned to this state of affairs as if it was completely acceptable. I mentioned that Islam demands the consent of a bride and they explained that they had to respect their parent's wishes and there was too much at stake for their family and they couldn't let them down: 'thing is, we have to respect our parents because that's our religion'. Fatima's mother in particular seemed very complicit in her daughter's misfortune, unable to separate her child's interests from her own. Yet Fatima did not hold anyone responsible for her personal history and was so fatalistic it made me despair. I was even more depressed to find that despite experiencing the tumult of divorce she was placing the requirements of her family above all other considerations in her quest to marry again. 'Well, my mum really wants me to be married, it's affecting her so much to see me divorced. I've said I can't marry someone from back home like before but she really stressed. She's only alright with it if he's from the exact same village and we know the family and like them.' I couldn't understand why two intelligent and articulate women would let their lives be managed so completely and when I expressed my amazement I was reassured that 'our parents know what's good for us. They know us and they are just trying to keep us on the right track.'

Asma was also at pains to tell me that it was highly unusual for her to be out on a Friday night. 'I'm never out, me. I go to work and I'll come straight home and that's it. I'm not giving anyone any reason to say anything about me. I keep myself pure and I'm not getting any kind of reputation because it doesn't just come back on me. I've got three younger sisters and it's bad enough that I'm getting divorced but I don't go anywhere or meet anyone so no one can say that I don't keep myself pure'. I was taken aback by her use of the term pure. Why would she live under seeming house arrest out of fear of aspersions on her character? Her response was that girls had to be more careful than boys. That's just the way it was. She was from nearby Keighley so had chanced an evening out in Bradford as it was less likely she would bump into anyone she knew. She and Fatima had a well thought out cover story if they were unlucky enough to be spotted.

The notion that the respectability of entire families is tied to the inferred actions of its female members is hardly restricted to Muslim communities. Yet both Asma and Fatima seemed convinced that this was all part of adhering to their faith. Are patriarchal attitudes really given justification in Islam? They seemed to believe so. I began to have my own doubts.

Later, such doubts increased during a trip to India. There was much discussion at the time of the increasing availability of mobile phones and the debauching influence they were having on girls. Most of the outraged moral crusaders were Muslim and it was apparent that this was a drive very much led by conservative elements within the Muslim community. One particular television news item depicted an outraged matron-esque woman with her *dupatta* (scarf) wrapped vigorously around her head, calling upon parents to prohibit the use of mobile phones among their daughters lest they use them to make illicit phone calls to boys and become embroiled in *haram* (sinful) activities. The emphasis again was on restricting the movement and choices of women in order to protect them from committing sin. I discussed this with a lovely young relative who surprised me by saying she fully supported the campaign. Her reasoning was that if girls these days 'were given small freedoms they would push it too far and get out of hand'. In essence she was explaining that if you give a bit of leeway to Muslim girls they would take advantage. This view that there is a need to 'police' female morality I found to be widely held not just by men but also by women. It seemed women themselves were often the enforcers of patriarchal norms. Such examples can feasibly be argued away as cultural corruptions of the teachings of Islam. But that does not explain why huge swathes of the Muslim world are so deeply immersed in misogyny.

Just a casual glance towards the Muslim world is enough to see how badly women are treated. In Saudi Arabia, they have to wear a black (the worst possible colour for that climate) abaya, often stick to the four walls of the home, always have a male 'guardian' when they have to go out, and are seldom allowed to be seen in public. Driving is a crime punishable by flogging. In Pakistan, rape victims are often accused of adultery and punished barbarically. In Afghanistan, the Taliban regularly ransack girls' schools. A women suffering serious illness cannot see a male doctor; and there aren't all that many female doctors as they are not allowed to educate themselves. In India, women can be divorced at almost any excuse simply with the husband uttering 'I divorce thee' three times; or he can send a text message if he can't be bothered to utter the words. In the Sudan, women are frequently flogged under Islamic law. In many Muslim societies, women are deemed inferior to men. Their testimony in court is worth half that of a man. Husbands who beat their wives, and there are plenty in our societies, are cheered. The list of horrendous abuse and denial of basic rights to Muslim women seems endless.

In the widely available literature that one finds in most pious households, women are depicted as a separate, inferior race, infantile and in need of proper management. Consider a classic: *Perfecting Women* by Maulana Asharf Ali Thanawi, a book still given as a present to new brides. The Maulana makes it totally clear that women have to be socially subordinate to men – this is the demand of Islamic law. The moral decline and degeneracy of Muslim civilisation is largely due to female misbehaviour. Indeed, it was the concern about 'ruination of the religion' caused by women, which had gone 'beyond the women and their children and in many respects even had its effects on their husbands', that he was forced to write a guide for good behaviour for the weaker sex. Women are prone to excesses – even at a wedding reception they can commit 103 different sins, such as celebrating the wedding by dancing. The Maulana urges strict seclusion of women and insists that they have to be controlled and managed.

Perfecting Women is not so much a guide to etiquette, more an insight into the paranoid world of conservative male scholars.

Another equally distinguished and widely read Maulana, Abul Ala Maududi goes even further. In his *Purdah and Status of Women in Islam*, the founder of the Jamat-Islami of Pakistan offers a 'scientific justification' of the inferiority of women. Apparently, we suffer from a 'biological tragedy' which makes us ever ready to be 'sexually licentious', we are forever corrupting men, and leading society towards hell. The hijab is the lonely but solid institution standing between us and a moral abyss. 'In the matter of the continuation of the race', writes Maududi, 'man has been entrusted with no other task except that of sowing the seeds. Afterwards he is utterly free to do whatever he likes in any walk of life. As against this, the whole burden (of procreation) has been put upon the woman, for the performance of which she is prepared from the time when she was a mere foetus in the womb of her mother'. It is worth noting that the great Maulana uses a mechanical metaphor for his analysis: God is a 'Master Engineer', the universe is 'a Factory', where machines do what they have to do. The female machine is designed to menstruate, get pregnant, and suckle and rear children. That is its sole function. It is not fit to do anything else; it can do nothing else. That is a law of nature: 'this is the division of work which Nature itself has made between the sexes of mankind. Biology, physiology, psychology and all the branches of social sciences indicate this division. A good civilisation is one which accepts this dispensation of Nature as it is. Once it is done, you may give woman her proper place, give her honour in the society, respect her justifiable cultural and social rights, but burden her only with domestic duties, while allot all outdoor responsibilities and the command of the family to man'. It did not occur to Maududi, of whom it could be argued that most of his arguments came from the sinister cannons of eugenics, that it was precisely this 'division' that leads Muslim civilisation hurtling down the plug hole.

The more I read about 'Women in Islam', in books that one can buy from any good 'Islamic bookshop', the more I began to feel that misogyny was indeed integral to Islam. Sure, they all said that men and women are equal in the sight of God, but when it came to the crunch women were always dangerous, not to be trusted, not very intelligent, and under no circumstance to be allowed away from the watchful eye of a male guardian.

As an example of how women have been objectified in Islamic religious literature, consider this gem from the otherwise celebrated eleventh-century religious thinker al-Ghazali, revered by one and all as one of the great scholars of Islam. In his *Counsel for Kings*, al-Ghazali devotes a whole chapter to 'Women and their Good and Bad Points'. 'The race of women consists of ten species', al-Ghazali tells us, 'and the characters of each (of these) corresponds and is related to the distinctive quality of one of the animals. One (species) resembles the pig, another the ape, another the dog, another the snake, another the mule, another the scorpion, another the mouse, another the pigeon, another the fox, and another the sheep.'

Which one am I? I ask myself. 'The woman who resembles the pig in character knows full well how to eat, break (crockery), and cram her stomach... She is heedless of her husband's rights... She always wears filthy clothes, and an unpleasant smell issues from her'. I quickly discount this species, along with the ape who is overly concerned with how she looks and 'her secret (self) is not the same as her (outward) appearance.' Probably not the dog either, 'who whenever her husband speaks, jumps at his face and shouts at him and snarls at him,' but probably my husband could answer this one. I wouldn't categorise myself as the scorpion either, who 'does her utmost to cause enmity and hatred' or the mouse who 'is a thief' or even the pigeon who 'flits about all day... and does not speak affectionately (to her husband)'. The fox seems to have some sort of compulsion to eat everything in the house when her husband is out and start a quarrel with him upon his return saying 'You left me (alone in the house) sick'. So that only leaves one option – the sheep, 'in which everything is useful. The good woman is the same. She is useful to her husband and to (his) family and the neighbours'. Al-Ghazali could have added: and very good for slaughtering.

Elsewhere in *Counsel for Kings* he urges Muslim men to jealously separate their womenfolk from unrelated men, to the extent that if a woman is forced to speak to a man she must imitate the voice of an old woman. She must also never lock gazes with a strange man even if he is blind.

At this juncture, I have to admit, Islam and I were on two different wavelengths. I mean if al-Ghazali thinks the best we can be is a sheep, and Maududi and others engineer us behind lock and key, what could one expect from the average *ulama* – the so-called religious scholars, the kind who populate the tedious 'Islam Channel' or issue fatwas on numerous on-line forums? What is this perverse obsession with a woman's monthly cycle? Why is modesty and honour written on our bodies? And are Muslim men all latent rapists, unable to control their desires? And who appointed the bearded ones as a fashion police: forcing and abusing women to 'dress properly', imposing the hijab as some sort of sacred relic whether we wanted to wear one or not? I have seen very un-sexy women in skimpy outfits walking through the streets of London. In the same field of vision my gaze meets hijabified females in skinny jeans and tight tops who are far sexier and much more likely to arouse the attentions of the hypothetical marauding Muslim male.

Most of this misogyny is justified on the basis of the Qur'an and the traditions of the Prophet Muhammad. The sections on 'Social System of Islam' in Maududi's book begin with the Quotation of verse 51:49 - 'All things We made in pairs' – and provide one of the most misogynist interpretations of this verse you will ever read. Al-Ghazali begins his chapter on women with the words: 'The Apostle, God bless him, stated that the best and most blessed of women are those who are most prolific in child-bearing, fairest in countenance, and least costly in dowry'. Could the Prophet of Islam, noted for promoting women's rights, have said such a thing – thus reducing women to mere commodities?

Frankly, I do not accept such misogynistic sayings of the Prophet Muhammad. They are manufactured products of dubious male minds. And I refuse to accept the conventional interpretation of the Qur'an that has remained unchanged, for centuries, with layers upon layers built on the interpretation of a long line of male scholars. This Islam is without doubt steeped in misogyny. But it is not the Islam of my parents who brought me up as an independent, trustworthy and critical person. Beyond the rigid and narrow conservative notions of such groups as Wahhabis, Salafis and various traditionalists, there are other Islams – more open to new understandings.

Even during my school days, I could detect that the Qur'an was there solely to be venerated. As a child I remember the Qur'an would be carefully wrapped in a delicate red silk scarf that smelled of incense and was placed at the top of a wardrobe to emphasise its elevated status. We could only touch it if we were in a state of cleansed purity (*wudu*), it could never be dropped or placed in the way of harm. It was sacred and I was taught to love this book and everything it symbolised. I was also a little fearful of it.

I was terrified of not handling it correctly, or, heaven forbid, letting it fall to the floor in a clumsy moment of absent-mindedness. Worse still I lived in perpetual anxiety of mis-pronouncing or making a mistake as I recited it. I particularly dreaded such an error, not just because I was told what a grave sin it was to recite the Qur'an incorrectly, but because I was warned the person listening to you recite will be punished even more severely if they do not identify your mistake and correct you. As more often than not it would be mum or dad listening to me read I was petrified of condemning them to languish in hellfire. And then as I entered puberty I would learn that I must never, ever, ever touch the Qur'an while menstruating. This led to a number of particularly excruciating situations. I can still recall my abject horror when my Religious Education teacher asked me whether I would be able to bring in a copy of the Qur'an for a lesson she was preparing on Islam the next day. I was beside myself trying to think of a way I could transport the Qur'an to school and back without actually touching it. And what if my teacher was also on her period! The potential to sin was just too vast. In the end I explained to her my dilemma to which she was extremely sensitive and said she would plan the lesson for the following week. That same year during a trip to Karachi I was confidently told by an aunty that a menstruating woman should not sit next to a man. There was no explanation as to why. As it turns out, I was soon to realise that if you happened to commit the faux pas of sitting next to a male in Pakistan, whether he was a close relative or a stranger, he would immediately jump up and seat himself elsewhere anyway. Such was the taboo of attempting to seat yourself next to a male full stop, it made the capacity for awkwardness during the monthly menses a moot point!

For a text to be venerated, the assumption has prevailed that its content cannot possibly be questioned by mere mortals, for to do so would be to challenge the word of God. The Qur'an is considered by Muslims to ostensibly offer a guide to living. It is assumed to articulate conduct in intense detail, whether it concerns financial dealings or etiquette in the bathroom. Every aspect of a person's life is covered and for the vast majority of Muslims the Qur'an, along with the recordings of the life and sayings of the Prophet, the hadith, provide a literal and absolute definitive interpretation, which apparently is all that is needed. The book is timeless, the message universal. To argue to the contrary is to veer towards apostasy.

After reading literature at university, it became apparent to me that the passive, literalist absorption of a text is an impoverished approach to reading. Yet this is what the traditional scholars offer as their interpretation of the Qur'an. The valuable contribution of traditional scholars is not in any doubt, but their commentaries have often epitomised the phenomenon of prevailing culture being interpreted through the medium of religion. It is also important that these scholars were men, suggesting the practice of the religion was inevitably framed in the interests of men. I think that is a fair assumption to make. The fact that Islamic classical scholars are exclusively male would explain why the prism of interpretation has been couched in patriarchy. The inevitable consequence of this has been the creation of an Islamic exegesis that is devoid of female input and therefore is heavily weighted in favour of patriarchal concerns. Male scholars had very little access to the lives of women during the classical period and so could not possibly justly illustrate their place in Islam. Women became subjected to commentary in translations and interpretations of the Qur'an and hadith with no way of representing themselves with an authentic voice. The classical scholars in turn influenced contemporary traditional commentaries by people like Maududi and Sayyid Qutb. We are thus caught in a cycle of misogyny that seems to perpetuate itself endlessly.

Reverence for traditional scholars has become an instrument for suppressing criticism. Who would dare criticise al-Ghazali today? Or other venerated luminaries such as Ibn Kathir, al-Razi or al-Tabari? Criticism is made even more difficult when the dominant thinking forbids any attempt to offer a personal perspective on the Qur'an. The seventh century jurist Sa'id ibn Jubayr quotes a hadith attributed to the Prophet's cousin Ibn Abbas who recalls him saying, 'Whoever speaks concerning the Qur'an according to his own opinion, let him expect his seat in the fire.' So there you have it: keep your mouth shut – particularly if you are a woman!

This disapproval of interpreting the Qur'an beyond the confines of traditional exegesis meant that the voices of women were pushed to the margins. As a result, traditional and patriarchal interpretations gained prominence, because society was, frankly, patriarchal. Other voices did exist, but were drowned out or ignored. The distorting effect of this omission is illustrated by a collection of sayings of the Prophet's wife Aisha. These were published by the fourteenth-century scholar Imam Zarkashi and at times contradict some of the statements of the companions and many other so-called sayings of the Prophet branded by the traditionalists. Zarkashi also quotes a hadith that implies every Muslim should take personal responsibility for his or her understanding of Islam: 'The Qur'an is malleable, capable of many types of interpretation. Interpret it, therefore, according to the best possible type.'

There are numerous examples of how misogynist interpretation has become part of Islamic theology. For example, in the Qur'an Adam's wife has no name, she is not held responsible for the transgression that leads to the couple being tempted by Satan to sample fruit from the forbidden tree. Both Adam and Eve share the blame and there is no charge that original sin lies solely at the feet of the woman. Yet in the exegesis of traditional scholars Adam's wife becomes Hawa (Eve) and thus to some extent the story revealed in Genesis is appropriated. The classical collections of hadith by the ninth-century Persian scholars Imam Bukhari and Muslim ibn al-Hajjaj, regarded as two of the most authentic and respected, make constant reference to Eve and depict her as the guilty party in the act of disobedience. They go even further and equate Eve's alleged lead role in the act as symbolic of the capacity of women for weakness and betrayal. Despite having no sanction in the Qur'an this episode has become accepted in traditional scholarship and is used to support a patriarchal and misogynist strand among followers of Islam. Perhaps the makers of SATC2 had consulted these weighty volumes when they came up with Samantha's Eve-like violation of the rules – rules that exist to save her from herself apparently. These manipulations add weight to the 'different but equal' mantra that often merely means that women must conform to society's expectations as, just like the mobile-phone wielding girls in India, they are likely to abuse or are unable to handle any opportunities and freedoms made available to them.

Another example relates to the Qur'anic verses about witnesses. The classical scholars have engineered a patriarchal reading of this verse to infer that a woman is worth half a man in terms of their reliability for testimony – thus further perpetuating the stereotype of the intellectually impaired, emotionally fragile and unreliable female. What nonsense! I cannot believe this is what God intended. The message here is obviously contextual. During the era of the revelation women were not involved in judicial, political and public affairs. They were subjugated and considered inferior. Islam set out to instil equality in society and the Prophet was an exemplar of this. He viewed women as equal in all senses to men. In light of his example and the spirit in which the Qur'an was revealed it seems obvious that the discussion of female testimony in the Qur'an is a technical solution to redress social norms, not a universal comment on a woman's reliability as a witness. In fact Islam set about encouraging women to step forward and give legal testimony. By calling on two women to bear witness, Islam was pushing for women in society to be engaged in greater numbers, to represent themselves and support each other. When considered in relation to the Prophet's overall attitude towards women, this interpretation seems to be the only sensible and fitting one.

Reading Muslim literature on women, one can be forgiven for assuming that Islamic history has produced no female scholars and there are no accounts of women by women. However there are significant examples of female scholars and students of Islam at the time of the Prophet. A tradition of female scholars was also very much present in early Islam and so-called 'alternate' perspectives presented by women were part of the original body of work from which *fiqh*, Islamic jurisprudence, was derived. A comparative reading of hadith alongside the prevailing attitudes held in society lay bare the lie that the Prophet was in any way misogynistic. Women attended consultations held by the Prophet in mosques and argued and debated with him. The level of openness to women and the seeking out of female intellectual input was unprecedented for the time. Sadly, this was never matched in subsequent centuries. We only have to look at the negation of facilities for women in mosques to illustrate how far contemporary Muslims have deviated from the example of the Prophet. The mosque was intended as much more than a place of worship. The Prophet worked to create a space accessible to both men and women that would disseminate advice and guidance. Philosophical and theological discussions, education, and the settling of disagreements were to be made available to all who visited the mosque. The idea that they should become male-only domains with no provision for women is in contradiction with the Prophet's aims. It seems that with the Prophet no longer alive to assert a pro-woman position, the prevailing cultural attitudes of the day meant that scholarship by women – works that are only latterly being rediscovered – became sidelined.

Prolific and influential women scholars included Umm Darda, wife of the well known companion of the Prophet, Abu Darda. She is one female luminary who is mentioned in al-Bukhari as possessing a vigorous intellect and producing great scholarly work. Ibn Kathir writes of her superior knowledge in matters of Islamic law and jurisprudence. Karimah al-Marwaziyyah was one of the later female scholars, and widely regarded as the singular authority on the interpretation of al-Bukhari during her lifetime. Despite her example she was, unfortunately, to herald the dwindling of female influence in the exegesis of the Qur'an as the list of women scholars diminished after her. The most abundant period of female scholarship was undoubtedly during and immediately after the Prophet's lifetime – proof of his rejection of misogyny and nurturing of female education, a tradition exemplified by his wives, all culminating in a blow for any Muslim who denies women an education on the basis of religious teachings. For example, Umrah bint Abdu Rahman was an eminent figure and an authority on the Prophet's wife Aisha's hadith, under whose aegis she had studied since childhood.

Early Islam's female scholars and the voices of the Prophet's wives, particularly Khadijah and Aisha, serve to reset the gender dynamic in the interpretation of Islam which had been so heavily weighted in favour of men. It has been argued, for example, that Aisha's narrative can be read as an illustration of the burdensome nature of polygamy. A growing body of opinion now points to a wealth of evidence indicating that polygamy is not in fact permissible in Islam. We may determine this by examining the historical context in which the Qur'an was revealed. Men in seventh-century Arabia thought nothing of taking tens, possibly even hundreds of wives whether as a result of war, peace treaties, trade agreements or the acquisition of slaves. Women were treated very dismissively and with little or no rights. The Prophet, directed by God, sought to alter this state of affairs. He did this by permitting the taking of more than one wife, up to a maximum of four, only if certain conditions were met. The conditions relate to the treatment of each wife – which must be equal in every respect down to the tiniest detail. Financially and emotionally, a man must treat each wife with unfaltering precision – he must love each woman absolutely equally and must spend the exact amount on each woman financially and materially. These conditions are insurmountable. However much anyone may seek to attest to the contrary I simply cannot believe that it is possible for any man to love more than one woman equally. This impervious pre-requisite renders the feat outside the spirit of Islam.

The Prophet Muhammad, the most exemplary of men and an example for all Muslims, did not find managing a polygamous family to be without its challenges. In her narrations it becomes apparent that Aisha struggled considerably with feelings of jealousy towards Khadijah. Hers was the jealousy of the new wife of a widower who cannot compete with the hallowed and irreproachable memory of a mourned first love. She repeatedly asked the Prophet whether he had reserved his greatest love for Khadijah. This is a further sign that polygamy is not encouraged in Islam, as even the Prophet was not always able to meet the conditions set down by God for polygamous marriage. Certainly, Aisha provides evidence that despite an individual's best intentions, taking more than one wife is not necessarily conducive to a harmonious and fulfilling family life. I am sure many husbands, including my own, would concede that in fact one wife is quite enough!

The Prophet remained monogamously committed to his first wife Khadijah for almost a quarter of a century. She was fifteen years older than him and already a widow, which made their marriage unconventional for that era. He was slow to partake in the pervasive practice of polygamy and only took further wives after Khadijah's death. These were marriages designed to strengthen alliances and establish peace. His devotion to Khadijah was unquestionable, yet Aisha is considered by many commentators to have been his favourite wife. There is a great deal of controversy surrounding Aisha's age upon marriage – which has been estimated between nine and 15 years old. Through twenty-first-century eyes it is shocking to think that the Prophet Muhammad, by now 50, could be betrothed to a child. However, during the Prophet's time marriage at such a young age was unremarkable, and Aisha had already been engaged to someone else. It is important to consider the social mores and culture of the society into which the Prophet was born before passing judgement on his actions or even before blindly imitating them.

This argument is similarly applicable to the much-maligned ruling on adultery. The Qur'an is unequivocal in its assertion that sexual relations should be conducted within the boundaries of marriage. And what of those who express their sexuality outside marriage? The punishment detailed in the Shariah, or Islamic law, is horribly barbaric. Could the Qur'an really sanction the stoning to death of women and men who commit adultery? Modern-day examples from Iran and Afghanistan would suggest that usually it is only the woman who is punished; and in Pakistan, it seems even if a woman is raped she is still considered guilty. Here we see the hypocritical corruption of the text. The Qur'an considers adultery (*zina*) heinous at a time when fornication and sexual proclivity was unbridled. It seeks to deter such chaotic behaviour, particularly because seventh century Arabian society was tribal, with great importance placed on bloodlines. Children and women were dependent on men so regulating sexual activity would increase the likelihood that a man would take responsibility for them.

Yet its method of dissuasion does not translate into actual punishment. This is because a successful conviction for adultery carries impossible conditions. In a similar vein to the appearance of sanctioning polygamy, punishment for adultery becomes a hypothetical charge. Four witnesses of sound mind must bear witness to the act of sexual intercourse for a charge of adultery to be upheld, or a confession from both parties be obtained. The punishment was simply never meant to be realised. In the case of rape, much misogynist hysteria has clouded Islamic jurisprudence. I would argue that the Qur'an makes clear a woman forced into sex is not to be charged with *zina*. The two acts are utterly incomparable and absolutely distinct. To tease out an Islamic ruling on rape, it is imperative to consider the overall message of the Qur'an, the pro-woman outlook of the Prophet, and the consistent efforts to protect women and celebrate sex within marriage. It seems obvious in light of such considerations that rape is not condoned in the Qur'an. To argue otherwise, and to punish a victim of rape as if she was a willing participant, is abhorrent. So why does Islam not position itself more clearly on this issue? I would argue that at the time of the Prophet accusations of rape were difficult to prove or disprove. Gang rape, and rape in public, were not uncommon. Conviction as a result of reliable testimony from four witnesses was therefore conceivable in such cases and rightly so. But we no longer live in pre-Islamic Arabia. Scientific advancement has completely revolutionised rape prosecution cases and it is important to remember that the Qur'an was responding to the specific societal condition of its time.

This is the crux of my argument. To liberate much that goes under the rubric of 'Islam', we need to read the Qur'an and the life of Prophet

Muhammad in the context of time. Throughout history, both the basic sources of Islam have been read through the lens of cultural practices of a seventh century society. Yet even a casual examination and consideration of the historical context of the original sources reveals that they are free from misogyny. The Qur'an cannot be read superficially and was never intended to be approached in such a way. Yet those who interpret the Qur'an in this manner do so to uphold their own agendas of patriarchal control and the oppression of women.

It is hugely seductive to regard the very first believers as the original and authentic Muslims, untainted by cultural baggage. In a world where many Muslims feel disaffected and demonised by the dominant global narrative, it is tempting to find a way to reject contemporary culture and everything it stands for, and to seek solace, direction and validation in a way of life removed from all that is around us. Looking to a romanticised 'perfect' past is by no means exclusive to Muslims. British politicians have long since banged this drum whether by shouting empty slogans such as 'Back to Basics' or by evoking a rose-tinted, post-war era where community spirit resounded and no one was yet bemoaning on the *Daily Mail* website that 'it's PC gawn mad'. However, this yearning to mirror life as it was lived in the Prophet's time seems undermined by a point rarely acknowledged: the Prophet and his companions, indeed the entirety of the early Muslim community, lived in a society in which customs and culture were already in existence. They did not live in a vacuum and it is hardly feasible that even as Islam was revealed and practised they were able to insulate themselves from the pre-Islamic culture into which they were born.

Islam was revealed in an era vastly different from the one in which we live today. We can only discover its meaning and relevance for contemporary times by lifting it out of its seventh century cultural context. I don't live, and don't want to live, in the seventh century. The traditional commentators and their contemporary counterparts do not speak to me or for me. Valuable as their work undoubtedly is, it must be read with an acknowledgement of the cultural attitudes and societal predispositions which they brought to the text. My own reading does not convince me that Islam is misogynistic. But then that's just my reading, compounded by my subjective experience of Islam. No less or more valid than yours, or even, dare I say, Samantha's.

I hear a new *Sex and the City* film is in the pipeline. It may be an idea to inform the Muslim males in Abu Dhabi and elsewhere that their work is cut out to ensure there's no further misunderstanding should the SATC girls choose to come their way. The question is how to pull Islam out of the mire of misogynist practice and interpretation and revive its pro-woman ethos. Not all Muslim males are misogynists; but there are some that definitely need help. After all, when you've starred in the worst film to come out in 2010, you know you've got a long road ahead. Don't tell me it's 'Orientalist stereotypes'. Islam does sex too.

THE TAQWACORE VERSION

Michael Muhammad Knight

I have a religion, and I call my religion Islam. I call myself a Muslim. But the truth is that I've made up Islam for myself. If this matters, if someone making up their own Islam seems unreasonable, you can skip past these pages.

The most frequent accusation that I've heard against my work is that I treat Islam like a buffet. People like to say that I take what I want and leave what doesn't suit my taste. I don't respect Islam, they say, because I only follow the Islam that I've made up, instead of the Islam that they've made up. Whenever my work draws nearer to the Islam that they've made up, or I am kind to the people and ideas that they hold dear, they say, 'Knight has matured as a writer. ' Otherwise, they tell me that I'm confused, that I don't understand real Islam, and that if I looked deeper into my heart, I'd find the truth—the truth, of course, being their truth.

Recently, I learned that one of my friends had passed away, and also that one of my friends whom I believed had passed away was in fact alive. I mention them here because they both represent Islams that work for me.

My friend who had passed away, Ari Said, was reportedly a half-Israeli, half-Palestinian who posed for *Suicide Girls* and called herself the 'Gaza Stripper'. She had 'WEST BANK' tattooed on her knuckles, and 'ANA HARAM' across her chest — meaning 'I am haram,' or 'I am forbidden, prohibited, illegal, sinful'. She died, along with her boyfriend, when they ran a red light and hit another car. I don't know which one was driving, but I had heard more than once that Ari was a crazy driver. Doesn't matter at this point. After her death, I learned that Ari was neither Israeli nor Palestinian, but just a white girl named Lauren who had imagined this conflicted personal mythology for herself and lived it out. For reasons that I'll never get to know, she reinvented herself as a blaspheming Muslim and an anti-Zionist Jew, and lived her new story until it became undeniably real.

The last time I had heard from Ari was over a year earlier, when she shared what she called a 'taqwa-epiphane' with me via Facebook:

right before easter i was sitting on the toilet at this dude's house drinking beers and listening to this guys shitty metal and a commercial came on for those cadbury easter eggs. I yelled out '**** JESUS' and then immediately wondered why the hell I yelled that. I don't particularly care for Christians, which i feel guilty for because all the reasons i have for not liking them you could really apply to any religion but i think maybe it was the fact that it was the commercialized bunny-ness of the whole thing. Then i felt sort of bad, like it's one thing to swear allah when i love allah but jesus is like, some people's god and i felt like i had done some sort of horrible blasphemy because it wasn't even my right to blaspheme that dude.

my mom is a christian convert and one of the most pure humans i know in regards to their spirituality. A week after my turret blasphemy, my mom had something really awful happen to her and i was comforting her and all of a sudden she just screamed obscenities at god and i thought 'wow, my mom is totally taqwacore right now.' And then it hit me that taqwacore isn't really about being muslim or punk but having such a pure relationship with whatever deity you value you can shout obscenities and know that at the end of the tantrum your whatever is still going to love you and love you despite of or for you saying fuck him.

This strange word that Ari used, 'taqwacore', was invented by me, for use in a work of fiction full of Muslims doing bad things. It comes from the Arabic *taqwa*, meaning consciousness of God, and 'core', the suffix for numerous subgenres of punk rock. The word has come to represent Muslim punk rockers, but more importantly, as Ari pointed out, a distinctly punk way of handling religion. A way of telling idols that you love them — and meaning it — before you smash them to pieces.

Ari was taqwacore before anyone had made up a name for it, and she was more true to taqwacore than anyone who liked to throw the word around. 'Rest in peace' won't work for Ari; if Allah welcomes her into the gardens of paradise, angels are getting their jaws broken.

Taqwacore held me together at a time when I did not know if I could count myself as a Muslim. My conversion experience was so typical that I'm now embarrassed that it hurt so much: you're mixed up, lost, trying to find your way in life, and then the ultimate truth comes and slaps you in the face, and then you give it everything that you have, and you push and push and think you're going to sprint the whole way, and then you fall. Instead of getting up, many of us just lie there watching the people who can still go, and we wonder what's wrong with us.

Whenever I'm asked to explain my first disillusionment with Islam, I give different answers. Yes, it was wounding to learn of the sectarianism and political turmoil that divided the early community, and it was confusing to read accounts of early Muslims doing things that don't vibe well with the world in which I live. The real problem was that I wasn't allowed to have problems; because Islam was the ultimate truth, and the Qur'an promised us that Allah had perfected our religion for us, questions were mischief. The mosque squeezed so tight that I just fell out.

After my initial failure as a Muslim, I started to hang out with the punk rock kids, and they taught me that I did not have to apologise for myself. I liked the punk mythology about being who you are and never compromising for anything, and hoped to mix up that spirit with what I had known as Islam in my mosque. So I wrote a novel, a sloppy, amateurish punk-rock novel with no serious plot, just confused Muslim characters who wanted things. This was the same year that my schizophrenic father revealed his belief that I was F. Scott Fitzgerald's reincarnation (though my father advised against using the word 'reincarnation'), so I had started reading a lot of Fitzgerald and desperately trying—as many people tend to do with schizophrenics, and problematically so—to find some brilliant mystery in my father's delusion, a big secret that would explain everything. The Fitzgerald fixation resulted in my Muslim punk rock novel doubling as an immature tribute to *The Great Gatsby*.

I started out distributing the novel myself in punk-rock DIY fashion, with photocopied and spiral-bound books in the trunk of my car. It brought me to some good and confused people, Muslims like Ari Said, Muslims who loved Islam even when they weren't sure if they believed in God, Muslims who drank and prayed, all kinds of Muslims. Sometimes we prayed to Allah, sometimes we prayed to nothing. We had no consistency, no platform, no shared ideas of where Islam should go; the only point was to have a space in which we didn't need to have answers and no one could impose a measuring stick upon us to see if we qualified as Muslims. In the taqwacore cipher, I've prayed with queer Muslims, pork-eating Muslims, atheist Muslims, and Hindus. I've smoked weed with good Muslim kids in the good Muslim uniforms, the right beards and headscarves.

In my experience of taqwacore, the whole religion was flipped upside down and pulled apart. There was no legitimacy or authority owned by anyone that could make a difference to us. Taqwacore wasn't about accepting or rejecting Islam, because who knew what we were accepting or rejecting? Taqwacore was like a tornado blasting through the mosque, knocking down the walls so that 'inside' and 'outside' ceased to have any meaning, and scattering all of the pages from all of the books. We just walked through the rubble, picking up pages and pieces of pages where we found them, with no clue where they belonged.

Confused kids like Ari Said would write to me to say that the taqwacore thing made them feel less alone. They had the same impact on me, because I had written my cheap book from a position of complete loneliness, wondering if I could ever wear the label of 'Muslim' again, and wondering whether the label even mattered. To find out that there were real taqwacore kids like Ari Said, who felt the same isolation and confusion and asked the same questions, did more for me than providing answers; it put the question to sleep, because nothing was at stake.

My other friend, the one who turned out to be alive after I thought that he was dead, was born near the end of the 1940s and named John Kennedy. In 1965, he was arrested for stealing a car and found to be mentally unwell. They sent him to a hell-hole called Matteawan State Hospital for the Criminally Insane, which was where he met Allah.

The particular Allah that he met was a man who had been born Clarence Edward Smith, and had become Clarence 13X after joining the Nation of Islam at its Harlem mosque, under the leadership of its then-minister Malcolm X. Before his own arrival at Matteawan, Clarence had left the Nation of Islam, renamed himself Allah, and began teaching his own doctrines to street kids and hustlers. When arrested and charged with possession of marijuana and swinging a piece of wood at a man's head, Clarence told the judge that he was Allah and that no one could charge Allah. The judge found Clarence to be insane and shipped him up to Matteawan.

The institution was notorious for its abuses and torture, and young John Kennedy found himself beaten and drugged into a coma. When he regained consciousness, he found Clarence standing over him.

It should be said here that Clarence, being a former member of the Nation of Islam, had been taught that black men were gods and white men were devils. And John Kennedy was a white man. Clarence told John, 'You are a righteous man.' John answered, 'You must be God.' Clarence told John that as a matter of fact, yes, he was God, and that he would teach John the knowledge of himself. He shared the secret Nation of Islam lessons with John and then declared John to be Azreal, his death-angel, whose divinely appointed role would be to capture the wrong-doers.

John Michael Kennedy became Azreal in 1966, and he has been loyal to the culture ever since. I found Azreal in Harlem in 2004 and he shared what he had been given, naming me Azreal Wisdom; in his teacher's number-play, 'Wisdom' signifies the number 2. So I'm the second Azreal, the heir to Allah's death-angel. I take the name seriously, because I know that the man was waiting forty years to give that to someone.

Clarence's teachings had spawned a whole movement, the Five Percenters. The name comes from a Nation of Islam lesson stating that while eighty-five percent of society would be the 'deaf, dumb, and blind, slaves to mental death and power,' enslaved by a bloodsucking ten percent, the remaining five percent could see through all the poisonous dogmas and liberate themselves and others. In 1967, when Clarence was released back to the city, he told his Five Percenters that he wasn't the only Allah; the Five Percenters had to be their own Allahs, because who can be your Allah but you?

The Five Percenters offered me a truth that I had already known, the same truth that I had attempted to express with punk rock, and they were able to wrap it up in a quasi-Islamic symbol system that spoke to my personal back story. The truth is this: you are God. There's no 'mystery god' over you; it's just you. Punk rock says, 'No gods, no masters', and the Five Percenters say, 'I God, I Master'. Allah, the man that I call Allah, taught that his name was an acronym for 'Arm Leg Leg Arm Head', pointing out the divinity in the human form. He taught that 'Islam' meant 'I Self Lord Am Master', meaning that no imam has any greater connection to the Mind of the universe than you.

As I read them, the Five Percenters offered an Islamic postmodernism, in which we can still have God even after realising that a word like 'God' had none of the transcendence that we assigned to it, that transcendence beyond our own histories and contexts was impossible. We are God because we cannot know God outside ourselves, because nothing can be interpreted without being changed by the interpreter. No one can claim possession of an absolute, immutable 'Islam'. There's only Islam as I know it and Islam as you know it.

There's an oral tradition claiming that the man known as Allah had allowed his Five Percenters to engage any religious tradition, as long as they knew that they were the ultimate power of that tradition, rejecting anyone's attempt to bring their minds 'under the capture'. The former Clarence 13X, an exile from his mosque, provided me with a new way of finding peace within mine; ironically, it was a man who called himself Allah who brought me to that other Allah, the more Abrahamic one.

My gatekeeper to the Five Percenter tradition, John 'Azreal' Kennedy, has spent most of the last fifty years between homelessness and various forms of incarceration. If I go long enough without hearing from him, at some point it becomes reasonable to think that he might be dead. When Azreal stopped checking in with the Five Percenters, we just took it for granted that he was gone. A couple years went by in what I thought was my post-Azreal life. Then, in the same weekend that Ari Said died, a Five Percent elder named Allah B let me know that he had heard from Azreal; Allah's death-angel was at a hospital somewhere in New Jersey. Allah builds and destroys and gives and takes away.

In these two figures — some girl named Lauren who became Ari Said, covered in Arabic tattoos and providing shelter to wayward Muslims, and John Kennedy, who met Allah in a sanitarium and become the angel of death — I have my own Islamic community that empowers me to both embrace and reject the tradition as I see fit.

I am often asked whether I consider myself a 'practising Muslim'. The question usually comes during interviews with non-Muslim journalists who somehow possess a remarkably clear idea of what 'practising Muslims' do. Assuming that I share in this understanding, they ask without giving the question any weight, treating it as a softball, nice and easy and requiring nothing more than a simple yes or no.

I tell them that I have no idea.

The truth is that I do call myself a practising Muslim, but this is strictly by my own calculations, which are socially and culturally meaningless. When people ask whether I'm 'practising', they only want to know how well I match up to what they imagine all other Muslims to be doing.

How can I answer them? The truth is that I don't know what constitutes Islamic practice, and these people never show me their own measuring sticks or explain their criteria. They just ask the question like it's self-evident.

I do my best. It at least seems reasonable to assume that by 'Islamic practice', they mean deliberate actions and behaviours that are distinctly and undeniably Islamic. This would mean that unless participation in a certain action could effectively separate Muslims from non-Muslims, it's not enough to make me a practicing Muslim. The Prophet spoke of a woman who was rewarded by God for being kind to her cat, and I try to display compassion for animals in remembrance of this story; but since Buddhism also teaches kindness towards animals, I can't call myself a practicing Muslim just because Islam inspired me to treat cats well. When I try to help people and give charity, it's with mindfulness of the twelfth century Islamic theologian and philosopher al-Ghazali, who wrote that we should strive to imitate the Qur'an's names for God, including attributes such as 'The Merciful' and 'The Generous'. However, if Christians are also encouraged by their tradition to be merciful and generous, my charity isn't 'Islamic' — at least not until I give to others in an Islamically structured way, such as the practice of *zakat*.

Islam says that we should not be assholes, and I often find this to be extremely difficult; but because most other religions also discourage people from being assholes, my efforts to resist being an asshole fail to mark me as a practicing Muslim. I couldn't answer the journalists with, 'Sure, I'm a practising Muslim, because I try to be a nice person'. People need something more clearly observable.

The matter of 'practice' often begins and ends with ritual. Do you put your head on the floor like a Muslim, at the times and places that Muslims normally do so, and do you say the right words at the right moments? I like praying with my brothers and sisters in Islam; but when alone, I do not pray with consistency. Nor do I always make a respectable effort to face the right direction. I have also prayed without properly washing first. When it comes to Islamic prayer, I guess I do practice, but poorly and without discipline.

It might be easier if I cared about things like *fiqh* (jurisprudence), which would allow me to unite my practices under a proper name and its established authority. On the occasions that I pray, I move and speak as I was taught, in accordance with one of the four major Sunni schools, but I am not sure which one. I'm guessing that I pray like Sunnis of the Hanafi school; but when I have access to a *turba*, a small clay disk upon which Shia Muslims prostrate their foreheads in prayer, I use it. Sunnis or Shias who exclude each other in claiming ownership of 'authentic' Islamic practice are not going to be satisfied with me bouncing back and forth between them. There's no legitimacy in the space between monoliths.

I have also prayed behind a woman imam, Amina Wadud. For many, many Muslim men and women, gender-integrated prayer is a clear rebellion against Islam; but I only do it because I am a Muslim. I have a need for Muslim community, to share in Islam with the people that I call my sisters and brothers, and to have a space in which our ritual acts correspond to the world and ethics in which we live. This 'rebellion' is nothing but Islam.

My most radical acts of subversion are thus Islamic practices, and what one group calls practice, another calls deviation. In one of the acts seen as most definitive of a 'practising Muslim', I performed *hajj*, the pilgrimage to Mecca. But I have also made other pilgrimages, visiting sites that many, but not all, Muslims would recognise as 'Islamic': the tombs of Sufi saints in Pakistan, Syria, and Ethiopia. Shrines remain a controversial topic in Islamic discourses; for Muslims that would get tagged with labels like 'Salafi' and 'Wahhabi', shrines encourage idolatry and are forbidden deviations from Islam. For others, these are the tombs of great Muslims who possessed spiritual and often physical lineages to the Prophet; if that's not Islam, what is? Muslims love these shrines, and Muslims also blow up these shrines. Whether shrine-hopping qualifies one as a practising Muslim, as with anything else, depends on who you ask.

'Are you a believing Muslim? '

To this one, I answer, 'Who gives a damn? '

Being Muslim isn't always about what I believe. I don't actually believe in a dude with wings named Gabriel who flies around delivering messages to people from the Creator of the Universe; but if someone recites the Qur'an, it can still bring me to tears. I don't know what that's about. I went to Mecca and blew eight thousand of my own US dollars on that trip just to walk where Abraham and Hajar walked, and I'd cry thinking of them, but I don't really believe that these people ever existed. I went back and forth between the two hills like Hajar, I went to the spot where Abraham's footprints are enshrined, and I threw stones at walls to imitate Abraham's rejection of the Devil; and the whole time, I regarded the stories as fiction. It was the meaning that I invested in these stories, not a belief in them as historical, that brought me to Mecca.

I feel as Muslim as ever, but I don't deal with belief so much anymore. I've gone up and down with it too many times; eventually I realised that I'd have to find a way to feel about Islam that did not depend on Islam's claims actually being 'true'. I do love Islam, and I love being Muslim; I love praying with my sisters and brothers, I love the shared world that we create for each other, and I love the inner language that Islam has given me. When I'm alone and I want to pray, or just sit in a field and freak out on God, I can only do it through the concepts given to me by Islam. Islam is my language, my script; to decide that I no longer have a right to claim Islam would be like deciding that I no longer wanted to understand the English language. At this point, it's not voluntary. Whether I speak belief or disbelief, it will always be as a Muslim.

For me to remain unstable on articles of belief has actually allowed me to see much more of Islamic tradition than many of my sisters and brothers who remain committed to one particular strand. I've lost any concept of 'orthodox' or 'mainstream' Islam; for me, Islam is Islam, and it's all Islam. I've been able to drift between Sunni and Shia, Five Percenter and Sufi, Salafi and progressive. Because I don't assign myself authority to declare anyone a non-Muslim, I can take the best from any mosque and leave behind what I don't want — which means that indeed, I do treat Islam as a buffet. Personally, I'm okay with this. I can't really defend myself against such a criticism if I don't actually see it as criticism. I sometimes want my Islam to be more, but for now, I do my best with what I have.

Islam gives me rituals that both bind me to my community and bring me into sacred space, symbols and texts that touch my heart, and stories that help me to become human. My life is better for being Muslim, for having access to this tradition. I am a better person for loving Islam. I might sort out the belief stuff later, insha'Allah; in the meantime, I think that my spiritual instability leads to a more pro-Islam position than any Muslim who treats faith as a zero-sum game. I asked myself a question that they won't bring themselves to consider, a question that creates possibilities beyond their vision: If this religion is just made up, can it still offer anything?

So that's my Islam right now. I hang out with crazy Muslim punk rockers and a guy who met Allah in a mental institution, I pray with the weirdoes, I have no sectarian attachments, or too many, and I don't always know what I believe. And this is the best that it has ever been. Seriously — I became Muslim just a hair under twenty years ago, and the peace is just starting to come in. I've worked long and hard to earn my flake-out time, my new golden age when all mosques are mine and no mosques are mine, when I can remain spiritually homeless but always find shelter somewhere. It's only now, after all the ridiculous fire of teen conversion, the soul breaking disillusionment, the obscene rebellions and heresies, the doubts and confusions and confessions, that I am finally holding myself to my own scorecard.

Two weeks ago, I received an email from a Muslim who has read one of my books, informing me that I do not qualify for his Muslim clubhouse, that I'm a *kafr* (unbeliever) and I don't know true Islam. I answered that I've my own Islam, and it works great, and he can have his clubhouse all to himself.

DO YOU BELIEVE?

Soha Al-Jurf

'Anyone who does not doubt will not investigate, and anyone who does not investigate cannot see, and anyone who does not see will remain in blindness and error.'

Abu Hamid al-Ghazali

I always thought that Islam is something in which you either believe, or you don't believe. If you want to call yourself a 'Muslim', it's sort of an all-or-nothing deal. You're either in or you're out. I thought that the path of a believer, particularly a Muslim believer, is a straight path. You're placed on it at birth, and you just start walking. You know precisely where you are going, and you know which steps to take to get there. You don't wander, veer in any direction, or get lost. Contrary to what I was actually experiencing in my own life, the path of a believer was not, as far as I understood, characterised by clawing one's way through a lifetime of doubt and disillusionment, hoping to arrive at a resting place.

The way that Islam was presented to me by many Muslims, it seemed that belief didn't come from a personal path of inquiry and revelation, but by accepting what others believed without challenging them – by simply offering one's mind as an empty receptacle for another person's views. It seemed that every time I questioned or expressed doubt towards the views of others on Islam, my views were typically perceived as blasphemous, and they were immediately dismissed. Or, rather, I was immediately dismissed.

Having been raised in a non-Muslim country, I may have been at a disadvantage when it came to finding an Islam that I could connect with. It's not that I was offered no education about Islam at all, I just got an abridged

85

version of it, imparted to me sporadically from various sources in my immediate and extended community. My knowledge of Islam was then subjected to filtration through a Western paradigm, and, since I am a woman, a Western feminist paradigm.

The issue of being a woman in Islam is an issue I contend with both inside and outside of my Muslim community. Between defending myself within my community and defending my community against the ignorance of people outside of it, I feel as if I am in constant battle. I battle against Muslim men who tell me how to dress and who harass me when I choose to dress differently. And then I turn around and battle against the so-called Western feminists who don't recognise that a Muslim woman's choice to wear the veil – when it is not forced upon her by men who are corrupting the actual dictates of Islam, which clearly state that men cannot force women to veil – is an expression of her personal freedom.

Beyond the challenges of sorting through the conflicting messages about a woman's rights and restrictions in a Muslim context, the day-to-day, moment-by-moment discourse within Muslim communities often devolves into debates about whether specific behaviours are or are not *haram*, that is forbidden. Topics range from trying to come to a consensus on whether or not and in what contexts men and women are allowed to share public spaces, to whether or not having statues or paintings in your home is a sin. These discussions are often presented as if they are intended to guide people towards righteousness. Personally, I experience these discussions as interminable arguments about what is or is not punishable by God, with little attention to whether these religious decrees bear any logic or relevance to living an ethical existence in our current social and cultural contexts.

By the time all of the fragments of information had gone through a process of interpretation by a long string of Muslim and non-Muslim individuals with very specific opinions about what Islam is and is not, what it requires of its believers and does not require, and what it exemplifies and does not exemplify, Islam had been reduced to a set of rigid, contradictory concepts that seemed to have nothing to do with anything holy at all. This was not a religion that I could relate to.

My difficulty in connecting with my religion was of course exacerbated by the fact that my Arabic is not strong enough to read or understand the Qur'an in its original language. When I read the Qur'an in English translation, I extracted virtually no meaning from it, in spite of the fact that people who read it in Arabic say that it is the most profoundly beautiful writing ever written. I'm always surprised and a little bit envious when people who convert to Islam say that they read the Qur'an in English translation and found the teachings to reveal a profound truth and beauty that they knew with all their hearts was the only path. So much so that they felt compelled to give up their own faith, often alienating their families and communities, to become Muslim. I admire their clarity and conviction. I want to experience that kind of knowing – I want to read the Qur'an through their eyes. I seem to be missing something that might lead to the settling of my heart.

It is a known phenomenon that it takes scholars many years of study to understand the complex language that is used in the Qur'an. Even those who can read it in its original language cannot fully comprehend it. All religions and spiritual traditions are, as far as I know, typically based on texts and rituals that are difficult for lay people to interpret, whether that is because they were written in complex or archaic language, or because of the historical contexts in which they were introduced. Followers of a particular faith rely on the guidance of religious scholars, spiritual teachers, schools, elders, and other members of their spiritual communities to 'translate' the religious teachings into principles and practices that can be understood and implemented by the community. As a result, it's difficult to separate a religion from the interpretation of that religion by its believers, particularly when they are quoting its sacred texts to support whatever claims they are making—whether those claims are sincere attempts to guide themselves and others towards an ethical existence, or corrupted views that serve dishonorable intentions. Islam is plagued by individuals who claim that they alone possess the 'correct' interpretation of scriptures.

Moreover, these believers are adamant that Islam is the One True Way and that its teachings must not be questioned or adulterated in any way but simply followed as written. But how can we follow what is written when there is disagreement about how to interpret the writing? Furthermore, it is difficult to know how much of what is written can or should be taken as symbolic, rather than taken literally. Thus, Islam is a religion that invites both contemplation and debate, while everyone simultaneously insists that there can be no contemplation or debate about something that is considered to be the Essential Truth.

I have often heard Muslims say, 'the moment you imagine or compare God to anything, then He (the candidate to Divinity) is not God'. In the Qur'an, it is written that, 'No vision can grasp Him...He is above all comprehension' (6:103). Can there be one true way for all human beings to interpret and implement communication from a Source that is unseen and, by definition, incomprehensible to the human mind?

Apparently, some people think there can be. Nowhere is this more evident than in people's persistent fixation on incessantly reiterating the punishments or rewards that await all of us in the hereafter. I recently read an article by a clearly well-intentioned and earnest Muslim writer that was part of a series on heaven and hell. The article I read happened to be one about hell, in which the author provided a detailed description of what awaits the sinners in the afterlife. The punishments included 'shoes made of fire that will burn your brain' and food that will 'boil the intestines like scalding water'. He stated that, according to a hadith in *Sahih al Bukhari*, 999 out of every 1000 people will go to hell, for behaviours ranging from murder to arriving late for prayer. 'A believer's life is based on both hope for Allah's mercy and fear of His punishment', the author wrote. 'Go through the Qur'an; nearly every other page contains something about Paradise and Hell, and the descriptions of both are equal...' This fact, he emphasised, is one of the numeric miracles of the Qur'an. So, I went through the Qur'an. Frankly, the descriptions of hell seem to predominate, although perhaps only because they are so much more vivid.

I later read one of the author's pieces about Paradise, which he said is described in a hadith as a place whose inhabitants 'will neither have differences nor hatred amongst themselves; their hearts will be as if one heart'. In the Qur'an, he continued, Paradise is described as a place where Allah 'will remove whatever is in [people's] breasts of resentment, so they will be brothers, on thrones, facing each other'. These concepts are beautiful, and they reflect a religion that I could easily identify with. But why do these images have to be balanced by visions of hellfire? What purpose does that serve?

Islam is replete with disturbing images, and, for some ill-fated reason, I seem to have been surrounded by people who revel in sharing them. It's almost as if people develop a strange fascination with this gruesome imagery, like watching violence on television or the aftermath of an accident on the freeway. Apparently these depictions, whether they are a true account of what awaits us for our 'sins' or not, are meant to keep us on the virtuous path. As far as I'm concerned, this type of teaching is like forcing children to watch war movies to instruct them about peace. It makes me want to close the Book and read something else. Something a bit more cheerful.

Of course, my questioning the Qur'an's messages about hellfire is precisely the behaviour that many Muslims find irreverent. But I don't intend my questioning as a subversive effort to revile God or that which is sacred or holy. On the contrary, my heart's desire to connect with that which is holy informs all that I do. I am somebody who wants to believe. I want there to be One Truth, by which all of humanity is guided. I want all of the pieces to come together and form a cohesive narrative.

As I was raised Muslim, I want to believe in Islam—that Islam is the path to the Oneness I seek. I know many people who find peace, comfort, and a sense of justice in Islam. But I've never been able to see how a system of punishment and reward, sins and good deeds, or fear of a Being who is described as Infinitely Compassionate, could lead my heart towards Union.

And so I separated myself from my religion. Years ago, I opted out. Or at least I tried to.

The problem is you can't really separate yourself from yourself. As strange as this may seem to people who view me as a progressive, Western-influenced woman, my attempts to extricate myself from my identity as a Muslim felt as if I was trying to remove myself from my own skin. I felt as if I was peeling myself away from something that I consider to be an intrinsic identity—I identify with being Muslim in the same way I identify with being Arab, Palestinian, or Palestinian/Arab-American. These are all identities I can choose not to cultivate, focus attention on, or feed in any way. But that will not change the fact that turning away from my religion or culture of origin means that I am living in opposition to, or at least, withdrawing from, these identities. Rejecting who I am does not mean I am no longer that person; it only means that I am rejecting who I am.

My ambivalence about how to reconcile my Muslim identity with how I wanted to live my life, both practically and spiritually, was evidenced in the language I started to use when people asked me about my religion. Rather than simply saying 'I'm Muslim', I would say: 'I'm a non-practicing Muslim'.

'I was raised Muslim'. 'My parents are Muslim'. But the ambiguity with which I tried to explain my experience of myself as a Muslim wasn't actually describing the complexity of my relationship to Islam in an authentic way. It didn't tell the whole story; it only expressed part of it. Sharing only a portion of the totality of my identity felt as if I was cutting myself off from parts of myself; it led to further isolation and feelings of separateness.

I cannot find freedom by locking up a part of myself and turning away from it as if it doesn't exist. Being separate, cut off, or cut out is the opposite of Oneness. Wholeness. Okay-ness. One of the predominant ways in which human beings punish or torture other human beings is to isolate them. Human beings were created in such a way that they rely on connection for survival—not just physically, but spiritually and emotionally as well. Separateness is the epitome of Hellfire, whether that separateness is from others, from oneself, or from God.

William Wordsworth describes our separation from God-Consciousness in his poem *Ode on Intimations of Immortality from Recollections of Early Childhood*:

Our birth is but a sleep and a forgetting;
The Soul that rises with us, our life's Star,
Hath had elsewhere its setting
And cometh from afar;
Not in entire forgetfulness,
And not in utter nakedness,
But trailing clouds of glory do we come
From God, who is our home:
Heaven lies about us in our infancy!
Shades of the prison-house begin to close
Upon the growing Boy,
But he beholds the light, and whence it flows,
He sees it in his joy;
The Youth, who daily farther from the east
Must travel, still is Nature's priest,
And by the vision splendid
Is on his way attended;
At length the Man perceives it die away,
And fade into the light of common day.

Wordsworth echoes the philosophy of many spiritual traditions in this poem: we come from God, and our path will lead us back to God. But the longer we spend in this world the more our egos become enslaved by their own defenses against the inevitable insecurities that result from the utter chaos that characterises life. As we attempt to negotiate the realities of war, the complexities of human relationships, and the mundane activities of daily living, it becomes more and more difficult to remember what we are trying to get back to. We are haunted by a nagging emptiness that signals a desire to return to someone or something or somewhere that would make us whole, but it doesn't occur to most of us in this modern world that what we are longing to return to is God.

Whether my desire to touch the sacred was within me as a result of religious teachings or in spite of them, there was restlessness in my soul that signaled a longing to reconnect with something from which I appeared to have drifted. Although I felt suspicious of religion, there was no question that I was seeking a path to Connectedness. But the very path that was known to me as a way to reach some form of a benevolent and eternal Source was betraying me. Islam, which was supposed to eradicate my separateness, was offering me no entry point – no basis on which I could build a foundation of faith.

When I shared my feelings of disconnectedness with other Muslims, they told me to pray. Prayer, they said, was the most profound way to connect with God. Certainly I could see the wisdom in stopping whatever I was doing, five times a day, to perform ablutions, dress in modest clothing, find a quiet place, and perform a ritualised pattern of movements with prescribed recitations. But when I prayed, I felt ridiculous. I didn't understand most of the words I was saying. I could never remember which *raka'a* I was on, whether it was time to kneel, prostrate, bend, or stand. Whenever I stood up after a prostration, I stepped on the hem of my prayer skirt, pulling it halfway down my legs. When I moved in any direction at all, my head covering slid off, revealing most of my hair. I didn't see how I could achieve an authentic relationship with God when I felt so self-conscious about His prescribed methods to reach Him. I kept coming back to the conclusion that Islam just did not work for me.

Yet, the more I tried to separate from Islam, the more fragmented I seemed to feel. Rather than finding freedom from the constraints of a

religion that seemed to be more punitive than compassionate, I was beginning to feel more and more imprisoned by the walls of separation I was
placing between myself and something that was elusive and not fully
known to me, but from which I thought I needed to distance myself. I
couldn't seek refuge in the very thing I was denouncing in hopes that it
would ease the pain of my denunciation. This fragmentation was what
caused me to become a seeker.

Like many people in the West who are seeking a spiritual practice that is
outside their religions of origin, I felt drawn to Buddhism. In the United
States, Buddhism has become known as a spiritual practice of peace and
compassion, based in loving-kindness, self-awareness, and the transformation of suffering that results from our attachments to the illusions of this
manifest world.

I studied the teachings of the Vietnamese Buddhist monk of the Mahay-
ana tradition, Thich Nhat Hanh, as well as Pema Chodren, who is an
American nun who practices Tibetan Buddhism, in addition to many others, through their books and recordings of dharma talks. They 'translated'
Buddhism into language that could be understood and practiced in a Western context. The language that Thich Nhat Hanh used to describe Buddhist
principles was particularly instrumental in the development of my understanding of compassion and self-transformation. In his *Five Mindfulness
Trainings*, he writes about the Buddhist precepts that command people not
to kill, steal, use false speech, engage in sexual misconduct, or ingest
intoxicating substances. These are all themes that recur throughout Islamic
texts, often with severe consequences for breaching them. Backbiting, for
example, is considered to be one of the most egregious behaviours in
Islam, and it is referenced frequently. In the Qur'an, the gravity of engag-
ing in gossip and slander is made clear by comparing it to 'eating the flesh
of your dead brother' (43:12). In a hadith in *Sahih al Bukhari*, the Prophet
Muhammad is quoted as saying, 'a man might speak a word without thinking about its implications, but because of it, he will plunge into the Hellfire
further than the distance between the east and the west'. Certainly, Islam's
sentiments are noble. However, I question whether these extreme descriptions are necessary to make the point. By contrast, Thich Nhat Hanh
phrases these same principles of right speech in the following words:
'aware of the suffering caused by unmindful speech and the inability to

listen to others, I am committed to cultivate loving speech and deep listening in order to bring joy and happiness to others and relieve others of their suffering. Knowing that words can create happiness or suffering, I am committed to learn to speak truthfully, with words that inspire self-confidence, joy, and hope. I am determined not to spread news that I do not know to be certain and not to criticise or condemn things of which I am not sure. I will refrain from uttering words that can cause division or discord, or that can cause the family or the community to break. I will make all efforts to reconcile and resolve all conflicts, however small'.

Finally, someone was speaking in a language that I could understand.

The principles of Buddhism are not focused on posthumous punishment or reward for one individual, but, rather, on every individual's place within the whole. Buddhism teaches that in order to live a peaceful existence and to support others in doing the same, we must transform our own afflictions. It is about being present. It is about connecting with the self, connecting with all that is outside of the self, and recognising that there is no separation or distinction between that which is self and that which is beyond the self.

Although the Prophet's teachings echo these sentiments, and references to the same principles about kindness, compassion, and right-living are abundant in Islam, Thich Nhat Hanh's teachings appeal to one's rationality, rather than to fear – if I am aware that my behaviours or thoughts cause suffering, either to myself or to others, why would I choose to continue those behaviours? We may need guidance to learn different ways to handle our afflictions and to re-connect with our true selves and our inner wisdom, but this can be accomplished without admonishing those seeking guidance.

Both Islam and Buddhism guide individuals toward seeing that our true nature is often veiled by the false self – the personality that has been crafted over the years as a buffer between the hardships of a human existence and our tender souls. Both emphasise that it is simply the nature of a human being to continuously return to the habit energies of anger, doubt, fear, jealousy, and despair. Both traditions focus on disciplined practices that are meant to transform our habituated suffering. If we don't transform it here, it keeps repeating itself, both in this lifetime and beyond this lifetime.

After several years of Buddhist practice, I became convinced that Buddhist and Islamic principles were not divergent, although their delivery often was. Although I continued to practice Buddhism, describing myself as a 'Buddhist' felt inauthentic; I still felt unsettled about my religious identity. At that point, I became 'a Muslim who practices Buddhism'. 'A Muslim whose beliefs are more in line with Buddhism'. 'A Muslim who does sitting meditation'. I was borrowing the teachings of another practice to compensate for what I felt was lacking in my own.

I've often thought there is purity, a naivety, a clean slate in coming into a religion or a culture that is not one's own. There is a built-in deference that comes from not knowing too much – it's what Buddhists refer to as 'Beginner's Mind'. Americans who convert to Islam as adults, for example, never experienced a lifetime of 'Being Muslim in America'. They were spared that legacy of shame. On some level, they are granted the freedom of non-attachment that comes from not having been raised with any of the baggage that comes along with exposure to the religion within certain cultural contexts. Although they may not realise it, this allows them to extract the parts of Islam that work for them and discard the rest. Without being fully aware of it, this is what I was doing with Buddhism. The fact of being an 'insider' in relation to Islam somehow made it so that I simultaneously knew too much, and not enough. I didn't know how to afford myself the freedom of choosing an Islam that I could believe in.

I have been indoctrinated to believe that, as a Muslim, any attempt to extract the parts that work for me and disregard the parts that don't make me a non-believer in the eyes of many Muslims, or, at least, a bad Muslim. Until recently, it didn't occur to me that I might have to struggle, both within myself and against the demands of others, to create, refine, reconsider, restore, or revitalise my beliefs over the course of a lifetime. My experience as a 'Muslim who practices Buddhist principles' gave me a context in which to begin to interpret Islam differently.

There is a verse in the Qur'an (43:36-37) that says, 'And whosoever is blinded from remembrance of the most Merciful – we appoint for him a devil and he is to him a companion. And indeed, the devils avert them from the way [of guidance], while they think they are rightly guided'. Many people, of course, choose to interpret this verse literally; I certainly did for many years. However, seen through the lens of some of the Buddhist principles I had learned, I started to interpret verses like this one as symbolic lessons about connection or disconnection from our Ultimate Source –

our 'devils' are our demons, our afflictions: our anger, our jealousy, our pettiness, our cravings, our despair. They take us away from our true nature — our God-Consciousness. They create an illusory world in which we become attached to the stories our minds create, losing sight of the purity of our own hearts.

As I delved more deeply into Buddhism, I began to see more and more parallels between the principles of Buddhism and those of Islam, partly by re-interpreting the language in which many of the teachings were transmitted, and partly by committing to reading and listening to more Islamic teachings, rather than turning away from them the moment I read or heard something that was in opposition to what I considered to be compassionate, heart-centred being. The more I learned about Buddhism, the more I realised that, like Islam, the same message can be perceived completely differently, depending on how language is used and interpreted, and the biases of the person who is interpreting it. Like Islam, Buddhism is a complex spiritual system that is drawn from historic events and intricate texts that are complicated to understand, and, therefore, subject to interpretation by scholars and practitioners. Buddhism is not a singular, unchanging belief system; it is comprised of many different traditions, schools, and methods that vary from teacher to teacher, community to community, and country to country. Buddhism, therefore, cannot be reduced to one set of practices and principles. Although various sects share commonalities in their underlying tenets, different Buddhist Schools often reach extremely divergent conclusions from reading the same texts and listening to the same stories.

With my Beginner's Mind, I was ignorant about the number of different sects within Buddhism that held divergent views from those I had been taught. In some sects of Buddhism, for example, there is a concept of hell, or purgatory, called a *Naraka*. *Narakas* are places of darkness and torment in the underworld, where souls are sent for expiation of their sins. Sins, in the Buddhist context, are typically defined in terms of karma — the results of one's inner and outer actions. Unlike the concept of hell in Islam, however, *Naraka* is not eternal. Once an individual has 'cleansed' his or her karma, the soul is reborn into another realm. Interestingly, a breakdown of the root word for 'hell' in Arabic (*jahannam*) translates as 'a place that

looks scary, is completely dark, and has no comfort'. Hell, in my experience, is not reserved for the afterlife.

In spite of the many references to torture and punishment for one's sins
that are made in the Qur'an, there do appear to be conflicting statements
within the Qur'an as to how people's actions will be judged in the afterlife.
Some of these statements give me hope. In 17:7, for example, we read:
'whoever is guided is only guided for the benefit of his own soul. And
whoever errs only errs against it'; and, earlier on in the same chapter: 'We
have bound each human being's destiny to his neck. On the Day of Resur-
rection, We shall bring out a record for each of them, which they will find
spread wide open, "Read your record. Today your own soul is enough to
calculate your account"' (17:13-14). Although many Muslims typically say
that 'each one of us will have to face God on the Day of Judgment', these
verses suggest that we will have to face ourselves. Each of us must take
responsibility for our actions, irrespective of how we define our faith.

Inevitably, we all develop our faith in the context of our personal experiences that occur in the span between birth and death. My faith – an
inexplicable trust that there is something incomprehensible and mysterious
happening outside of the realm of this earthly existence – came into being
when my mother's sister was killed by an Israeli soldier in the West Bank
in 2002. Although I felt no connection to Islam at that time other than a
residual ambivalence, when my aunt was killed I had an experience that
confirmed my belief in something. It wasn't completely in line with my
perception of the teachings of Islam, but it wasn't out of line either.

When I heard that she had died, the first thing I wanted to know was,
did she have time to say the *shehadeh*? Muslims, before they die, are
instructed to say 'I bear witness: there is no God but Allah, and Muhammad is the Messenger of Allah'. It may seem strange for that to have been
my first thought, since my relationship with Islam was an ambivalent one,
but I knew it would have been important to her. I was told that she died
smiling, and, apparently, knowing she would die, she had said it. I felt
relieved. It meant her passing was a peaceful one.

In the days following my aunt's death, I experienced an intensity of
grieving that I can only describe as complete surrender. The fact of losing
someone I love, combined with the violence by which her life was taken,
led to a feeling of sadness that obliterated certain boundaries. In a way,

grieving was its own unique experience of Oneness. The night after she was killed, I was sitting with friends, eating dinner. While I was sitting at the table, unfocused and bleary-eyed, I had the thought, 'I wonder where she is'. Immediately upon thinking this thought, a soft, almost imperceptible light seemed to emerge from the corner of the room – obviously in my mind, but as if it was actually in the room. An image of my aunt's smile appeared as though it was infused into that light. Suddenly, everything was filled with this light. The walls, the table where we were sitting, the food we were eating, my own body. Everything around me appeared to dissolve into light molecules. Nothing was solid. The deepest experience of love, beyond what I had ever imagined, settled into me. I felt completely at peace. 'What is this?' I asked silently. 'Are you in heaven? Are you with God?' 'God is Love', she said. And then the image faded. I was left with that feeling of expansive love and light for days. Although the grief had not completely faded, I was simultaneously being carried by this unfathomable experience of love.

After a few days, that feeling began to fade, and, once again, I was left with only grief. 'Where did you go?' I asked. 'Have you transitioned into another realm?' I was driving my car at the time, and, once again, I had the experience of everything around me – the dashboard, the steering wheel, the road, the trees, the birds – becoming molecules of light, and I was filled with peace. A few days later, that feeling was gone. After about ten days, I could no longer seem to access it.

Later that week, I met a friend for coffee. He didn't know that my aunt had died. I asked him, 'What happens when we die? Do we go to some sort of heaven? Some sort of hell?' 'Well, obviously I can't know for sure', he said, 'but I had an acquaintance who died recently. He was severely depressed and he ultimately drank himself to death. After he died, I was sitting in a café, drinking hot chocolate. I had this thought, "I wonder where he is". All of a sudden, I was filled with sadness. Everything around me became heavy and dark—like the whole world was covered in a black, tarry substance. The heaviness stayed with me for days. I couldn't shake it'. 'So, what was that? Was he in hell? Was that some sort of reflection of hell?' 'I think we create our own heaven and hell', he said. 'Right here on earth'. That our hell might be something we create on earth made sense to me. Once again, there are Muslims who will say it is blasphemy to question

whether the fires of hell refer to our own journeys on this earth or to literal inevitabilities in the afterlife. My experience with my aunt's death, and
my friend's recounting of the experience of his suffering friend, suggested
that both might be true. The experience gave me a glimpse into something
that connects this realm with something that is beyond this realm. It seems
to me that there is an accumulation of energy that we create through our
thoughts, beliefs and actions here on earth, and we somehow take that
energy with us once we transition out of our physical form.

In his book *Peace Begins Here: Palestinians and Israelis Listening to Each Other*,
Thich Nhat Hanh writes, 'if we are not reconciled with our killers at the
time of death, it is extremely painful to die'. At the time of death, the
moment of death, we move out of this manifest world and into something
far greater and more vast than the pain and violence of this life, and it is
therefore necessary to transition with clear heart and conscience. That is
not to say that pain, evil and injustice should be discounted as insignificant
parts of human experience, or that joy and love are not meaningful. But
most spiritual traditions seem to agree that we transition into some form
of eternal afterlife, or that we simply transition into some other form,
perhaps to bring that form back into the manifest world.

The practices and principles of spiritual traditions are meant to help us
transition with clear heart, mind and soul. Taking anguish or anger into the
next life is in conflict with what in Islam is referred to as our *taqwa*, our
God-consciousness. The totality of our spiritual being is so much greater than
even the greatest evil we face in this manifest world. This makes our existence on earth both completely inconsequential, and profoundly important.

I have since discovered that what I experienced when my aunt died is
described quite similarly in many different spiritual traditions. And the
idea that we carry what our souls have gathered here on earth into the next
realm – into something that is beyond this plane of existence – seems to
be common to many traditions. It is also in line with both Buddhist philosophy and Muslim principles that our actions on earth will be carried
with us after death. And that death is a beginning of another journey; it is
not the ultimate end.

The last time I was in Jordan visiting my extended family, I heard something that gave me a context for re-interpreting the orthodox teachings of
Islam about what happens after we die. It was Ramadan. I wasn't fasting

because at that time I was still committed to my resistance to Islam. During Ramadan in Amman, where most of the members of my mother's family live, we would sit out in my aunt's garden after *iftar* and listen to a member of the family talk about a verse from the Qur'an or a hadith. One evening, my uncle quoted something from a speech by a religious scholar he heard on television a few nights before. The scholar said that this notion of committing good deeds in order to avoid the fires of hell is misguided. All of us will end up in the fires of hell. But, those who know the path (from their practice and study of religion) will find their way out of it. The 'believers' will recognise the path the moment they hit hellfire, and they will hurry across the bridge that will lead them out of there. Others, who have some degree of faith and practice, may wander a bit, hesitate a bit, but make it across eventually. Still others will fall right over the bridge into, I assume, the fiery pit, and never make it out.

Life is like this. We must know how to find our way out of our own hell. We must know how to break our cycle of suffering, how to release our attachments to things that bring us suffering rather than joy. We must choose whether we will cycle in the depths of our own self-created hell, or find a pathway out. It's difficult to seek a path out of our hell and into alignment with God outside of the context of religion, or to know if, indeed, there is a path to God that has nothing to do with religion. Is it only through religion that we know of the presence of God? Or has a known presence called 'God' decreed that we must follow His religion? Is my purpose as a spiritual being here on earth to connect with a particular religion, or to connect with God?

In Islam, it is believed that every individual has access to a direct relationship with the Divine. Many Sufi practices in particular are geared towards facilitating that direct relationship, perhaps more so than in orthodox Islam. Sufism, which is often referred to as the inner, mystical side of Islam, seems to combine the principles of Buddhism and Islam in many ways – by focusing on disciplined practices that are intended to maintain union with the Divine while simultaneously working to cleanse the heart of its impurities and to overcome the afflictions of the false self. Although Sufism is sometimes discounted by orthodox Muslims as an illegitimate form of Islam, it is, in theory, a tradition that embodies the pure heart of Islam. It rests on the border between religion and philosophy; it is drawn from Islam but not confined by it. Sufism represents a reaction against the excessive emphasis on Shari'a (Islamic law), in favour of focusing on Spirit and *Tariqah* – the Path. Sufism appears to draw from the depth of Islam's lessons about compassion and self-actualisation.

Orthodox Muslims will say that I am manipulating the tenets of Islam if I draw solely from what I perceive as the religion's beauties while discarding the aspects that go against my own beliefs and intuitions about what supports, and what interferes with, my relationship to the Divine; that I am a hypocrite to call myself a Muslim if I don't accept all of it. But is developing my own relationship to Islam the same thing as making up my own interpretation, and therefore invalid or blasphemous?

In his *The Knowing Heart: A Sufi Path of Transformation*, the Sufi author Kabir Helminski writes: 'there is a saying of Muhammad that is quoted by [the Sufi poet] Rumi: "Follow your heart, even if the religious judge offers a different opinion"'.

Ultimately, it is Love, not Fear, that will guide my heart towards righteousness. It is in the presence of Love that my Soul will find its resting place. Of this I have no doubt.

HERETICS

Carool Kersten

In 2009, the Moroccan-born Anouar Majid, a professor of English at the University of New England in Maine, capped off his earlier pleas for a critical rethinking of the rhetorical use of religion and the political exploitation of national and civilisational heritages with *A Call to Heresy:Why Dissent isVital to Islam and America*. A highly personal meditation building on his earlier writings on the place of Muslims in a postcolonial and polycentric world, the book's intentionally provocative title does not imply a rejection of Islam. On the contrary, it is meant to give Muslims a morale boost to face the challenge of modernity without fear. Majid contends that Muslims have the emotional and intellectual maturity to 'confront their own contradictions'. They should display a confidence that 'is robust enough to allow for troubling questions to be raised'.

Majid's invitation to entertain heretical views by equating them with dissenting opinions is not new. In fact, his stance is reminiscent of the one taken by Peter Berger in *The Heretical Imperative*. Returning to the etymological origins of the word 'heresy' – from the Greek word *hairein*, which means 'to choose' – Berger takes it as his point of departure to interrogate the theological possibilities offered by liberal Protestantism's openness towards human experience. Confronted with the plurality of worldviews that is the hallmark of modernity, humankind must shift from a resigned acceptance of fate towards an ability to make considered choices, relying on the human faculty of thought and reflection. It is very much the same for Majid: 'modernity, in its Islamic sense, is no more than embracing the right critical method and ensuring a society that doesn't punish difference or proscribe intellectual pluralism'.

Historically, the introduction of critical thinking into religious discourses has always been controversial and not exactly risk-free. However, in a review of Majid's book, the American anthropologist of Islam Daniel Varisco also notes that 'the ashes of the heretics … have bred significant reforms to bring religious traditions into relative harmony with the inevitable pace of culture change'. The animosity towards religious dissent is not surprising. Calling into question people's most deeply-felt convictions will obviously invite hostile reactions on the part of believers who feel threatened by ideas that undermine their world view. It can also pose a challenge to the author-ity of religious institutions or establishment figures. This kind of provocation has even graver consequences, because such organisations or individuals have the power and the means to sanction those whom they regard as infringing on what is perceived as an exclusive domain. They simply cannot tolerate ideas impinging on areas which they have declared off-limits to the common believers. The maverick Muslim scholar of Islam Mohammed Ark-oun designates those parts of a religious heritage that are excluded from critical examination as 'the Unthought'. Usually that is not the end of it. A 'thought police', consisting of administrative office holders assisted by a collaborating clerical class, can effectively bar any interrogation of such intellectual no-go areas by defining and formulating an approved and sancti-fied body of learning. The hegemony of this 'Official Closed Corpus' turns everything else into the realm of 'The Unthinkable', and critical minds who venture there do so at their own peril.

Proponents of critical thinking, on the other hand, argue that it is neces-sary to expose religious tenets to such critiques, because criticism results in the kind of creative interpretations which lead to a radical and urgently needed rethinking of long-held and often unquestioned beliefs and doc-trines. This way criticism actually contributes to the revitalisation of reli-gious traditions, increasing their versatility and enabling them to adapt to changing historical circumstances. In the face of the rapid changes of modernity and post-modernity such flexibility is all the more vital to their survival. That is why the French historian Lucien Febvre quoted Paul's Letter to the Corinthians when he defended the iconoclasm of the *Annales* School of history-writing, which he founded together with Marc Bloch between the two world wars: 'We must have heresies'. In Christendom heresy was used to qualify doctrinal positions which had been rejected at episcopal meetings or councils during the early church era. Later, when Roman Catholicism had established its supremacy, this was expanded to interpretations of doctrine which did not adhere to what had been proclaimed as official church dogma by the Papacy. Heretics were considered deviants. Their views were officially condemned, while the perpetrators were convicted for entertaining and propagating 'heterodox beliefs', and then often put to death.

In contrast to Christendom, the Muslim world never developed a hierarchical ecclesiastical structure geared towards enforcing formalised procedures for declaring what is orthodox and what is not. Consequently, it is much more difficult to determine what constitutes 'official' doctrinal positions or dogma. That does not mean that such authority was never claimed or assumed. Accusations of heresy were frequently levelled and execution of those held liable and condemned not uncommon. However, those in charge of safeguarding the purity of the faith in the *Dar al-Islam* – the Abode of Islam – operated in a more fluid setting. The status of the *ulama*, or religious scholars, did not necessarily depend on some form of formally invested authority, for example, by appointment to a public office. Generally, it depended on peer recognition, a communal esteem for learning, and a high regard for an individual's piety. Then there were those who assumed – and still assume – that responsibility on their own accord, motivated by a personal sense of duty, although in some cases it was simply a matter of opportunism. In fact, the body of Islamic learning accumulated over the centuries contains many works with titles that begin with the words: 'the different opinions of the religious scholars' on this or that issue. In the absence of any institution receiving sufficient recognition as a final authority over what is to be considered as 'proper' Islamic doctrine, heresy has remained a rather ambiguous concept in Muslim contexts. The Caliphate never held the kind of authority needed to make any definitive statements on doctrinal points; its role was to ensure law and order and thus to create the right conditions for the believers to lead a proper Islamic life. As a government it did not have any formal deciding power over the distinction between proper and improper; that authority rested with the religious scholarly class, who also acted as the 'watchdog' keeping an eye on the government's conduct.

This ambiguity is already manifestly present in Islam's earliest sources and can be traced back all the way to the Traditions of the Prophet. On the one hand, we encounter a hadith claiming that the prophet had once said that: 'The disagreements of my community are a blessing' – apparently condoning some benign form of pluralism. On the other hand, we find grim warnings against serious doctrinal disputes because of the risk of political dissension and communal splits. There is even an ominous hadith predicting the fragmentation of the Islamic community into seventy-three sects. This story circulated widely and received great currency in Islamic writings on sectarianism. In fact, it governed the categorisation of Muslim heresiography or literature on deviant sects. In one of the most renowned contributions to the genre, *Kitab al-Milal wa'l-Nihal* or the *Book of Sects and Creeds*, the twelfth-century historian of religions Shahrastani divides his discussion accordingly into a first part, dedicated to Abrahamic (I assume this is better than scriptural because the Hindus, etc also have scriptures) religions, where he also discussed the seventy-three sects, and a second part for all the other religious beliefs and practices including Indian religions, the Sabean creed, and the religious beliefs and practices of the pre-Islamic Arabs. However, he relegated some Muslims to this second part, those philosophers he accused of challenging the need for revelation. Shahrastani introduced a specific term for this last position: *al-istibdad bi'l-ray* — the exclusive and wilful use of personal opinion, which was tantamount to denying the veracity of prophecy and prophethood. Effectively, proponents of such ideas were beyond the pale of Islam, exposing them to the much graver charges of unbelief, atheism, or — worst of all — apostasy.

The ambivalence surrounding the issue of what constitutes heresy, apostasy and unbelief is also reflected in the terminology used to describe these perceived deviancies. There are a number of terms which can be considered as equivalents of heresy, although initially the difference between heresy and apostasy or *ridda*, the actual renunciation of Islam, was not always that clear-cut.

One of these terms, *ilhad*, is found in the Qur'an (VII: 80; XXII: 25; XLI: 40). According to the venerable *Encyclopaedia of Islam*, the word's root meaning is 'to deviate from'. Like *Ridda*, it came into use under the Umayyad Caliphate to designate the desertion from the Muslim community — the *ummah* — or for rebellion against Umayyad rule. Abdallah ibn al-Zubayr, a nephew of the Prophet Muhammad's wife Aisha, was accused of perpetrating *ilhad* when he — and his supporters — rose up in revolt against three successive Umayyad caliphs, seeking refuge in Mecca, and effectively proclaiming a counter caliphate. After being killed in battle in

692, he was posthumously beheaded and his corpse crucified. During the same time frame, in a battle of words, the imperial poet laureate claimed that the Kharijite leader al-Dahhak al-Shaybani was followed by every mulhid in the realm, while – as a kind of tit for tat – the Kharijite bard Isa al-Khatti dubbed the Umayyads themselves tyrants and deviators.

According to the encyclopaedia entry, it was not until the Abbasid age that *ilhad* began to be applied to deviant religious beliefs, 'not so much the mere adherence to a false religious doctrine as a rejection of religion as such, which implied a materialist scepticism or atheism of sorts' (EI VIII: 546). The eponymous founder of what came to be known as Asharism, Abu'l-Hasan al-Ashari (874-936), used *ilhad* as an umbrella term for a broad range of heterodoxies incl   uding proponents of Hellenic cosmologies, dualists, deniers of God's attributes, and even the *Barahima* – a diffuse and obscure collective that has been thought to refer to Hindus (Brahmins) as well as Muslim freethinkers who denied the existence of a Creator-God or the need for Prophecy. In later centuries the Isma'ilis were also referred to as *mulahida* (plural of *mulhid*). During the Mongol age, the term had become so widespread as the common designator for Nizari Isma'ilis that both European and Chinese travellers took it to their home countries, assuming it was the actual name for the Nizaris. Much later, the Ottomans began employing *ilhad* for certain doctrines circulating among Sufis and Shiites which they deemed subversive, while in the nineteenth century, the scholar Ahmad Djewdet Pasha (1822-1895) qualified the ideas propagated by the French revolution as *ilhad*.

Another designation that found wide currency among Muslims was *zandaqa* and *zindiq*. These terms of Persian origin were initially used to describe Manichaeism and its followers, who had been denied *Dhimmi* status under Islamic law – the legal protection accorded to the adherents of other scripture-based Abrahamic religions, such as Jews and Christians. Its use then shifted to designate various forms of free-thinking and even atheism. Eventually it evolved into a generic and often indeterminate term applied to unspecified heretics, renegades, and unbelievers. In effect, it was used as a synonym for *mulhid*, *murtadd* and even *kafir*, or infidel. Dismissive of the value of the mostly verbose refutations of Manichaeism produced by its Muslim detractors, the Islamic heritage also contains numerous examples of applying the term *zindiq* to literary figures and mystics whose views were regarded as controversial. By invoking the charge of Manichaean dualism their Islamic credentials were automatically called into question. In this regard, scholars have drawn attention to the parallel with the German and Dutch words for heretics: *Ketzer* and *Ketter*, which initially referred specifically to the Cathars, a medieval heretical sect in Southern France famously discussed in Emmanuel le Roy Ladurie's superb *Montaillou*. However, it soon became the generic German and Dutch term for heretic. Within the Muslim world the accusation has been levelled against, for example, Ibn al-Muqaffa (d. 756); the Muslim Aesop or Lafontaine, possibly because the translator of the fables of *Kalila wa Dimna* was a convert to Islam from another Persian religion; Zoroastrianism. The blind Syrian poet al-Ma'arri (d. 1057/8), composer of a vast body of often scandalous poems, was suspect in the eyes of many of his contemporaries because he was vegetarian – which was also a requirement for the Manichean elect. Even a mystic such as the martyred al-Hallaj (d. 922) faced the charge of *zandaqa*, in spite of the fact that the Sufi outlook is diametrically opposed to the Manichaean worldview.

Zindiq, *mulhid* and *murtadd* were thus often used as synonyms and applied in a rather cavalier manner, not just to denote heretics, but also apostates. These conflations of terms and meanings show not just the difficulties of determining who was a heretic and who wasn't but are also indicative of differences in opinion as to what constituted mistaken or wrongheaded interpretations of Islamic tenets, and what was regarded as a renunciation of the faith altogether. Clearly those whose views no longer fitted within the scope of the seventy-three sects mentioned in the hadith – and then picked up by Shahrastani – were considered to be beyond the pale; but even that distinction in itself often was a matter of dispute.

To complicate things a bit further, there is yet another relevant term in circulation; the juridical classification of *bid'a* or 'unlawful innovation'. Even though the *Encyclopaedia of Islam* entry contains a caveat, saying that *bid'a* must be distinguished from the accusation of heresy, that charge is nevertheless often implied. Strictly interpreted, unlawful innovation should be reserved for 'matters which have been introduced in disagreement with what has come down from the Prophet'; either as a result of confusion or a mere arbitrary decision without basis in the proper foundations of jurisprudence rather than wilful deviation or rebellion. Within this narrower context of legal thinking it may have been circumscribed more clearly as ideas which ran contrary to the teachings of the Qur'an, traditions of the Prophet or the consensus of the scholarly community, and therefore a danger to the integrity of the wider Muslim community. However, the introduction of beliefs or practices for which there was no precedent in the time of the Prophet was in effect also often regarded as heretical. History has shown that this fear for dissenting opinions and the spectre of a fragmentation of the *ummah* into sectarianism was not unfounded: after all, within a few years of the prophet's death, differences over the right to succession led to political rivalries and eventually the splits between Sunnis, Shiites and Kharijites which are still affecting the Muslim world of today.

It is also true that, even without any formal legal basis , caliphs on occasion tried to impose or push through certain doctrinal positions, forcing everyone under their jurisdiction to acknowledge these as dogmatic truth. The most notorious episode occurred during the Abbasid period. In the early decades of the ninth century, the son and successor of the legendary Caliph Harun al-Rashid of *Arabian Nights* fame, *al-Ma'mun* (d. 833), made a short-lived attempt to declare the teachings of a rationalist theological school known as the *Mu'tazila*, encapsulated in five *usul* or 'foundations', as the only legitimate doctrine. The *Mu'tazila* had been heavily influenced by the legacy of Hellenist philosophy. Thanks to the efforts of the so-called *Bayt al-Hikma* – the House of Wisdom, a translation school established under Abbasid caliphal patronage – the Muslim world became privy to Greek learning. Although the vast majority of texts made accessible in Arabic as a result of this herculean translation exercise dealt with practical subjects such as medicine, geography and the other natural sciences, some religious scholars also saw great potential in the philosophies of Plato, Aristotle, and Plotin for providing Islamic tenets with a rational foundation.

While they managed to win the support and protection of Caliph al-Ma'mun -- who fancied himself a bit of philosopher – Mu'tazilite thinking was and remains very controversial. Consequently, the Caliph's decision was met with fierce opposition when he turned against his main detractor, the defiant and popular preacher Ahmad ibn Hanbal (780-855). Al-Ma'mun died shortly after instituting a kind of Inquisition called the *Mihna*; his policy was upheld by successive caliphs and the *Mihna* was used to repress acts of political rebellion. *Fitna* or 'chaos' was abhorred in Islamic legal and political thinking and it is ironic that later-day followers of Ibn Hanbal's position, the Hanbali school of law, would be among the staunchest advocates of avoiding political fragmentation and challenges to the ruler at any cost. However, within fifteen years of al-Ma'mun's death, Caliph al-Mutawakkil became wary of the population's resentment of Mu'tazilite intellectualism and of the people's outrage over the government's ill-treatment of its opponents, especially the troublesome Ibn Hanbal. Anxious to avoid further political unrest, the caliph withdrew his support. This effectively turned Mu tazilism itself into a heresy and earned Al-Mutawakkil the honorific 'Restorer of the *Sunna*'. Anyway, in the ensuing backlash against Mu'tazilites, it was not so much the supporters of Ahmad ibn Hanbal as the rise to prominence of the scholar al-Ash'ari, who had started his career as a Mu'azilite, that brought down this rationalist form of Islamic philosophical theology. Al-Ash'ari set the stage not only for an alternative theological school that bears his name but for a much wider movement known as the *Ahl al-Sunna wa'l-Jama'ah* – 'the adherents of tradition and consensus'. This broad-spectrum trend comes closest to what could be considered a mainstream Islamic orthodoxy during the classical era.

In the debates between Mu'tazilites and Ash'arites both sides made claims to representing the proper interpretation and understanding of the core tenets of Islam. A much more challenging instance of critical Muslim reflection, however, is represented by the so-called 'Freethinkers'. Their intellectual adventurism was considered so radical that it put them beyond the pale – that is outside of the sphere of the seventy-three sects mentioned in the prophecy attributed to Muhammad himself. The most infamous exponents of this category were Ibn al-Rawandi (815-860/912) and Abu Bakr al-Razi (865-925/35). In her study of these two medieval Islamic Freethinkers, Sarah Stroumsa criticises the arbitrary use of the term 'freethinking' in Western academic scholarship on Islam, accusing fellow Islamicists of casting their nets too wide. Majid Fakhry and Josef van Ess, for example, have somewhat flippantly called freethinking 'innovative nonconformism' or 'eccentricity', while Dominique Urvoy's use of the French equivalent *Penseurs Libres* creates the wrong suggestion of some kind of association with the independent thinking along the rationalistic ways of the *Lumières* of French Enlightenment.

Instead, Stroumsa tries to circumscribe the term Freethinking in the context of the Muslim world, and suggests limiting it to 'those intellectuals who, in opposition to other heretics, did not adhere to any scriptural religion'. Most of what we know of these intellectual mavericks has reached us through the heresiographies of their detractors, but it is from the surviving fragments of Ibn al-Rawandi's most notorious composition, the enigmatic *Kitab al-Zumurrud* or *The Book of the Blinding Emerald*, that the Freethinkers come across as 'advocates of autonomous reflection on the major metaphysical and human issues, with no commitment to the monotheist tradition'. The controversy surrounding their thought is focused primarily on their denial of prophetic intercession in revelation. With the acknowledgement of Muhammad's prophethood forming the second part of the Muslim Creed, it is not surprising that 'the danger presented by freethinkers was felt by Muslims as profound and pressing, out of all proportion by their actual number and real strength'. Paradoxically, this interpretation at the same time turns Freethinking in its most radical form into 'a typically Islamic phenomenon, a heresy whose particular character developed in response to the centrality of prophecy in Islam'. Another irony is how other philosophers joined the orthodox assault on individuals such as Ibn al-Rawandi and Abu Bakr al-Razi in order to deflect attention from their own often equally controversial ideas.

However, when speaking of controversy, it is no exaggeration to say that throughout Islamic history no group has had a more mixed reception than the Islamic mystics or Sufis. On the one hand, the giants of Islam's spiritual or mystical tradition are revered for the powerful ways in which they manifested their piety. On the other hand, their attempts to give creative expression to the core tenet of Islam — *Tawhid*, or the absolute oneness and unity of God —also exposed them to the gravest charges of heresy and subjected them to the most terrible forms of persecution. In most instances this was because of the outrage caused by the often shocking statements they made while in a state of ecstasy. These rapturous exclamations are known in Arabic as *shatahat*. In his essay collection *Sufism and Surrealism*, Adonis — the Syrian-Lebanese avant garde poet — offers a different and highly original interpretation of the *shatahat* of the great Sufis by presenting them in juxtaposition with modern symbolist poetry. In this book — more literary criticism than study of religion — the great pioneer of free verse in Arabic draws interesting parallels between such figures as the Sufi al-Niffari and the French poet Paul Valéry.

Abu Yazid al-Bistami – in the Turkish parts of the Muslim world better known as Bayezid – survived his scandalous personal identification with the transcendent, but Abu Mansur al-Hallaj was less fortunate. His sufferings for refusing to retract the exclamation '*Ana al-Haqq*!' – 'I am Truth!' – have been powerfully recounted by the French Orientalist Louis Massignon in what is still considered the authoritative work by a Western scholar on the martyr-mystic and a masterpiece in the canon of what Leonard Binder called 'good' Orientalism. His magisterial *La Passion d'al Hallâj* (1922) also betrays glimpses into his own mystical inclinations, which in the final decades of his life led him to found the spiritual order of the *Badiliya* and seek ordination as a priest in the Melkite tradition. Mary Louise Gude's *Louis Massignon: The Crucible of Compassion* convincingly shows the hybridity of Massignon's spirituality, combining elements of Christian mysticism, Sufism, and a Gandhian understanding of the principles of *Ahimsa* and *Satyagraha* – non-violence and truth force. Pope Pius XI referred to him even as a 'Catholic Muslim', which was meant as a compliment. Massignon's influence on Pius XI and successive pontiffs is evinced by the Vatican II *Nostra Aetate* (1965), the 'Declaration on the Relation of the Church with Non-Christian Religions'.

Throughout the classical age, critical Muslims have continuously looked for creative ways of airing their controversial ideas. The use of parables by the philosopher Ibn Sina, or poetry like al-Ma'arri's and Jalal al-Din al-Rumi's, offered ways of expressing theological, philosophical and spiritual preoccupations. These literary genres or motifs were often not only safer but, in Sarah Stroumsa's assessment 'perhaps also intellectually more rewarding. For rather than forcing these thinkers into a head-long collision with the notion of prophetic religion, these new ways made it possible to integrate transformed echoes of freethinking into the Islamic legacy'. But in spite of his attempts to disguise his potentially explosive ideas in allegorical tales, even an intellectual giant such as the philosopher Ibn Sina (known to the West as Avicenna) did not escape the wrath of the self-appointed righteous. The challenge to his ideas by Abu Hamid al-Ghazali, a man who was certainly his match in terms of cerebral prowess, in the highly polemic *Tahafut al-Falasifa – Refutation (or Incoherence) of the Philoso-*

phers — reflects the entrenchment of Ash'arism as mainstream doctrinal orthodoxy and the rejection of speculative, and even critical, thinking, captured in their slogan '*bi-la kayf*' — 'don't ask how'.

In other instances the whole political climate was so intolerant that any hint of religious non-conformism constituted a real danger. One such example is the so-called Zahiri School of Islamic Law established by a religious scholar and man of letters from Muslim Spain named Ibn Hazm (d. 1064). Like the better known Hanbali School, Zahirism advocates a strict adherence to the literal meaning of the Qur'an and the Hadith collections. It gained tremendous influence in the Muslim west after it was adopted by the Berber dynasty of the Almohads, who swept across north-west Africa and conquered large parts of the Iberian Peninsula known as *Al-Andalus*. Thus, Zahirism became the officially endorsed school of law. Thinkers such as Ibn Tufayl (d. 1185) and Ibn Rushd (d. 1198), who both worked for the Almohads as court physicians and jurists, were forced to take recourse to varying rhetorical and stylistic ruses in order to avoid being regarded as heretics, or worse. As Leo Strauss has explained in *Persecution and the Art of Writing*, coining one's thoughts in the guise of a literary genre or even adopting the position of one's detractors has been a generic practice among scholars and thinkers working under repressive or totalitarian regimes of all places and ages. As examples, Strauss cites Ibn Tufayl and Ibn Rushd's Jewish contemporary Maimonides (d. 1204), and the seventeenth-century Portuguese-Dutch philosopher Baruch de Spinoza.

Ibn Tufayl adopted the same medium as Ibn Sina, basically retelling the story of *Hayy ibn Yaqzan*, who was abandoned on a desert island but managed to develop a religious understanding of the world on the basis of relying solely on the faculty of reason, coming to insights and conclusions which were not in conflict with revealed religions. Also the last Andalusian representative of rationalist philosophy, Ibn Rushd (to the West better known as Averroes, the great commentator of Aristotle), had to resort to trickery or deception. As *qadi al-quddat* or chief justice of the Almohad emirs, he used the format of a fatwa to present his critique of Ash'ari hegemony and to ventilate his own philosophical alternative. The *Fasl al-Maqal* or *Definitive Statement* was conceived as the coup de grace for Ghazali, finishing the more blatantly open attack he had earlier initiated in *Tahafut al-Tahafut* — *The Refutation of the Refutation*. Through this duplicity

Ibn Rushd managed to discredit the eleventh-century *Hujjat al-Islam*, while simultaneously presenting to a privileged few rationalist thinking and demonstrative proof as a parallel affirmation of revealed knowledge.

Aside from 'hard' Averroist rationalism, Muslim Spain also produced *Shaykh al-Akbar*, the 'Great Shaykh' Muhyiddin Muhammad ibn Ali ibn al-Arabi (1165-1240). Born in Murcia, the young Muhammad was a prodigy who allegedly met Ibn Rushd when still a child, telling him where his philosophy went wrong. Claimed by a wide array of Sufi orders as their spiritual forefather, Ibn al-Arabi's theosophy – a philosophical synthesis of the tenet of *Tawhid* with a neo-Platonist understanding of the universe – is intimately tied up with a mystical understanding of Islam. The ontology and cosmology Ibn Arabi developed on the basis of his theophanies is as sophisticated and complex as it is controversial. Those who subscribed to his doctrine of *Wahdat al-Wujud* or 'Unity of Being' have always been met with suspicion. Scholars and biographers who have examined Ibn Arabi's life and thought, such as father and daughter Michel Chodkiewicz and Claude Addas, relate the controversial episodes of an alleged death sentence pronounced by a Cairo judge on unspecified charges of heresy, and a persistent legend of his execution, or rather assassination, in Damascus. In her *Quest for the Red Sulphur*, Claude Addas dismisses the Cairene story of the imposition of capital punishment but recounts the story of Ibn Arabi's alleged murder at the hands of his Syrian detractors, a story told to every visitor to Damascus inquiring about Ibn al-Arabi's final days there.

In any case, Ibn Arabi's heretical doctrine of the 'Unity of Being' survived and was taken up by later-day mystic-scholars such as Abd al-Karim al-Jili (1366-1424) and Mulla Sadra (1571-1641). It was not only instrumental to the formulation of the former's theory of *Al-Insan al-Kamil*, or 'Perfect Man', but also crucial for the introduction of Islam in Southeast Asia. Although Islam probably made landfall in the Malay-Indonesian archipelago as early as the seventh century, because trade relations had existed even in pre-Islamic times, it did not gain a foothold among the local population until the thirteenth or fourteenth century. This coincided with the spread of the 'Unity of Being' and 'Perfect Man' doctrines along the maritime trade routes which also served as conduits for trans-national Sufi orders such as the *Qadiriyya*, named after al-Jili's ancestor Abd al-Qadir al-Jilani (d. 1166). Apparently these ideas struck a chord with the Malays who inhabited insular Southeast Asia and gave rise to centuries of lively debates. Echoes of these ideas were also discernable at the Mughal courts of Akbar and Dara Shikoh.

As Ibn Arabi's doctrine remained controversial, Shaykh Ahmad Sirhindi (d. 1624) one of the most important religious scholars of the late sixteenth and early seventeenth century and according to some the *mujaddid* or Islamic renewer of his age – offered a compromise He suggested it was more appropriate to speak of *Wahdat al-Shuhud* or 'Unity of Witnessing', instead of 'Unity of Being'. This softening of the radical implications of Ibn Arabi's thought also served to advocate a more sober Sufism, recognisant of the importance of upholding and adhering to the *ibadat* or acts of worship. Sirhindi's conciliatory suggestions prefigure the more forceful attempts towards Islamic reformism which began to take shape in the course of the eighteenth century on the eve of the onslaught of modernity on the Muslim world. He stands at the beginning of the comprehensive attempts by the sage of Delhi, Shah Waliullah al-Dihlawi (1703-1762), to salvage traditional Islamic learning and revitalise the study of the Qur'an through its translation into Persian, but it also connected to the uncompromising and regressive scripturalism of the dour and austere reformer of the Arabian interior, Muhammad ibn Abd al-Wahhab (1703-1791/2).

However, the confrontation with modernity, which hit the Muslim world like a tsunami in the wake of European colonialism in the nineteenth century, soon drove some Muslim reformists back to the Islamic tradition's rational heritage. This does not mean that Islamic reformism represents a uniform picture. Far from it; even among Islamic modernists we find accusations of heresy. There is the notorious instance of the renowned Pan-Islamist activist Jalal al-Din al-Afghani (1838-1987) siding with the detractors of Sir Sayyid Ahmad Khan (1817-1898). Al-Afghani was an anti-Darwinist who attacked Sayyid Ahmad Khan's attempts to reconcile advances by the Western academe in the natural sciences to the Qur'an in a tract called 'The Refutation of the Materialists' – a thinly-veiled accusation of heresy.

More recently, innovative and pioneering Islamic thinkers have become more defiant, and it is no longer uncommon among contemporary Muslim intellectuals to adopt derogative designations as a badge of honour. For instance, the philosophy of the Mu'tazila has made a comeback. In 1968

the Indonesian scholar Harun Nasution, educated in Saudi Arabia, Egypt
and Canada, submitted a doctoral thesis at McGill University arguing that
the Islamic reformism of Muhammad Abduh could be qualified as a revival
of Mu'tazilite thinking. He then went on to become a leading tertiary
educator in his home country and was eventually put in charge of redesign-
ing the entire Islamic studies curriculum at the network of Indonesia's
Islamic State Universities. Not only did he insert the teaching of various
'heterodox' schools into the official programme, he also put the works of
Western scholars of Islam and other 'orientalists' on the prescribed reading
lists. Moreover he had no qualms about being identified as a neo-
Mu'tazilite himself. A parallel development is taking place with the recov-
ery of Ibn Rushd's legacy. Since the 1970s there has been a renaissance of
his methods for the development of an Islamic rational thinking led by
Arabic-speaking philosophers such as Egypt's Hasan Hanafi and the Moroccan Muhammad Abid al-Jabiri as well as the Algerian-French historian of
Islam Mohammed Arkoun and others. Collectively they are already
referred to as 'Arab Averroists' or, perhaps less elegantly, 'neo-Ibn Rushdi-
ans'. In this respect it is important to stress that this adoption or embrace
of Mu'tazilite and Averroist ideas is based more on the grounds of their
philosophical rigour than on their theological and juridical import.

Even though it now appears possible to self-identify as a Muslim heretic
in the relative safety of the West, or to be a self-confessed neo-Mu'tazilite
in contemporary Indonesia ,incidents abound to demonstrate that being a
critical Muslim is still not devoid of danger. The undeniable polarisation
between Muslims and non-Muslims, and – more importantly– between
Muslims themselves, comes on the back of what is called the 'Islamic
resurgence', but which, as James Beckford has suggested, would be more
accurately described as a new 'salience' of religion. The fact that since the
late 1970s and early 1980s the presence of religion in public life has
become more noticeable – not just in the Muslim world, but globally –
does not mean it hasn't been there all along.

The examples of the fatwa against writer Salman Rushdie and the case
of Bangladeshi author and women's rights activist Taslima Nasrin immediately spring to mind. The saga of Rushdie's years of living under police
protection at undisclosed locations following Ayatollah Khomeini's fatwa,
effectively a death sentence, received extensive media coverage.

Against the background of an increasingly antagonistic climate pitching radical Islamists and uncompromising fundamentalists against more moderate Muslims, writers have been challenged on grounds of the (perceived) religious implications of their artistic work. The near-fatal stabbing of the revered Egyptian novelist and Nobel Prize laureate Naguib Mahfouz in 1994 clearly shows how emboldened the proponents of a narrow understanding of Islam had become. While such physical attacks or threats are indicative of a worrisome hardening of positions, challenges to literary figures on religious grounds are in themselves not new, as the earlier examples from Islam's classical era have shown., In the 1920s Taha Hussein (1889-1973), a leading Egyptian intellectual and figurehead of the Arab Renaissance and the modernist movement in Arabic literature, was challenged over his controversial theory that the celebrated *Mu'allaqat* or 'Golden Odes' of the pre-Islamic era were actually fabricated by Muslims in order to give more credibility to the mythological episodes in the Qur'an. At that time nerves were still raw from the shock of Atatürk's abolition of the Caliphate in 1924, and the subsequent publication of *Islam and the Foundations of Governance*, in which Azhar scholar Ali Abd al-Raziq (1988-1966) claimed that there was no doctrinal basis for any Islamic political institution, including the historical caliphate. Consequently, Taha Hussein's study entitled *On Pre-Islamic Poetry* was more than the religious establishment could stomach, and they fell on the blind literary critic and novelist. A relentless campaign led to his dismissal from the post of professor of literature at Cairo University in 1931.

Any controversial treatment of the Qur'an continues to be hazardous in Egypt. In 1995 Qur'an scholar Nasr Hamid Abu Zayd was forced to leave his homeland when his innovative methodology for a critical textual examination of the Qur'an was condemned as unbecoming to Islam's Sacred Scripture by scholars from al-Azhar Islamic University. More radical Islamists saw this as a license to go after the man himself. Charging him with apostasy, a number of zealots filed court petitions to have Abu Zayd forcibly divorced from his wife on the grounds that an unbeliever cannot be married to a Muslim woman. Being declared not merely a heretic but an apostate put his life in immediate danger because in the view of Muslim extremists his blood was now halal or 'permitted to be spilled'. This was no imagined or empty threat. Aside from the botched attempt on Naguib

Mahfouz's life two years earlier, Islamic extremists had succeeded in assassinating the journalist and writer Faraj Foda in 1992 because of his criticism of the Islamist preacher Shaykh Kishk. With the help of Fred Leemhuis, director of the Dutch Institute in Cairo, Abu Zayd and his wife found refuge in the Netherlands, where he became a visiting professor at Leiden University. Not until 2010 did he dare to make his first public visit to his home country, only to die rather unexpectedly in a Cairo hospital.

Less dramatic, but nevertheless sufficient grounds for serious concern, were the troubles faced by one of Abu Zayd's former teachers, the philosopher Hasan Hanafi. Following a lecture at the newly established library of Alexandria in late 2006, in which he likened the Qur'an to a supermarket where one takes what one wants and leaves what one doesn't want, Hanafi quickly found himself at the centre of a scandal. Once again, the religious establishment was swift in its condemnation, with one scholar accusing Hanafi of being a Marxist while another called into question the professor's sanity. Hanafi was no stranger to controversy. As an upcoming scholar in the late sixties and early seventies his writings on the future role of religion in Muslim societies had already drawn the attention of the Egyptian security apparatus, and in 1997 his bold reinterpretations of Islam caught the ire of both Islamists and their sympathisers at al-Azhar, leading to demands for his removal from Cairo University. Ironically the same security authorities who in earlier years had been monitoring Hanafi's activities now considered it prudent to put him under police protection.

This antagonism has also spread to Southeast Asia, a part of the Muslim world traditionally associated with softer, pluralist and cosmopolitan exponents of what Robert Kaplan has recently dubbed 'tropical Islam'. In Malaysia, yoga was declared 'un-Islamic' in 2008 because it contains Hindu elements that might corrupt Muslims. In Indonesia too Islamists have become more assertive in the undeniably more open political climate of the post-Suharto *Reformasi* era, emerging in the wake of the fall of the military-controlled New Order regime in 1998. While in the eighties and early nineties, as rector of Jakarta's Islamic State University, Harun Nasution was able to push through a radically progressive, inclusivist and open-minded curriculum that encouraged students to think critically, in 2005, barely a month before succumbing to a protracted liver condition, Indonesia's leading Muslim intellectual, Nurcholish Madjid, was faced with a fatwa from the country's Council of Muslim Scholars (MUI) in which his liberal interpretation of Islam were condemned.

In his younger years, from 1967 to 1971, Madjid had made a name for himself as chairman of Indonesia's Muslim Student Association (HMI). Initially regarded as the anointed successor of Muhammad Natsir, the country's leading modernist Islamic politician, Madjid caused a furore with the launch of the provocative slogan 'Islam Yes! Islamic Party No!' He was not only disowned by the modernist Islamic establishment, but his 'accommodationist' attitude towards the newly installed military government even led to accusations that he was a stooge of General Suharto's New Order regime. In spite of Islamist challenges, Nurcholish Madjid -(also affectionately known as 'Cak Nur') managed to build up a reputation as a Muslim public intellectual and scholar of Islam able to bridge the divide between traditionalists and modernists. After obtaining a PhD from the University of Chicago under the direction of the renowned Pakistani-American Islamicist Fazlur Rahman (a fascinating study of Ibn Taymiyya) he returned to Indonesia to establish the Paramadina Foundation.

The Paramadina Foundation was a think tank cum publishing house dealing with issues such as the place of Islam in a secularising society, religious tolerance and plurality. Cak Nur used the organisation as a platform for reaching out to an upcoming middle class of well-educated and increasingly well-heeled Muslim urbanites, as well as to the political elites. Having achieved material success and political influence, many of these professionals, bureaucrats and politicians found themselves landed in a spiritual vacuum. The Paramadina Foundation filled that void with study groups and seminars, often conducted at Jakarta's five star Hotels. Nurcholish Madjid also became one of the advocates of what has been alternately presented as 'urban Sufism', *tasawwuf positif*, and 'Sufistic spirituality'. Obviously this contributed to a 'commodification' of religion, but it definitely also led to what in Indonesian is called the *Penghijauan* or 'Greening' (green referring to the symbolic colour of Islam) of Indonesian society.

Eventually this spread to the highest echelons of the political establishment, with generals underscoring their Islamic credentials by publicly displaying their personal piety. In 1991 it reached the very top when President Suharto and his family performed Hajj accompanied by an entourage of military top brass and advisers, and the aging general adopted the first name 'Muhammad'. Another indicator of the penetration of Islam into Indonesian society was the establishment of the Association of Indonesian Muslim Intellectuals (ICMI) under the patronage of Suharto's personal protégé, his long-serving minister of technology and eventual successor Dr. Burhanuddin Habibie; and based on articles of association written by Nurcholish Madjid. A few years later, Madjid again made political head-lines by negotiating Suharto's resignation, thus avoiding bloodshed in the face of a popular uprising and increasingly insistent calls for his departure following the government's mishandling of the 1997 currency crisis which crippled Southeast Asia's once booming economies.

Whereas the demise of the New Order regime, and the disappearance from the political scene of Suharto and care-taker President Habibie, her-alded possibilities for unprecedented liberalisation, democratisation, and opportunities for open debate never seen since independence, there was a darker side to this political sea-change. The government's collapse in 1998 also left the armed forces in disarray as they tried to adjust to a new and less prominent political role within the Indonesian state structure. As a result of the ensuing breakdown of law and order, tensions that had been repressed for decades burst out into the open; in the eastern parts of the archipelago it came to violent clashes between Muslims and Christians, while on Borneo indigenous Dayaks attacked migrants from the congested and over-populated islands of Java and Madura.

The Islamists smelled a chance to re-enter the political arena and dust off their agenda for turning Indonesia into an Islamic state. Those in favour of political Islamisation turned against the proponents of the more tolerant and open cultural Islam fostered in the 1970s, 1980s and 1990s. They quickly set their cross-hairs on Nurcholish Madjid as well as younger advo-cates of Islamic liberalism. Successfully mobilising the MUI, the Islamists managed to obtain a condemnation of secularisation, pluralism and liberal-ism as being in contradiction to the teachings of Islam. The resulting fatwa was used to unleash a sharp polemic in sympathetic media and Islamist publications. Critics of Nurcholish Madjid and intellectual-activists such as Ulil Abshar-Abdalla spoke of a 'virus of liberalism' having infected Indone-sia's Islamic higher education system, accusing them of spreading '*sipilis*' – anacronym for secularism, pluralism and liberalism and a pun insinuating an association with the venereal disease.

At the time of the fatwa Nurcholish Madjid was no longer conscious, and soon afterwards he died in a Singapore hospital. But the younger generation of intellectuals would have to confront their critics. Individuals such as Ulil Abshar-Abdalla, who had founded the *Liberal Islam Network* (JIL) and had already been exposed to death threats following an earlier controversial fatwa by the radical *Forum Ulama Umat Islam* in 2003, remained defiant. He did not refrain from speaking up in favour of the principles of secularity, pluralism and liberalism. He has continued to argue that these are not incompatible with the interpretations and practices followed in his native Eastern Java, the heartland of Indonesia's traditionalist 'tropical Islam'. Ulil and his *Liberal Islam Network* were joined by other articulate intellectuals associated with such organisations as Syafii Anwar's International Centre for Islam and Pluralism (ICIP), the Wahid Institute, the Freedom Institute and others. Until today they stand by their principles of religious tolerance and pluralism as a moral compass for critical engagement and creative interpretation of the Islamic heritage. They also continue to support the rights of minority sects such as the Ahmadiyah, even in the face of condemnation by the Indonesian Ulama Council and calls by the country's Minister of Religious Affairs for its disbanding.

Although the antagonism between moderate and radical Muslims has not subsided, the increased political stability under the current government, led since 2004 by President Susilo Bambang Yudhoyono, has resulted in substantial progress in the political democratisation process and a growing respect for the freedom of expression. In the wake of the 'Arab Spring' of 2011, Indonesia is increasingly showcased alongside Turkey as a possible model for other Muslim countries to follow. Despite the mixed track records of the Turkish AKP-led government and Indonesia's Democrat Party, they nevertheless provide the most recent successful examples of critical engagement with religion in Islamic contexts.

It is in this vein that we have to understand Anouar Majid's provocative call for heresy. Aside from the defiant tone strikes in the face of atrophied and conservative Islamic traditionalism, a regression into uncompromising scripturalism and intolerant political Islamism, as well as the anti-Islamic rhetoric issuing from certain quarters in the West, there is another reason for using the term heresy and it's adjective. By returning to the original meaning of its root word *hairein* as 'choice', the designation can be appropriately applied to those Muslim thinkers who have adopted an eclectic approach towards the intellectual legacies of both the Muslim world and the West. By selectively using aspects and elements from the Islamic civilisational heritage, or *turath*, and Western strands of thought, in particular recent advances in the humanities and social sciences, they are mapping new avenues for future Islamic critical thinking. Some, like Hasan Hanafi and Muhammad Abid al-Jabiri, opted for developing overarching and comprehensive philosophical systems, while others such as Mohammed Arkoun and – to an extent – Nasr Hamid Abu Zayd, chose to become what the late Claude Lévi-Strauss called *bricoleurs* – intellectual 'handymen' who cobble together new, pragmatic ways of thinking primarily based on ideas, concepts, theories, and methods which they have come across on their own intellectual wanderings. What they share is a desire to restore the rich Islamic tradition of critical inquiry and interrogation of received knowledge.

COSMOPOLITANS AND HERETICS

NEW MUSLIM INTELLECTUALS AND THE STUDY OF ISLAM

CAROOL KERSTEN

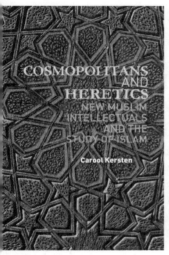

'Kersten's sharply written study examines the contributions of three cutting edge Muslim scholars who engage creatively with the main currents of twentieth-century thought: Nurcholish Madjid, Hasan Hanafi and Mohammed Arkoun. This is intellectual history of the highest calibre that should be read by anyone interested in modern Islamic thought. Outstanding.' — **John Calvert, Professor of History, Creighton University and author of *Sayyid Qutb and the Origins of Radical Islamism***

Dramatic political events involving Muslims across the world have put Islam under increased scrutiny. However, the focus of this attention is generally limited to the political realm and often even further confined by constrictive views of Islamism narrowed down to its most extremist exponents. Much less attention is paid to the parallel development of more liberal alternative Islamic discourses and the emergence of a Muslim intelligentsia.

Cosmopolitans and Heretics examines three of these new Muslim intellectuals who combine a solid grounding in the Islamic tradition with an equally intimate familiarity with the latest achievements of Western scholarship in religion.

9781849041294 | Available Now | Paperback | £22.00

41 GREAT RUSSELL STREET, LONDON, WC1B 3PL
+44 (0)20 7255 2201
WWW.HURSTPUB.CO.UK
WWW.HURSTBLOG.CO.UK

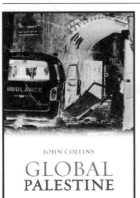

COUSIN TROUBLE

Ben Gidley

Judaism and Islam are in many ways the closest of cousins. Sharing a rigorously monotheistic faith as articulated by a shared canon of prophets in related Semitic tongues, tracing their common origins to the patriarch Abraham, their destinies have been inextricably intertwined. In dispersal in western countries such as Britain or France, Jews and Muslims have together occupied the ambiguous position of being constructed as both 'ethnic communities' and 'faith communities' at odds with their normatively Christian wider societies; both have suffered forms of racism and persecution, been accused of dual loyalties, condemned for refusing to integrate, stereotyped as terrorists.

The kinship of Judaism and Islam is most concisely evoked (and it has become clichéd to do so) in the bear-homonymy of the Hebrew and Arabic words for peace: shalom and salaam. And yet, today more than ever, Jews and Muslims live largely in a state of enmity, characterised by mutual distrust. Hearing more about each other than perhaps ever before, it seems that Jews and Muslims might know less about each other than at any time in their histories. There is widespread Islamophobia amongst Jews, widespread antisemitism amongst Muslims. Arguably, though, it is not each other that they fear, but the idea of the other. How do these ideas form? I would like to looks at this question, focusing especially on the Jewish idea – or, rather, ideas – of Islam.

A century ago, a significant proportion of the global Jewish population lived amongst Muslims, either in Muslim lands under Muslim governance or side by side under British or French colonial rule. Around a third of a million lived in Turkey, and another third of a million in North Africa. There were also sizeable communities in Persia, one of the oldest sites of Jewish life, in the Arabian peninsula (including the ancient community of Yemen), in Kurdistan, and in the mountains of central Asia. In British

India, Jews tended to live in either Christian or Muslim areas; cities like Karachi and Peshawar had thriving synagogues and Jewish associations.

Ottoman cities like Salonika and Sarajevo had long been key Jewish cultural centres. In Baghdad, Jews lived lives densely interwoven with Muslims and Christians in the city's complex multiethnic tapestry. In many of these lands, the Jews spoke Judeo-Arabic languages, forms of Arabic written in Hebrew script and containing Hebrew and Aramaic words; in others, they spoke Ladino, the ancient Spanish brought into exile when Jews were expelled from Spain in 1492 and spread across the Middle East.

In these contexts, the Jewish idea of Muslims and the Muslim idea of Jews were of course mediated by inherited prejudices, religious traditions and colonial narratives, but these ideas were also shaped by day to day, face to face experience. In Baghdad or Cairo, Jews and Muslims were tenants in the same buildings, business partners, friends; in other contexts, such as Yemen, a strict division of occupations kept Muslim and Jewish communities in symbiotic relationships with each other.

Now – after the turbulence of the twentieth century, and especially the nationalism catastrophically exported from Europe to these lands – the map looks very different. Apart from Israel, whose six million Jewish inhabitants live surrounded by predominantly Islamic countries, there are only a handful of places where Jews and Muslims see each other every day, in the flesh as opposed to on the television. Where eight of the eighteen largest Jewish populations in 1900 had been in majority Muslim countries, today there are none. There are still tens of thousands of Jews in Iran, in Turkey and in Uzbekistan, but most Jewish populations across the Middle East and South Asia have dwindled to four figure numbers or less.

In the former imperial metropoles – inner and outer city districts of Paris where Jews and Muslims of Maghrebi descent share the same spaces, or neighbourhoods like London's Redbridge where the socially mobile children of Ashkenazi and Bangladeshi immigrants have moved from the old East End – newer modes of living together have been forged, sometimes peaceful, sometimes tense. The scholar Sami Zubaida suggests that it is in London and Paris rather than in the Middle East, where Middle Eastern cosmopolitanism most authentically survives, but the politics of Israel/Palestine overshadows Jewish/Muslim relations just as powerfully here as closer to the conflict zone.

The pull of Zionism and the push of increasingly ethnically exclusive anti-colonial nationalisms, often accompanied by antisemitic riots, led to a massive transfer of the Jewish population from countries like Iraq and Algeria to the new-born Israeli state after 1948. In Pakistan, for example, a community of a couple of thousand departed between independence and 1953, leaving just 500. All in all, around 800,000 Jews were made refugees in that period across the region.

Some commentators have called this 'the Jewish Nakba', taking the Arabic word for catastrophe used by Palestinians to refer to their dispossession when the state was founded. The term is controversial, arguably offensive; by taking the name of another people's trauma, it denies the singularity of each. But it names the way in which the ethnically exclusive nation-state was a catastrophe both for the masses of people caught on the wrong side of the new borders and for the cosmopolitan idea that we might simply live together in casual, quotidian conviviality across lines of difference. Thinking of the ethnic cleansing of Jews from Arab lands as the other side of the coin of the Palestinian Nakba (instead of heroic narratives of emerging nascent statehood or tragic narratives of victimhood) also connects Jewish history to some of the other catastrophes of that post-war, post-Holocaust moment – notably the Partition of British India along religious lines.

If Jews in the last half century have been living in the shadow of the loss of that catastrophe, how are the older times, when Jews and Muslims shared spaces differently, remembered? Broadly speaking, Jews commemorate this history in one of two ways, mapping roughly on to (and over-determined by) attitudes to Israel/Palestine today.

Convivencia

One roseate view sees the lost world of Jews in Muslim lands as characterised by tolerance, vibrant cultural creativity and generous intercultural sharing. The ur-text in this mythology is al-Andalus, Moorish Spain, the period long seen as a golden age of Jewish culture, which was brought to an end by the Christian Reconquista and the subsequent Catholic Inquisition and expulsion of both Jews and Muslims. Just as some Palestinian families displaced in the Nakba have carried the keys to their lost homes for six decades, some Sephardic families ('Sephardic' refers to the branch of the Jewish people dispersed from Seferad, Spain, after 1492) have handed down keys to Spanish doors over six centuries. The key term used in describing that golden age is *convivencia*, living together.

Now, Jewish tourists flocks to Cordoba and Granada to see where the great Jewish philosopher Maimonides discussed Aristotle with his Muslim and Christian friends, to visit the lovingly restored Moorish synagogues, and to dine at the expensive restaurants serving the fusion food of Umayyad Andalucía. Maria Rosa Menocal's *The Ornament of the World: How Muslims, Jews and Christians Created a Culture of Tolerance in Medieval Spain* of 2003 was a popular academic text on the Spanish golden age, contrasting the pluralism of Islamic rule to the intolerance of medieval Christendom. Although Menocal is not Jewish, her book was well received and widely reviewed in Jewish periodicals, just one example of the nostalgia for Islamic al-Andalus that has become a stock in trade of the Jewish public sphere. The beautiful Jewish cookbooks of Cairo-born Claudia Roden have put the hybrid foods of Islamic lands back on the fashionable Jewish table; the haunting music of Yasmin Levy has made the Andalucian Jewish golden age vividly alive for Israeli and diaspora Jews; and Joann Sfar's graphic novel, *The Rabbi's Cat*, has captured North African Jewish *convivencia* in gorgeous colour.

This narrative dramatises the contrast of the pluralism and tolerance of Muslim rule with the genocidal intolerance of Christendom (it was the Ottoman sultan who welcomed the Jews who fled the Spanish terror). Thus it aligns its liberal Jewish narrators with the European underdog, compensating for any association with an Israeli state seen as an extrusion of Western imperialism. Similarly, statements by the fashionably iconoclastic intellectual Slavoj Žižek about the Balkans, contrasting Islamic tolerance to Christian intolerance, are widely circulated among anti-Zionist Jewish commentators; Žižek has suggested that the Jewish/Islamic symbiosis was so powerful historically that it makes more sense to talk of a Judeo-Muslim civilisation than of a Judeo-Christian one.

Most recently, Jewish writers have recast the pre-1948 Jewish Middle East in the same roseate light as al-Andalus. This started in the 1990s with the scholarly and political interventions of Sephardic writers like Ella Shohat, Smadar Lavie and Ammiel Alcaly, who reclaimed an identity as 'Arab Jews', who participated in a shared, multi-ethnic Arabic-speaking Levantine culture, erased in Israel by a Zionism that was hegemonically European. (Although some anti-Zionists, such as Moshe Machover, have argued that this move, stressing Zionism's Jewish victims, sidelines the suffering of Zionism's 'real', and really Arab, victims.)

These writers have challenged the standard Zionist historiography of Israel's heroic rescues (with codenames like Operation Magic Carpet for Yemen, and Operation Ezra and Nehemiah for Iraq) that supposedly redeemed the scattered Jews' proto-Zionist longing for return. The new identity politics instead stresses the erasure of the rich Middle Eastern Jewish culture in Israel and the racism faced by Jewish Arabs at the hands of a European Zionist elite.

In the last few years, this *convivencia* narrative has been popularised by a wave of books and CDs celebrating and commemorating Jewish life in cities like Baghdad and Cairo, in overwhelmingly celebratory terms. One in three Baghdadis in 1941 were Jews, mostly seeing themselves as Iraqi and Arab at least as much as Jewish. Sasson Somekh's *Baghdad, Yesterday: The Making of an Arab Jew*, published in 2003, recalls the lost world of Iraqi Jewry, and located the Jewish community in Baghdad as very much an Arab community. As reviewer Adam Schatz put it, it is 'an elegy for an experiment in coexistence, rather than a Zionist parable about its impossibility'.

Similarly, Violette Shamash's 2008 *Memories of Eden* is the memoir of a member of the Baghdadi Jewish elite who recalls what she calls her native land as literally a paradise, spiced with the smells of the river Tigris which flowed past her father's palace, the smell of the apricot trees in the garden and the kebabs grilling on the wood oven. For Shamash, an antisemitism imported from abroad and wholly alien to Iraqi culture brought about the demise of this paradise: 'All the communities lived together peaceably, teasing each other good-naturedly and without inhibition about their religion, [until] the poison of Arab nationalism and Nazism entered the bloodstream.' Shamash's book, not written with any anti-Zionist agenda, subverts standard Israeli histories of the Middle East narrative, and has been praised by anti-Zionist Jews such as Baghdad-born historian Avi Shlaim.

Nissim Rejwen's memoir, *The Last Jews of Baghdad*, published in 2004, told a similarly nostalgic story. Rejwen came from a lower middle class family, but through his work as a journalist and bookseller became part of the Iraqi intelligentsia. Shamash's family had left Iraq before the creation of the state of Israel, but Rejwen stayed to the last possible moment: after a series of anti-Jewish edicts from 1948 to 1950, the Kingdom of Iraq announced that Jews had a year to renounce their Iraqi citizenship and leave. Rejwen landed in Tel Aviv in 1951. His escape was part of the Israeli state's Operation Ezra and Nehemiah, but his account stresses the ill-treatment of the Iraqi migrants, their material and cultural impoverish-ment in their new Israeli exile – and thus upsets the Zionist narrative of the in-gathering of the exiles by the new Jewish state.

The British journalist Rachel Shabi has probably produced the most politicised version of the *convivencia* narrative in her book *Not the Enemy*. Shabi has claimed that recovering 'the long, vibrant experience of Jewish life in the Arab world' is 'deeply unfashionable', a claim belied by the popularity of the books and CDs I've mentioned here. Shabi's intent in recovering this memory is, as she puts it, 'a way of seeking templates for how to make things right again'. That is, historical Islamic *convivienca* might be a model for pluralism today, and if Israel could re-connect with its Middle Eastern self it could have different relations with its neighbours.

One problem, though, with the Jewish philo-Islamic narrative is that it collapses together 1400 years of Muslim history into a monolithic story. The pogroms in 1940s Iraq obviously do not reflect the essential character of Islam, but they did not come out of nowhere, as some of the memoirs suggest. The roseate history of Jews under Islam only works if it edits out the times and places when Muslim rulers were less than tolerant of their Jewish subjects; as with all historical narratives, it requires a systematic forgetting of some things in order to remember others, even if in this case the forgetting is benign and forgiving.

Dhimmitude and the Lachrymose Account

In flattening Islamic history, the Jewish philo-Islamic narrative exactly mir-rors a second Jewish narrative, a narrative which has little space for forgiving. This has been named (by historians such as Mark Cohen) the 'neo-lachry-mose' conception of Jewish history, a term which nods to Salo Baron, a great twentieth century Jewish historian and sociologist. Baron complained of the tendency among Jewish scholars to focus on European Jewry's history of discrimination, persecution and pogroms – instead of on the ordinary lives

Jews led between the attacks: the everyday instances of survival, creativity, joy, interaction and integration. The 'lachrymose story' Baron identified was often used ideologically to argue for the need for a Jewish state, as the only relief from Christendom's apparently congenital antisemitism. A similar lachrymose story has more recently emerged about the Islamic world, and again this has been harnessed ideologically by pro-Israeli hawks.

In the last decade, several groups representing Jewish refugees from Muslim lands have stepped onto the public stage in the Jewish community. The World Organization of Jews from Arab Countries, Justice for Jews from Arab Countries, the Association of Jews from the Middle East and North Africa (Harif) and Jews Indigenous to the Middle East and North Africa (JIMENA), have agitated for Jewish dispossession in Muslim lands – and Muslim antisemitism – to be remembered and redressed. A series of Israeli, French and American films about the exile of Jews from these lands, such as *The Forgotten Refugees* and *The Silent Exodus* (both 2004) and *The Last Jews of Libya* (2007) have been widely circulated in Jewish communities and screened at human rights events.

Although their position has challenged one of the key myths of modern Zionism – that Jewish migrants to Israel were willing, drawn by the pull of Zionism – the history of persecution these organisations and films stress fits in well with another of Zionism's myths, that antisemitism is an eternal affliction, only countered by a Jewish state. The movement emphasises justice for Jewish refugees, and insists that their experience mirrors that of Palestinian refugees.

One author who played a key role in formulating the neo-lachrymose counter-narrative is Bat Yeor. In her writings on the Middle East, she coined the term 'Eurabia' and popularised the neologism 'dhimmitude'. A Jewish refugee from Egypt to Israel, she has described the pogroms of the 1948 period as part of both an age-old subordination of dhimmi Jews by Muslims, and a deliberate strategy of rising political Islam. Her work shows the intersection of the neo-lachrymose narrative and a clash-of-civilisations worldview, and the global 'counter-Jihad' movement has widely disseminated the concept of 'dhimmitude'.

In the neo-lachrymose counter-narrative, a prominent role is given to the Farhud, a violent anti-Jewish pogrom which took place in Iraq in 1941 after the fall of the short-lived Arab nationalist government of Rashid Ali al-Gaylani, and carried out by Rashid Ali's supporters. The Jews were scapegoated for supporting the British who intervened against Rashid Ali's coup; the coup government had been both antisemitic and closely linked to Nazi Germany. The commonly accepted death toll is close to 200, with many more injured, although recent accounts have suggested higher casualty figures.

The neo-lachrymose narrative of the Jews of Arab lands sees the Farhud as significant for two reasons. First, it preceded the creation of the state of Israel and thus cannot be seen as an 'anti-Zionist' backlash but only as a purely antisemitic incident, thus indicting Arab nationalism as inherently anti-Jewish. Second, it establishes a connection between Arab antisemitism and Hitler's Holocaust.

This latter connection is even stronger in another story which features prominently in the neo-lachrymose narrative, that of Rashid Ali's backer, Haj Amin al-Husseini. This Palestinian cleric, the Grand Mufti of Jerusalem from the 1920s to the 1940s, was influential in the development of Palestinian nationalism but he also became closely connected with Hitler and the Nazis during the Second World War. The Mufti's role in collaborating with the Nazis has been given considerable attention in the Jewish media, as evidence for the nexus between Islamism, Arab nationalism and vicious antisemitism. The most extreme accounts go so far as to claim he suggested the Final Solution to Hitler.

Islamophobia, Antisemitism

These two ways of seeing the Jewish past in Muslim lands are in a sense both true – but, in denying large elements of the truth, both are also false. Jewish-Muslim relations, like Jewish-Christian or Muslim-Hindu relations, have varied enormously across the great sweep of time and space in which Jews and Muslims have lived together. An honest history of our interactions would reveal the systematic exclusion and denigration of dhimmi minorities under some Muslim rulers – and the relative prevalence of tolerance and pluralism compared to many Christian polities. It would commemorate the golden age of Jewish life in the Caliphate of Cordoba – but it would also recall the pogroms that periodically rocked Muslim Spain after 1090, and that Maimonides himself eventually fled. It would remember the Jewish worshippers killed in Hebron by Muslim militants in the riots of 1929 – and the many more saved by Muslim neighbours. It would recall Arab nationalist complicity in the Nazi Holocaust – and the 'righteous gentiles' of the Muslim world, from Albania to Morocco, who saved Jewish lives amidst the genocide, and the half million Muslim soldiers of the Indian army who fought against the Nazis in World War II. As Roi Ben-Yehuda has written, 'The history of *convivencia*, or coexistence, teaches us that while some history is worth repeating, we can only ignore the dark side of Jewish-Muslim coexistence at our own peril.'

The two ways of seeing the Jewish past in Muslim lands appear incommensurate because they almost always, in the heat generated by the Israel/Palestine question, immediately invoke two different ways of seeing the Muslim other. For example, although there is considerable evidence for the Grand Mufti's Judeophobia, historian James Renton has argued that 'this has been used to de-legitimise his whole career and the cause of the Palestinian Arabs in general', showing how the politics of Israel/Palestine today are projected back onto the Muslim-Jewish past in unhelpful ways.

In the UK, the heat generated by Israel/Palestine is intense: a pair of peace activists, one Palestinian and one Jewish Israeli, who toured British universities together in 2009 to advocate for peace, said that UK campuses seemed almost more polarised than Israeli/Palestinian society – the Israeli, for example, said 'Here in Britain the pro-Palestinian students are more hostile than the people I meet in the West Bank.' The last couple of years, since Israel's Operation Cast Lead offensive in Gaza, several joint Muslim-Jewish events – such as a performance of the Sheshbesh Arab-Jewish Ensemble at a networking evening for Arab and Jewish business leaders – have been cancelled after pressure from activists of one or the other side.

In this context, the Western Jews who commemorate an idealised, nostalgia-soaked, cosmopolitan past often do so (and this is most explicit with activists like Rachel Shabi) to place a stake on the future: Jewish/Muslim co-existence is not only possible but the historical norm, and thus a just peace in the Middle East is within reach – with Zionism as the main obstacle to it. On the other hand, those who document a lachrymose past of constant Islamic Jew-hatred are also making a claim on the future: the Jewish people, and its tiny state, Israel, must gird their loins and secure themselves against the might and mass of global Islam.

And the two incommensurate ways of seeing the Muslim other, the roseate and the lachrymose, in turn all too often determine two incommensurate (and equally wrong-headed) attitudes towards antisemitism and Islamophobia.

Those who hold to the roseate view of Muslim-Jewish relations tend to downplay contemporary antisemitism. They locate antisemitism in a Christian past (contrasted negatively to the Muslim past), minimise Muslim antisemitism, and emphasise Islamophobia as today's most pressing prejudice.

Last August, for example, the *Guardian's* Comment is Free carried an article by an American-Israeli journalist, Mya Guarnieri, entitled 'Islamophobia: the new antisemitism', concluding: 'In the past, there was antisemitism, roiling just below the surface. Now, there is Islamophobia.' Israeli historian Shlomo Sand made the same point, in an article entitled 'From Judaeophobia to Islamophobia' in the *Jewish Quarterly*. Across the Atlantic, Daniel Luban wrote an article in the Jewish magazine *The Tablet* entitled 'The New Anti-Semitism: Recent attacks on Islam in the United States echo old slurs against Jews', noting that 'The problem for the ADL is that there simply isn't much anti-Semitism of consequence in the United States these days.... At the same time, many of the tropes of classic anti-Semitism have been revived and given new force on the American right [but] their targets are not Jews but Muslims.'

More sophisticated accounts of Islamophobia as the new antisemitism have been developed by Jewish academics such as Matti Bunzl, who argues antisemitism is largely 'obsolete' while Islamophobia is a phenomenon of the now. Antisemitism, he suggests, was a creature of the age of the nation-state; Jews were the paradigmatic other of nations. Today, in the new Europe, he claims, we are in a post-national moment, and it is Islam that is demonised as the paradigmatic other for Europe as a whole. Jews, he says, 'no longer figure as the principal Other but as the veritable embodiment of the postnational order'.

The emergence since the 1990s of Islam-hating 'Euronationalism', the pan-European far right ideology directed mainly at migrants and Muslims, provides some evidence for this argument, especially as some Euronationalists have appeared to eschew Jew-hatred and embrace Israel. Further evidence comes from the more recent development of a disparate counter-Jihad movement (from the English Defence League and Geert Wilders to the terrorist Anders Breivik), with motifs drawn from the Crusades and the Habsburg defeat of the Ottomans at the gates of Vienna.

However, the Islamophobia-as-new-antisemitism argument is flawed conceptually and weak empirically. Conceptually, as Muslim scholar Abdelwahab El-Affendi has observed, Hannah Arendt, the great theorist of totalitarianism, argued that antisemitism intensified at the time of the decline of the nation-state, and that Nazism was in some senses post-national. And the rise of supra-national Europe has not called the death knell for the nation-state, which is as strong as ever. Empirically, some of the most vicious Islamophobes across Europe are also highly Eurosceptic and not Euronationalists, while the pro-Israel and non-antisemitic posturing of right-wing parties is often skin deep and merely rhetorical.

Further, by relegating antisemitism to the past, it denies the very real contemporary manifestations of antisemitism, including both discursive and violent physical manifestations. The annual monitoring by the Community Security Trust provides ample evidence for the persistence of antisemitism, sometimes alongside and inextricable from anti-Muslim racism, sometimes perpetrated by Muslims – and indeed provides some evidence for a rise in antisemitic incidents since Bunzl set out his argument at the start of the century.

The narrative of Islamophobia replacing antisemitism also promotes a kind of zero sum approach to different racisms, a perverse calculus by which racisms are measured against each other, the intensity of one necessarily diminishing the value of the other. As the scholar Christine Achinger has written, 'To shy away from noting differences for fear of establishing hierarchy between different forms of hatred and exclusion, though, does not further the anti-racist cause, but damages our ability to understand and confront either of them.' Belittling antisemitism as a mark of respect for the victims of Islamophobia is not much better than one-upmanship amongst victims as a policy for anti-racists. And, as sociologist Veronique Atglas has suggested, the way in which Islamophobia and antisemitism are always placed side by side in this victimhood competition positions the British state as a neutral arbiter – and Muslims and Jews as always outside the British state and British society, petitioning it for recognition of our grievances.

Beyond Islamophilia and Islamophobia

In fact, hatred against Muslims and hatred against Jews are often expressed together, by racists who see both minorities as closely connected or even as two sides of the same coin. You can see examples of this in one recent Community Security Trust annual report on antisemitic incidents, such as some neo-Nazi literature distributed in East London which concluded: 'JEWS AND MUSLIMS OUT OF REDBRIDGE'. This suggests a potential Muslim interest in combating antisemitism and Jewish interest in combating Islamophobia. This in turn points to a need for an anti-racist politics of alliance between Jews and Muslims.

If we want to combat anti-Jewish and anti-Muslim racism together, we need to attend to the commonalities and continuities between them, as well as the contrasts and specificities which make each of them distinct and in some senses unique.

There is some evidence too that being honest about histories of antisemitism, without falling into the paranoid hysteria of the neo-lachrymose school, might generate more meaningful interfaith dialogue than sugar-coating the story of Jewish-Muslim relations. The blog Point of No Return, which tells the story of the Middle East's Jewish refugees, has had its highest numbers of comments on posts about the death of the Jewish community in Pakistan – and the comments have overwhelmingly come from Pakistani Muslims coming to terms with the antisemitism in their country's history. Similarly, Shmuel Moreh's memoirs of Jewish life in Iraq in the 1940s paint a far less rosy picture of Muslim-Jewish relations than the others mentioned above, emphasising the violence of the Farhud, but their publication in Arabic in the Saudi-funded online magazine Elaph has generated huge numbers of comments from Arab readers, describing a mix of shame and nostalgia. The kinds of relationships created in these moments are surely more meaningful than those created when anti-Zionist Jewish writers reproduce comfortable clichés of co-existence.

This complex reality requires a complex politics. We need to stop competing in the victimhood stakes and recognise that both racisms are important and dangerous. We need to attend to Islamophobia in the Jewish community and to antisemitism in the Muslim community. And we need to be vigilant about the blurry line between taking sides on Israel/Palestine and taking up antisemitic or Islamophobic themes. Once Jews and

Muslims recognise they have a common stake in fighting both racisms then we can begin to build a world free of antisemitism and Islamophobia.

Even as the Israel/Palestine conflict continues to corrode Jewish/Muslim relations, there are some small reasons for hope. A report commissioned by Alif-Aleph UK, which promotes grassroots Jewish-Muslim dialogue, concluded that the 'commonly held assumption that Muslims and Jews in Britain have no contact with each other, know little about each other and fear or even hate each other [is wrong]. Dialogue is happening between Muslims and Jews at every level, all around Britain... Mutual respect usually develops quickly when Muslims and Jews come together to address common issues.'

Without glossing over the difficulties, especially prejudice and the fear of extremism, on both sides, the report showed that Jews and Muslims were highly motivated to come together, for a variety of reasons: a concern with anti-Muslim and anti-Jewish prejudice, a desire for Middle East peace, a shared sense of being part of a religious minority, a sense of the essential commonality of the Abrahamic faiths. There are also pragmatic concerns, such as combating legislation that threatens halal and kosher slaughter. Or, perhaps more mundanely, shared issues facing East End market stalls have led the Bengali Traders Association and the Jewish Traders Association to work together.

And these lead to countless grassroots initiatives, way below the radar of the mainstream media, from dialogue groups to exchange visits, joint seminars on religious texts to student campaigns for campus prayer rooms, interfaith football teams to joint cookbook projects. They even exist in the most religiously conservative communities, such as around Stamford Hill in Northeast London, home to many ultra-orthodox Jews, where regular co-operation between elders on shared local concerns belies the image of closed, parallel communities of distrust. There is a long way to go – much interfaith work is done by religious leaders and not lay community members; it often focuses on theological dialogue rather than building this worldly solidarity – but the journey has started.

I noted earlier that going beyond our monochrome ideas of the other towards an honest account of Jewish-Muslim relations would recall that the great Jewish philosopher Maimonides thrived in Islamic Cordoba – but also that he was forced to flee his home under the harsh rule of the ultraconservative Muwahhidun. However, as the Iraqi Jew Sasson Somekh has noted, 'in the end, he found comfort and glory in another Muslim city, Cairo, where he flourished and became the leader of his people and the friend of Muslim rulers and writers like Al-Qadi al-Fadil, a writer and poet who was the confidant of the ruler Saladin'. I believe that Jews and Muslims alike need to develop a better sense of the complexity and contradictions involved in our evolving story, to acknowledge both the shadows and the light. As the Israeli novelist Amos Oz says, justice demands that we remember while forgiveness demands that we forget. Real dialogue and meaningful alliances require both to be kept in play.

ESSAYS

THE TYRANNY OF PROFIT

Stuart Sim

In the MacTaggart Lecture at the Edinburgh International Television Festival in 2009 the media tycoon James Murdoch delivered a devastating attack on the BBC, and by implication public services in general, arguing that there 'is an inescapable conclusion that we must reach if we are to have a better society. The only reliable, durable, and perpetual guarantor of independence is profit'. It is a view neatly summing up an entire lifestyle that goes under various names: neoliberalism, market fundamentalism, globalisation, or to bring out its negative side more forcefully, 'casino capitalism', as it was dubbed by the political economist Susan Strange. If people in Murdoch's position are telling us that profit is the primary motivator of human action then so are their many media outlets. That has a far-reaching effect on the public consciousness, encouraging us to believe this is our true nature and free-market capitalism our destiny as a species. In the aftermath of the phone-hacking scandal we are all only too well aware of just how far the Murdoch media empire was willing to go in its pursuit of profit, which puts an interesting spin on what James Murdoch means by 'independence'.

The dismissive tone Murdoch adopts towards public service can only be depressing to anyone who thinks there is more to life than its economic aspect, and in its vision of society as primarily a means for generating profit for *homo economicus*. In other words, we cannot really trust anyone, or any institution, which is not concerned to make a profit out of their activities – in the public sector no less than the private. Yet tacitly or otherwise we go along with this notion in our everyday affairs in the West, where the profit motive now dominates in so many areas, even in those in which its impact is at best highly suspect, perhaps even counter-productive. This is certainly so in healthcare and education, for example, neither of which would seem to be all that well suited to the application of such a regimen. We are all living under the tyranny of profit these days and the notion that competition must apply in every area of human affairs. The line that is taken by the most vocal advocates of profit is that we are all naturally competitive. Recent studies in neuroscience (as outlined in the Royal Society for the Encouragement of Arts, Manufactures and Commerce's 'Social Brain' project), provide little in the way of evidence for this contention. In fact, the Social Brain project tends to suggest that human society functions better if we are cooperative. It really is time to start investigating why the pursuit of profit has managed to cast such a spell over us.

We can turn to philosophy for help in trying to understand why we have allowed this spell to have such power over us. Specifically to the work of the Slovenian philosopher, critical theorist and post-Marxist thinker Slavoj Žižek and his concept of the 'fetish'. This describes how people can be said both to know and not know something at the same time, and how this can lead them to going along with things that are not necessarily in their best longer-term interests. Thus in communist states when the Soviet empire still held sway, the citizens could still offer a measure of support for the regime despite being aware that it was signally failing to deliver on most of its promises, particularly in the economic domain. They both knew and did not know that this was the case; in a sense, it was just too painful to admit the former to themselves, because ostensibly there was so little that any of them could do about it at the individual level.

The concept of fetishisation captures the working of a very human trait, which could be described in colloquial terms as 'making the best of it'. If we find ourselves unable to do anything very much about our surroundings, political as well as physical, then we just have to learn to adapt to them somehow or other – even if we would rather not have to. Dislike of a tyrannical regime is thus internalised; not just that, but hidden away under apparent support for that regime. As Žižek puts it: 'one knows the falsehood very well … but still one does not renounce it'. The fetish can be considered 'the embodiment of the lie which enables us to sustain the unbearable truth'. It's my contention here that, in effect, we are currently doing something similar in the West, by accepting huge public spending cuts in order to help save the profit-obsessed system that has landed us in the economic mess we now find ourselves. Most of us don't want these cuts, but have difficulty envisaging a lifestyle not based on constant economic growth fuelled by financial speculation on the markets. Speculation bankrolled by a financial industry who put profit at the very top of their agenda, and can be ruthless about how they achieve it. We make the best of it, knowing the falsehood of this decision but still not renouncing it. (Interestingly enough, the situation is not quite the same in all of the Islamic world, as I'll go on to discuss later.)

Profit has been so fetishised by Western culture that views like Murdoch's can attract little adverse notice (even if the BBC, Murdoch's main target, did take offence and come back at him). Prime Minister David Cameron can also find it quite unexceptional to campaign for action against the threat posed by global warming on the grounds that there are potentially huge profits to be made by those willing to invest in developing green technology: 'I passionately believe that by recasting the argument for action on climate change away from the language of threats and punishments and into positive, profit-making terms, we can have a much wider impact'. The statement carries the implication that if profit were not forthcoming then the exercise would not be worth bothering about. Certainly not an issue for the business sector to concern itself with anyway.

When we look at the impact of the profit motive on areas such as healthcare and education, however, its detrimental effect soon becomes abundantly apparent. Never mind the disasters that can unfold in areas where profit is the acknowledged objective, such as banking and the finance industry in general. There are lessons to be learned from this fetishisation of profit and they need to be brought more fully into open public debate, because most governments and politicians in the West would seem to be in denial about the underlying cause of the financial crisis of 2007-08 – financial greed. Nothing much of consequence has been done to reform the way the markets and financial industry works in the aftermath of the crisis, and they are still treated as the major route to economic growth. The dominance of the profit motive in our lives is not really being questioned as it should be, and politicians continue to believe that it holds the key to stimulating the economy. If anything, they appear determined to make it play an even greater part in human affairs. That is why we have the current governmental campaign to introduce a greater degree of privatisation into the NHS, and so allow private healthcare organisations and their shareholders to profit out of human illness. All this despite the ample evidence available from countries like America that a profit-based healthcare system is both inefficient and elitist. The 50 million Americans without any coverage at all in case of sickness can stand as eloquent testament to that.

Yet neoliberals cannot bring themselves to give up their commitment to the profit principle, no matter what evidence may accumulate of its detrimental effect on human relations and our general quality of life. On the contrary, to them life is all about profit and nothing must get in the way of that project. What I am arguing here, however, is that we should be resisting this ideologically-driven project as strongly as we can. Resisting on the grounds that we are capable of being more than a self-interested *homo economicus* with a one-dimensional view of existence focused on personal gain.

The Public and the Private

The profit motive has been applied to more and more areas of our lives by our political classes, such that the 'business model' has become the major criterion by which almost all public services are judged; judged, and then all too often found badly wanting by those same classes, and thus cast as candidates for wholesale reconstruction. Privatisation is consistently held up as the solution to all our public service needs. Public utilities such as water and electricity are systematically being hived off from the public sector internationally, with very mixed results in terms of both efficiency and cost to the consumer. One has only to consider the fiasco over water privatisation in Bolivia in 2000, where massive price increases led to a popular uprising in the city of Cochabamba. The 'Cochabamba Water Wars', as they have come to be known, were subsequently brutally put down by the authorities at considerable loss of life – all in the name of creating more profit for the private sector that had moved in to take control of the utility.

The necessity for profit-creation now exercises an effective tyranny over the public sphere, no area of this seeming immune from its influence, and it is increasingly intruding into the private as well. Education and personal self-development are currently being encouraged mainly on the basis that they can improve one's earning power. Hence the Murdoch doctrine – the more profit you can show from your activities, the more free you are assumed to be as an individual. Profit from this standpoint guarantees you independence, an emotive argument in a society like ours with its cult of individualism. Profit, in fact, has become fetishised by almost all of us. Even socialist-inclined governments throughout the West think primarily in its terms of reference these days, having largely given up the idea of engineering any truly fundamental change in the system. They content themselves instead with instigating minor reforms to it, which activity alone is enough to bring down on them the ire of the neoliberal lobby. Neoliberals want no tinkering with the market at all.

The assumption is that the more profit that is generated in a society, the more of it will filter down the social chain, leading to improved living standards for us all – eventually anyway. Pragmatism is to the fore in such cases, with the system's (assumed) beneficial effects being taken to excuse any accommodation that has to be made with it ideologically. Leftist politicians in the West have long since made their peace with capitalist economics. In the words of Peter Mandelson after the Labour party's UK election victory in 1997, the left is now 'intensely relaxed' about the rich becoming ever richer, and no longer feels the need to rein them in. That this is a development for the overall public good is now all but an article of faith amongst Western politicians, few of whom will ever venture publicly to challenge the hegemony that has been established by neoliberalism lest this scare away international investors. In an age of globalisation, such investors will simply shop around for more congenial national markets – and, sadly, will always find them.

We would appear to have something of a consensus as to macro-economic policy across the West, with profit right at the very centre: the doctrine of neoliberalism. Neoliberalism represents a particularly purist interpretation of laissez faire economics, so it is not in itself new in its drive to make this a world fit for market trading: the capitalists of Marx's time would recognise it immediately, and be entirely sympathetic to its goals. Yet the extent to which this ethos has become an end in itself, rather than a means to improve the human lot, is rarely addressed. Instead, we have fetishised the concept of profit and effectively bracketed any qualms we may have had about this cultural shift. While there are some on the far left who still speak out against economic exploitation, and the increasing disparity between the income levels and wealth of those at the top and bottom in Western society in general, the political mainstream has long since turned a blind eye to them.

Part of the reason for this blindness to the faults of neoliberalism is that, as so many of its supporters have claimed, it's now 'the only game in town'. Socialism is not much in evidence around the world these days, and even social democracy has been in steady decline for some time now. There is no doubt that socialism as a political ideal has been tainted by the failures of various regimes in the twentieth century, most notably those going under the banner of communism. Communism tried as hard as it could to remove the factor of profit from our economic lives, with the state deciding how these would be conducted and what our respective allotted roles in the process would be. This was the era of the command economy, when central planning took over from competing organisations only interested in their own performance and the dividends they could provide for their shareholders through increased profit margins. The assumption was that if the state took over the means of production then any surplus value created would be used by the authorities to improve the lot of the population at large. In reality, however, living standards in the communist world failed to keep pace with those in the West, and the command economy failed to deliver reliably even the most basic goods that an advanced society required. Food shortages, for example, were a common occurrence under communism right up to the collapse of the Soviet empire.

Socialism and communism are not entirely the same thing, but there is no doubt that they share at least some of the same ideals, such as a desire for greater economic equality throughout the population. In which case, communism was not exactly a great advertisement for that ideal, as opponents like neoliberals have kept pointing out. Communism's implosion has meant that we are now, as the sociologist Zygmunt Bauman put it after the break-up of the Soviet empire, 'living without an alternative' in the political realm. Under the circumstances it's easy to see why so many of the population has decided to make the best of it, and go along with a system where profit rules. So where do we go from here?

The Empire of Profit

First, we have to profile our enemy. Where do we come across the tyranny of profit these days? Just how far does its empire extend in our society? It is there in the business world certainly, and that is only to be expected in an activity where profit is almost the sole raison d'être, but it is also present in a wide range of less expected areas that at one time were thought to be safe from its pernicious influence. In higher education profit has now become the new criterion of value, overshadowing such phenomena as the desire for self-development or the wish to make oneself useful to society through the dissemination of one's knowledge to others. One is now encouraged to regard higher education primarily as a route to higher lifetime earnings. So the idea is that one no longer goes to an institution of higher education to develop one's latent talents or broaden one's mind, but rather to invest in one's economic future. It has all become so very narrowly personal. Money spent now will guarantee a higher return later, and as it is your money, handed over to educational institutions in ever-increasing amounts as course fees, then you have every incentive to focus yourself on that goal above all other considerations. Knowledge equals hard cash.

Murdoch's MacTaggart Lecture is a ringing endorsement of the profit ethic as an integral part of the democratic lifestyle. Its sentiments are straight out of the school of the controversial American economist Milton Friedman, arguably the main architect of neoliberalism's recent rise to global political pre-eminence. Friedman advocated the abolition of any government intervention in the workings of the market, and a minimal public sector. His ideas were enthusiastically adopted by such influential politicians as Ronald Reagan and Margaret Thatcher, as well as by the powerful international organisations the World Bank and the International Monetary Fund. Murdoch's specific target is British official broadcasting policy, although its arguments can be made to apply to almost any area of business. The problem with the policy in place, for Murdoch, is that it is based on central planning, with the government laying down rules as to who can broadcast and what they can and cannot do once granted a licence. As Murdoch sees it this is a repressive system, and the 'result is lost opportunities for enterprise, free choice and commercial investment'. What is at risk under the current system, Murdoch contends, is 'the provision of independent news, investment in professional journalism, and the innovation and growth of creative industries'. Without these the public suffers, as indeed does the very concept of democracy.

Murdoch certainly works hard throughout his speech to promote an image of commercial broadcasting (and commercial media in general) as public-spirited, in giving the public what it wants and offering it a diversity of views that is critical to the health of a democratic society. It is a mixture of government intervention and BBC power that is preventing this diversity, this free circulation of opinion, from being as available in the UK as it should be. Murdoch wants this barrier to be removed – for the greater public good as he conceives of it. Competition is an absolutely necessary element of democratic life for someone of Murdoch's outlook, and in pretty well any sphere of it that you care to name. For the right-wing historian Niall Ferguson in *Civilisation: The West and the Rest*, it is also one of the critical factors that has led to global domination by Western civilisation, in which case the profit motive takes centre stage in the development of modern history.

Even if one accepted that Murdoch really was more interested in protecting our democratic freedoms than in the pursuit of profit for its own sake (a big 'if' I would suggest, as it must be with any major business tycoon) his argument still falls down on several counts. Diversity is not always what you end up with when advertising revenue is the main source of funding for media companies. Advertisers are notoriously conservative in their views, and generally prefer to deal with companies that appeal to the popular market without causing any controversy that might affect their jealously-guarded public image. This tends to encourage a convergence of style and content between all the companies targeting that market, since that is the obvious way to increase advertising revenue, and thus of course profit margins. Diversity from this perspective can come to mean just several versions of much the same thing, with companies unwilling to take chances that might alienate their audience, leading to a fall in viewing figures and a consequent fall in advertising revenue. That market is cut-throat at the best of the times, and the aftermath of an economic crisis is plainly not the best of times, so the pattern is to play as safe as possible and produce copies, or variations, of whatever happens to be drawing large audiences at any one time. Choice can be a rather dubious concept under such circumstances. One could argue that in real terms commercial companies have far less independence than entities like the BBC, because they are in the final analysis beholden to advertisers. The BBC does not have this kind of pressure, subtle though it may be, to worry about.

It is all too convenient for Murdoch to argue that profit is a means to a democratic end, when in real terms profit is an end in itself for organisations such as his family's media empire — as 'hackgate' only too clearly announced. The management of any organisation with shareholders will soon find themselves being asked awkward questions if they start pursuing wider social goals at the expense of their profit margins, the latter being their primary responsibility towards those shareholders (enshrined in company law, tellingly enough). It is a view put with characteristic bluntness by American neo-conservative Milton Friedman in an article entitled 'The social responsibility of business is to increase its profits'. There, he argued that businessmen who 'believe that they are defending free enterprise when they declaim that business is not concerned "merely" with profit but also with promoting desirable "social" ends', are in fact 'preaching pure and unadulterated socialism'.

The point needs to be made that Murdoch's outlook is the dominant one in the business world and it cannot simply be discounted as an instance of professional jealousy on his part about the power and success of the BBC. The vast majority of those in positions of business power sincerely do believe that '[t]he only reliable, durable, and perpetual guarantor of independence is profit', and are not really open to any arguments to the contrary. The mere existence of organisations like the BBC constitutes an affront to their ideology, and it will always be vulnerable to such sniping. Much the same goes for the NHS. It is not a matter that the Murdochs of this world can let rest: the supposed virtues of profit must be proclaimed at every opportunity.

The stock market represents the profit ethic taken to its extreme, and the extent of its influence on our lives has grown immensely in recent years as the search for ever greater profit margins ('alpha', in the market traders' jargon) has drawn entire countries into its orbit, making their economic survival contingent on its whims. Iceland, Ireland, and Greece are outstanding examples of the process in operation. And who knows how America will fare in the next few years?

In a sense, the stock market itself is a gigantic confidence trick, as no-one really thinks they are going to lose when they buy stocks and shares and play the market. Certainly, no-one plans to lose, no matter how much the mantra that 'the worth of your stocks may go up as well as down' is repeated. So it is a confidence trick that we are all playing on ourselves, and seem content to go on doing even in the aftermath of catastrophic stock market crashes. Somehow we are able to convince ourselves that each occurrence of collapse is an anomaly, rather than a sign of an underlying instability that will keep recurring, regardless of how much technological progress we may achieve in the interim. One of the main reasons for the recent crisis is that financial institutions were willing to take huge risks on their borrowing to expand their business. The assumption behind this policy was that the stock market would continue on ever-upward and that today's borrowing would be rendered insignificant by tomorrow's increased profit returns. We all know where that mistaken belief has landed us.

An Islamic Alternative?

Islamic societies do not necessarily have the same attitude to profit, and are more motivated by metaphysical concerns than their counterparts in the West tend to be these days (it was different in pre-secular times of course, when Christianity was the basis of the ideological paradigm). This can result in theocratic regimes, especially in those polities that espouse Shariah law, which imposes a religious dimension on all human conduct. The West has long since rejected theocracy, and I am by no means recommending its re-adoption, nor any other such expressions of religious fundamentalism. Nevertheless, Islam does provide us with an interesting example of a lifestyle based on factors other than the economic that appears to satisfy a significant percentage of the globe's population, even though many of them are living in some of the world's poorest countries. This is not to say that there is no class conflict or desire for political change in such societies. Indeed, the disparity of wealth between rich and poor is often even more marked there than it is in the West. But it is notable that any revolutions that have been occurring in the Islamic world tend to be against the ruling classes and their abuses of power, rather than against Islam itself. We have to concede that not all of humanity sees profit as its destiny and that lifestyles can be constructed on the basis of other reasons. Although there is more than a certain irony in the fact that those Islamic countries with large oil reserves (as in the Middle East) do make enormous profits out of selling this natural resource to the West, and as a result contain some of the world's richest people.

Nevertheless, Islam as a system still finds profit problematical, and Islamic banks are forbidden to charge interest, leading to some complex regulations about how loans are administered that have to accord with the terms of Shariah law. To quote the Institute of Islamic Banking website:

> Islam argues that there is no justifiable reason why a person should enjoy an increase in wealth from the use of his money by another, unless he is prepared to expose his wealth to the risk of loss also. Islam views true profit as a return for entrepreneurial effort and objects to money being placed on a pedestal above labour, the other factor in production. As long as the owner of money is willing to become a shareholder in the enterprise and expose his money to the risk of loss, he is entitled to receive a just proportion of the profits and not merely a merely nominal share based on the prevailing interest rate.

Islamic banking is thus committed to a partnership system in which profit has to be morally justified. This would seem to call for a practice which is a far cry from the wilder goings-on of the money markets in the West, particularly in the latter days of the pre-credit crisis boom period. In fact, that crisis sparked an upturn of interest in the world financial system about Islamic banking, given that it seemed far less sensitive to market turmoil than Western banks clearly were.

Although Islamic banking is widely practised in the Islamic world, it still consitutes only a small share of the global banking industry. How true it always is to Qur'anic principles in all its business dealings is a matter of conjecture. It can hardly avoid contact with the Western banking system altogether in an era of globalisation, and that invites at least a degree of pragmatism to be shown, quite possibly leading to some slippage from doctrinal purity. Yet Islamic banking remains an interesting phenomenon in having to justify its practices in terms of religious doctrine rather than just purely commercial ones. This might be seen as some kind of safeguard against the anarchy that we otherwise experience in the West. There is an element of social responsibility implicit in Islamic banking that is sadly missing in its Western counterpart, and we could well learn a lesson from it. Anything that holds out the promise of making credit crises less likely to happen has to be worth investigating, because they do seem to be looming up on the horizon yet again.

Challenging the Empire of Profit

There are signs coming to light around us, however, that we are becoming increasingly aware of the downside of the lifestyle that a profit-obsessed neoliberalism promotes and that a sense of dissatisfaction is beginning to make itself felt. Evidence for this can be found in anti-globalisation campaigns, anti-capitalist movements and public protests in countries like Britain, Greece, and Ireland against swingeing public service cuts. If the tyranny of profit is to be challenged then these are to be encouraged as much as possible, particularly at local level. Social networking has its role to play too in helping to organise practical protests, such as sit-ins and occupations of services about to be cut, like libraries, local hospitals, advice centres, or youth centres. Even if these activities do not prevent closures from occurring eventually, they are worth conducting to draw attention to what is happening at local level because of national government decisions, and to stir up publicity. The more fuss that is made the better. Fuss gains media coverage and we need more and more of that if we are to make people in general reconsider their lifestyle. Scope is also there to develop single-issue political groupings to contest local elections, where the monopoly of the big national parties is easier to challenge than it is in general elections.

There has also been a highly symbolic campaign against bankers' bonuses in Holland, which has been so successful in rousing popular support there that it has prompted the Dutch Parliament to pass a law against the practice in those cases where banks have been bailed out by the public purse. The Netherlands, as one newspaper report put it, 'is now vying for the title of Europe's most bonus-hating country'. This is a lead well worth following, since it was only the threat of a mass withdrawal of deposits that made the banks and the politicians realise that something had to be done to placate the public. The Dutch banks have since apologised for being 'insensitive' to public opinion on this issue, whereas in the UK their counterparts are content to repeat the threat that their senior staff will move elsewhere if such a policy is ever instituted (one does wonder where, given their sorry track record of late).

Consumer boycotts of this kind have been under-utilised to date, and can be turned against any company that the public feels is taking advantage of it. 'Clicktivism' offers a useful tool by which to mobilise action quickly on such fronts. If a company exploits developing world labour in order to produce cheap clothing (or cheap whatever), then stop shopping there and publicly exhort others to do the same so that the company is forced to take notice and amend its policies. Public shaming of irresponsible business practice is an option we can all exercise: we are all potential clicktivists in this respect. Perhaps Holland is more egalitarian-minded than countries like the UK, but there is no reason why campaigns of this nature could not take off elsewhere in the same way. The Dutch anti-bank campaign started as exchanges on Twitter and simply grew from there. It is eminently copyable.

We should campaign for banks to be turned into public utilities, like water and electricity supplies used to be. The privatisation of the latter throughout much of the West should have taught us an important lesson on the latter score. It has merely encouraged the new owners to see how far they can push costs up, as it is clearly in their interests, and those of their shareholders, to do so. The goal should be to remove the profit motive from such services as much as possible and to move power away from shareholders, who can only regard the general public as a source to exploit – as sickness and illness is for private healthcare companies.

Eventually, what all such activities should be encouraging us to do is to stop thinking like consumers. We've become so indoctrinated by this notion that we almost automatically assume that role, when all it does is to extend the empire of profit ever further, making it seem as if that is an essential, indeed inescapable, part of all human relationships. It is as if Thomas Carlyle's 'cash nexus' were the normal state of affairs nowadays, and not something to criticise, as he famously did. The point to remember is that where there are consumers, someone, or some company, is benefitting financially, and that is the only reason for their involvement. There is never anything altruistic or public-spirited about it, everything else is subsidiary to the accumulation of profit. Companies and entrepreneurs care about things like democracy only inasmuch as they make it easier for them to shift their product.

We've got to stop thinking of money as something which has to be put to work for us (as banks continually tell us in their advertising campaigns, as if we should feel guilty if this is not a perpetual concern for each and every one of us), but rather to treat it as what enables us to live. Other than saving a certain amount, and needing to be protected to some extent against inflation diminishing our savings' value over time, most of us have no need to seek out extra profit in this way. If we are shareholders, but perhaps beginning to feel sympathetic towards the anti-profit cause, then we should use that position to call our company to account if they are being ethically irresponsible. Annual General Meetings can provide a platform for this sort of criticism to be voiced, and shareholders can start campaigns amongst other shareholders to make the argument weightier and more difficult for corporations to sideline with vague promises of reform. Milton Friedman notwithstanding, there is a concept in the business world entitled 'Corporate Social Responsibility' (CSR) that most large corporations claim to be supporters of and that is supposed to go farther than the mere generation of profit. Although in far too many cases 'claim' is the operative word and companies are paying it little more than lip service. Breaches of ethics occur rather too frequently for comfort in the business world, with the practice of outsourcing alone generating a host of these, much to the discredit of the Western corporations involved.

A recent case involving Apple indicates just how problematical outsourcing can be on an ethical plane. Foxconn, the company that produces Apple iPads in Shenzhen and Chengdu, China, has been the subject of a scandal over its working practices. As a report on the company in the Western press put it, these reveal 'a Dickensian world of work that would be considered shocking in the West'. In order to keep up with the huge worldwide demand for iPads, assembly line employees can find themselves working 12-hour days, with only one day off every thirteen days. Basic daily wages can be as low as £5.20 before overtime. So bad are the conditions that seven workers committed suicide in 2010, and their deaths did create an outcry around the world. The only substantial reaction of the company, however, has been to install anti-suicide netting around the workers' dormitories and to insist that workers sign a contract to the effect that they promise not to commit suicide while in the company's employ. The contract is less concerned with the individual employee's welfare and more to do with avoiding lawsuits from bereaved families.

Shareholders in companies caught out in the way Apple has been, can hardly hide behind excuses such as different labour laws being in operation in different countries. What is happening in this instance is a clear breach of any concept of Corporate Social Responsibility (except for Friedman's), which means that a company should never countenance this kind of treatment of workers anywhere that it is involved. If globalisation really is a force for good, as neoliberals are always so quick to claim, then things like this should never happen. Western corporations ought to refuse to be party to such practices being carried out in their name and monitor their suppliers closely to ensure that they are complying. Apple has to be held culpable therefore, and its record overall with its supplier network is not at all good.

Yet the saddest aspect of this case is that Apple is by no means unique. Few outsourcing schemes would bear much close scrutiny; it is the system itself that encourages such a cavalier approach to the ethics of work in its search for ever-lower production costs. Outsourcing is driven by the desire to maximise profit, not to improve the lifestyle of the developing world's workforce. Neither are the profits that accrue from the policy negligible: in the first quarter of 2011 alone Apple showed a profit of $6 billion. The notion of 'fair trade' does not really seem to have caught on in the computer industry.

Employees of a company that is guilty of ethical breaches ought to think seriously about resorting to whistleblowing to make these public, difficult though this undoubtedly can make their life thereafter. Whistleblowing is deeply unpopular with managements, who are most likely to close ranks against anyone doing this and treat them as the enemy. Co-workers might even do the same, since their jobs may well be threatened by any subsequent action taken against the company by the authorities. There is no denying that it constitutes a career-threatening move, but the loyalty of the socially-conscious individual has to lie elsewhere – with the public, and his or her conscience, instead of with the employer.

At some point we would have to address the issue of civil disobedience when countering the relentless pressure exerted on social relations by the empire of profit. In the developing world violent protest is often the only way of making the ruling powers pay any attention to your plight – as the

Arab Spring only too graphically revealed. When events like this happen, then the privatisers (who are all too often Western-generated multinationals, as they were in the Bolivian water utility fiasco) surely have a duty to back down and leave the stage. Whether one agrees or disagrees with the principle of civil disobedience, it is always likely to occur in cases of desperation, bringing the possibility of violence in its wake. It has to be considered a symptom of what is wrong in terms of social relations rather than a cure, whatever political radicals may think. Ideological fault-lines are exposed at such times, and any victory that results will ring hollow to some extent if it is achieved at the cost of violence and loss of life. In cases like this, however, the real culprit is neoliberalism, which is creating the conditions for such a sense of desperation to arise. Civil disobedience will always be the last resort of the disaffected, but if neoliberalism acts in a cavalier enough fashion, as it is well capable of doing when untapped sources of profit come into view, then it runs the risk of triggering just such a response.

The Profit Addiction

The tendency of late in the West is to assume that almost all our needs must be subordinated to the economic, that once this dimension is sorted out then everything else will more or less fall into place. Most politicians are obsessed with the economy as their primary responsibility, regarding it as central to their electoral success. That is even the case at present when political parties are having to admit that cutting the national deficit, and hence the living standards of the majority of the population, is a necessary step to take post-credit crisis. The line generally taken is that once this has been achieved, then we can move back to economic stability and resumed growth, which must always be our paramount concern as a society. Hence the drive to ensure that public institutions are opened up to the profit motive, the argument being that this will be to our greater benefit; they will become more efficient, more entrepreneurial in spirit, thus less costly. Profit, profit, and more profit must always be the goal. Indeed, we could say that the West has now turned into a profitocracy.

Yet we know that societies can be run differently, as history amply demonstrates. In terms of the contemporary world, Islamic society is notably less consumer-conscious and while this does have its bad points as far as the general living standards of such society is concerned, it does at least indicate that life can be organised on grounds other than the relentless pursuit of profit: on something other than the Murdoch doctrine, in other words. Even if we accept that the profit motive is not likely to disappear altogether, we can nevertheless alter how profit itself is used and shared around – and in a general sense, how it is perceived. Profit is not our god, and we have no need to treat it as such: however, it is our addiction, and we do need to treat it as such.

I was in the final stages of completing a book recently entitled *Addicted to Profit: Reclaiming Our Lives from the Free Market* (forthcoming from Edinburgh University Press), when I discovered that there is actually a website named 'Addicted to Profits', which takes this to be a positive trait for investors to have. It includes interesting tips on how to profit from financial crises like the globally destabilising one we have so recently gone through, almost as if it relished the prospect of another one occurring. The message is that there is even profit to be made out of human economic misery, and that the investor's only concern should be to get a share of this while it's available, paying no need to the suffering. At times like this, neoliberalism can seem beyond parody, but perhaps this is where the Murdoch doctrine inexorably leads us. The existence of such a website means that we can't say we haven't been warned of what profitocracy has in store for us. It brings out some of the worst aspects of human nature, but we are not bound to follow its dictates. We can choose to emphasise the cooperative side of our nature instead, and that would be to the benefit of the population worldwide. Profitocracy does not have to be our political destiny, but it may well be if we do not start fiercely challenging the system of ideas on which it is based.

ALL THAT MUSLIM JAZZ!

Andy Simons

'Jazz album by Pakistan music veterans tops western charts'. Underneath the heading, the *Guardian* article of August 2011 declared: 'The rich strains of eastern music have for centuries wafted across the rooftops of old Lahore. But listen today and you might hear something new: jazzy riffs and bossa nova beat'.

That made a refreshing change. For the past few years, I've read one article after another announcing that jazz is dead. When you enter the few record shops still standing, you will note that the only jazz still selling, or rather, still being pushed, is Miles Davis, Ella Fitzgerald and all the other late legends. Bear in mind that the Universal record company conglomerate and, to a lesser extent, Sony and Fantasy, are pushing the vast catalogues of perhaps over-recorded stars to potential newcomers to the jazz market. Even music school graduates write their stuff in the manner of Wayne Shorter, the saxophonist who was a mainstay in Miles Davis's 1960s band and who later formed the successful jazz-rock fusion group Weather Report, a huge success in the 1970s. Younger players, graduates of music schools since the 1980s, still hold up 1960s and 1970s innovators as their role models. If jazz is not quite dead, it is certainly stuck in the the twentieth century.

I'm not bothered that jazz has become a repertory genre, replicating what was sparkling new in the 1920s or the 1970s. My gripe is that it distracts us from looking in the right direction. So where should we be looking? Certainly beyond the conventional West. In particular, I would suggest we turn our gaze towards the Muslim world – the Middle East and South Asia.

The Sachal Studio Orchestra is the latest in a long line of Jazz greats that prove my point. The Lahore band offers an imaginative interpretation of Dave Brubeck's *Take Five*, blending violin with sitar and tabla. The album, which includes versions of *The Girl from Ipanema*, *Misty* and *Desafinado*, reached the top of iTunes jazz charts in the US and the UK.

The success of The Sachal Studio Orchestra, to some extent, is an internet phenomenon. The orchestra's video has attracted a flood of hits. Even in the pre-internet days of the 1980s, when Sony bought American Columbia (CBS Records), I had hoped that the cultural steering wheel would move away from Manhattan. But despite the corporate marketers of recorded music having local branches throughout the world, the industry was still dominated by New Yorkers setting their table for the perceived American appetite. EMI had always been a poorly-run firm, but the private equity financiers who took them over in the mid-2000s were even worse. Despite having a musically rich Asian and Middle Eastern catalogue, they wasted the last years of retail record shops by not exploiting this canon in the West the way they had pushed Western music to the Orient.

Although the malleable jazz genre has been increasingly difficult to define, it started out as exciting dance music, a vehicle for human expression. This could take the form of clever tricks of arrangement, melodic or rhythmic riffs, instrumental or vocal emphasis in front of the rest of the ensemble, or improvised solos. Surely African-American music wasn't the only scene to generate this, but it was the most readily available source for the American music industry to promote. In fact, such expressive aspects of music are, and have long been, plentiful from Baku to Cairo. The Muslim regions embraced saxophones, trumpets, pianos and Hawaiian guitars to their middlebrow bosoms decades ago. Yet, they've still retained only local identity.

Things could have been different but for an accident of history. In America, the Jewish camp was well represented in the commercial success of jazz in the 1930s. The Andrews Sisters and Benny Goodman's Orchestra had hits with *Bei Mir Bist Du Shön*, and other Jewish-flavoured numbers influenced swing-jazz considerably. *Bie Mir* had been a strictly Yiddish musical stage number when it was redone in jazz time at Harlem's Apollo Theatre. And Yiddish swing itself had a small radio audience in the immigrant New York City neighbourhoods of the 1940s and 1950s, a musical halfway house on the path to Americanisation. This was mostly because Jewish-Americans had a population advantage over Arabs and Asians in the American record market. If Arab immigrants had been nearly equal in numbers, they'd get to

claim popular influence too. Today's jazz-orientated musicians in Israel/
Palestine don't argue claims of musical acreage – they're just grateful to
collaborate on recording sessions, the Jewish Israeli double-bassist Daphna
Sadeh's CDs providing a good example. Israel's jazzers are generally enlightened, but cross-cultural collaboration only goes so far. You've got to be an
Israeli Palestinian, not a resident of the West Bank, Gaza or Jerusalem, to be
able to record in Tel Aviv and travel internationally.

As it happened, jazzy American Jews of non-Arab descent had to shoul-
der the music of the Muslim countries, whether they understood this or
not. Composers have always looked towards the mythical Orient to inject
some impressionistic novelty into their personal canons. The public wanted
exoticism and hungry musicians served it up. The Jewish jazz composer
and later electronic music innovator Raymond Scott (aka Harry Warnow)
had a huge hit with the impressionistic *Twilight in Turkey*, recorded by his
own small band in 1937 as well as by various large swing bands of the day,
including the big band of Tommy Dorsey. And the trumpeter Dizzy
Gillespie wrote *A Night in Tunisia* for the Boyd Raeburn Orchestra in 1944,
grasping for a North African essence, which he did achieve melodically.
But jazz in the main had to wait until the late 1950s, when there was some
interest in facing East.

This was due to some honest searching, such as the pianist-and-quartet-
leader Dave Brubeck's 1958 album devoted to a perceived Asian culture,
Jazz Impressions of Eurasia. Brubeck, now past his 90s, was the inspiration
for The Sachal Studio Orchestra. The Lahore band, he told the *Guardian*,
had produced 'the most interesting' version of *Take Five* he has ever heard.
The *Eurasia* session, however, was mostly European in intent, but had
grains of globalism. In *Nomad*, Brubeck tried to illustrate rural Turkish life,
with Joe Morello trying to get a *darabuka* (a goblet-shaped finger drum)
sound from his tom-tom.

But the most significant impetus for looking towards the Muslim world
came with the Black Muslim movement, who were not just significant in
numbers but also avid consumers of jazz. Curiously, Elijah Muhammed's
movement didn't promote black music the way Marcus Garvey, the leader
of Black Nationalism, had done in an earlier era. The Nation of Islam never
quite fulfilled its promise of having their own co-operative food shops,
restaurants and record stores; even Minister Louis Farrakahn, who has sev-

eral calypso albums to his name, failed in his 1980s attempt at marketing a line of personal care products. One would think that in the United States, the haven for indie record labels, the Nation would have tried starting a record company, signing up players with new Muslim names, but no!

Around 1960 some African-American jazz players, whether Muslim in outlook or not, set their lamps towards the Middle East and North Africa. This was a mixed quest, spurred on by religion, racial affinity with newly-independent African states, and a longing to unlock the door of their own history by going further back than the generations of slavery in the Americas. So a handful of American Black musicians changed their names: the saxophonist Eddie Gregory became Sahib Shihab, and the saxophonist and academic William Evans became Yusef Lateef. But their quest wasn't particularly authentic, for even when they had help from African musicians their attempts today seem somewhere between New York City jazz and Hollywood soundtracks.

An important Muslim jazz player we need to know about is Ahmed Abdul-Malik (1927-1993), a double-bassist and oud player. He worked most notably with pianist Thelonious Monk, who famously incorporated conventionally-wrong notes and out-of-place beats into modern jazz. Abdul-Malik was born with his Muslim name because his father was Sudanese, and the future bass ace was raised in an Arab neighbourhood of Brooklyn. His oud wasn't virtuoso and so he was best on simpler things, like the familiar blues walks or by simply setting up the theme for a number. And his Muslim jazz brothers really struggled as they had no feel for what he was trying to convey. Back at the dawn of the 1960s, there was racial resentment by some African-American jazz adventurers against the white-controlled 'Jazz Police Central Office'. So for these individuals any effort to be both musically and culturally 'outside' was important. This had nothing to do with pitting Islam against Christianity – religion simply didn't enter into it. While it's amusing in hindsight to observe some top Black players, stars of great quality, finding themselves adrift when out of their culture, their attempts are to be applauded.

The best of Abdul-Malik's Middle Eastern-slanted output is 1958's *Jazz Sahara*. The compositions are modal Arabic, but unremarkable and rather dull when compared to the Rahbani Brothers' classics for the Lebanese singer Fairuz of the same period, even though they were Parisian-influenced. Most importantly, the composer hasn't grasped the quarter-tones that add so much soul to Middle Eastern music, even though these bent notes sound out-of-tune to the conventional Western ear. Fortunately, Naim Karacand, Abdul-Malik's fabulous violinist, did understand. On the other hand, the tastily aggressive tenor saxophonist Johnny Griffin hadn't a clue. There, I've said it. Hard to imagine but this exhilarating saxophone god was totally confused on this session, leaning heavily on Dizzy Gillespie's 1940s bebop novelty *Salt Peanuts*, grasping for Richard Rodgers' Oklahoma evergreen *Surrey with the Fringe on Top*, and that saxophone key fluttering device used by every beginner from Bill Clinton to the bloke busking under the bridge on Sunday afternoons. Although *Jazz Sahara* is typical of the cheap'n'cheerful, unrehearsed 'blowing sessions' we expect from the Prestige Records output of the time, it must have been considered ground-breaking in its wearing of non-Western dress.

By the 1960s, the jazz LP market was expanding and other artists entered the 'exotic' arena. While Ahmed Abdul-Malik and his oud were tried on a John Coltrane session, the saxophonist Yusef Lateef (1920-) made a whole album in 1961 titled *Eastern Sounds*. His use of flute and the shehnai-like oboe on the otherwise blues-based *Blues for the Orient* is a good meeting point between cultures. *The Three Faces of Balal* shows off Lateef's virtuoso talent on a wooden flute. What makes it ring true though, is that the tracks are mostly modal. Meanwhile, *Jazz 'Round the World*, Lateef's 1963 album for the better-distributed ABC-Paramount corporation, was all over the cultural map. His amazing 1983 Nigerian *Hikima* LP is impossible to buy nowadays but you can download it easily. Lateef's motivation was cultural and musical, but certainly not separatist. As a convert to Islam in his late 20s, an awareness of the *ummah* probably had something to do with his wanting to scope the wider Muslim world through the musical lens.

An important player at this time was the flautist Herbie Mann (1930-2005). This white Jewish New Yorker with a goatee beard started out on tenor sax but soon found flute to be his main means of expression. But playing conventional jazz wasn't enough for him, for he liked a wide range of music and was a great favourite at Harlem's Apollo Theater because he always ran a racially-mixed stage and his playing was indeed right in the groove. His record company was Atlantic Records, founded by Ahmet and

Neshui Ertegun, two Turkish-American brothers who loved jazz as well as rhythm'n'blues.

So it was natural for Herbie Mann, who had experimented with Arabic music, to record, in 1966, *Impressions of the Middle East* and, a year later, the equally hip *The Wailing Dervishes*. The latter is live, with oud, darabuka, and even the black Philadelphian brother Rufus Harley, a peace advocate and jazz master of the Scottish bagpipes.

Scottish bagpipes are, of course, staple instruments of police and military bands. But when Cairo Jazz Band was formed by Salah Ragab in 1968, the bagpipes were dropped and the military uniform was kept. Gamal Abdul Nassar was in power and, as in former British colonial territories, if one had to serve in the forces the best militia gig was to play in the band. The crew was, to look at them, a standard big band jazz orchestra. However, their recordings from 1968 to 1973 (into the era of Anwar El-Sadat) represent a North African re-weaving of American styles by being both funky and melodically 'out'. So the result is determinedly Egyptian.

In the Middle East, Cairo seems to function like New York. Just as jazz musicians from Arizona, Mississippi or North Dakota gravitate towards New York — because that's where the studios are and consequently where the media will support a career — Cairo serves as a magnet for a wide range of musicians – from serious to pop. It's the centre of the Arabic film industry and the prime site of music. Not surprisingly, it is also the hub of Arabic jazz.

The Cairo Jazz Club opened in 1997 and has catered to a wide variety of styles, from traditional New Orleans jazz to Herbie Hancock. The club is also a magnet for up-and-coming local groups, including Eftekasat, a modern sextet which includes piano, bass, drums, guitar, the oud, the nay (flute) and qaraqeb (iron cymbals). Naturally, they've been supported by the United States Embassy!

At a casual glance, Eftekasat appears to be a pedestrian jazz-funk-rock fusion, but it is tightly arranged for compositional sense and not self-consciously athletic. However, congas, the Indian tabla and the nay don't transform it enough for me. Western-focused Cairo never experienced Weather Report or, to my mind, the superior African-American commercial music renaissance of the 1980s that was infused with rich jazz chords and melodies in service to the groove. So the ensemble's audience, at least at the time of their 2006 album, hadn't much of a barometer to use. One can always hope they catch up with their own now-elastic post-Arab Spring Egyptian culture. We learn as much from disappointing sessions as we do from winners.

Arabic Jazz by melodic drummer Ahmed Radie is much better. Radie plays a finely-tuned kit and writes his own stuff, although you wouldn't know it from the image on the CD cover. This would be a drum-bass-piano-guitar outfit except for the very prominent *quanoon*, which is the world's most sophisticated hammer dulcimer. It is a live recording, which I suppose was cheaper than buying studio time, but that only makes the soloing more pressured and risky. If you don't appreciate any jazz-rock fusion, you won't like this, but it's a spellbinding performance.

The king of Cairo recording studios is the percussionist and producer Hossam Ramzy. The young Ramzy considered Egyptian music to be too old fashioned. Perhaps he had a point. Egyptian music, when not for full orchestra, is for dancing, as swing music was back in its heyday. And just as 1930s-1940s swing is often still marketed as 'music for jiving dancers', the Egyptian grooves are promoted as a backdrop to belly-dancing. If you find any modern recordings sold with veiled hips but exposed midriffs, it's probably a solid, improvisational jam. So Ramsey took up jazz drumming in London in the early 1980s. But he was encouraged by his outward-thinking saxophonist-bandleader, Andy Sheppard, to go back to Cairo and his original culture and move it onward.

The 'Sultan of Swing', as he is known, has made at least twenty albums, many of them with cameos by particular instrumentalists. So a quarter-tone sax master such as Rafat Misso, the quarter-tone accordionist Farouq Mohamed Hassan, and the ubiquitous *qanoon* ace Maged Serour get plenty of solo time on these albums. These are important players who may have never approached jazz if not for Ramzy himself. The rhythms are in non-Western yet utterly infectious time signatures. I won't con the followers of jazz scripture here; you simply might not accept it as jazz. But if you have a bold brain and artful ears, it will surely give you a healthy heart. To truly discover the fundamentals of Egyptian urban and rural grooves, one would have to do a full-time course in Cairo. But Ramzy's 2-CD *Rhythms of the Nile – Introduction to Egyptian Dance Rhythms*, on which he narrates and plays a variety of grooves, in 8/4, 4/4, 2/4 and even 5/4 times, is the best aural substitute.

But Cairo does not get all the jazz glory. It has a strong competitor in Beirut, where Incognito has flourished as a pan-Arab distributor of less commercial music, books and films. Their early signing, the Cairo band Masar, combines piano, oud, double bass and rhythm on their 2006 album *El 'Aysh Wel Melh*. A second release, *Things That I Miss*, under the name of oudist Hazem Shaheen, is less collaborative. They'd be more jazz-like if they had a trumpet, sax, clarinet, or flute, an instrument that plays extended notes. But they're a band to watch, if still together.

Incognito's other most Arabic-jazz act is Sign of Thyme, whose 2007 *Zad* album is also appealing, especially as half their repertoire is of oud-led versions of American modern jazz classics. Their first CD, *Like All People*, released in 2006, was entirely of original numbers – they've obviously got a lot to say. With a trio format of oud, electric bass and Middle Eastern percussion, they don't set a foot wrong and are overdue for a new release. The label has other strongly cross-cultural crews too, of which the Syrian group Hewar, catchy and inventive, is probably the best and most-recorded.

Beyond the Middle East, there is another, rather surprising, bastion of Muslim jazz. It is to be found in Azerbaijan, the oil production state on the Caspian Sea. Azerbaijan was the centre for the jazz movement in the USSR. At the close of the Second World War, Stalin imposed a prohibition against certain arts and this included jazz. Until his death in 1953, even so-called Western instruments were not encouraged, but, due to the vagaries of the oil export business, Baku, the capital, was more cosmopolitan than other Soviet cities.

The most important musician to come out of Baku was the post-war pianist Vagif Mustafa Zadeh, one of the best jazz keyboard artists ever. He was well-educated musically because the Soviets encouraged sinuous classical music education and gave lip service to promoting regional ethnic cultures, even if it meant bending the formats to fit the Kremlin's tastes. The Soviet bureaucrats were famous for concocting regional ethnic ensembles that didn't really exist, in order to promote the image of a happy union of cultures. The young Vagif Mustafa Zadeh took in jazz broadcasts of the in-ten-tion-al-ly-slow-speak-ing Willis Conover on the shortwave radio station, Voice of America. They actually met, so perhaps some of Conover's later programmes were personal favours to Vagif. Mustafa

Zadeh's exceptional skill and adventurous compositional genius melded all of this to create 'Mugham Jazz', a local variation based on traditional rhythms and modal scales.

Soviet tolerance only went so far. Unfortunately, Mustafa Zadeh wasn't able to tour Europe. Rather, he was continually sent further east and died from a heart attack on tour in Taskhent in 1979, aged only 39. His Melodya Records vinyl LPs and taped local broadcasts survived, and were published in a 2004 CD set. And his daughter Aziza Mustafa Zadeh took up her father's mantel. Rightly known as 'Princess of Jazz', Aziza plays Mugham Jazz with classical and avant-garde influences. There are now a plethora of jazz musicians in Baku, many featured on the double-disc-with-book release by Sony, *Jazz in Azerbaijan*.

Muslim migrants to Europe are also making their presence felt on the jazz scene. Two immigrant bands have made a particular impact in recent times. Stephan Athanas' Switzerland-based ContempArabic Jazz Ensemble, a septet, is just as you would expect: a thoroughly modern mix of European sensibilities with those of the Middle East. The approach on their *Souk* CD is respectful of the arrangements of the bassist, who happens to be the leader. The charts emphasise dynamics and the narrative of each number, but there's still improvisation. The chords formed by the added classical chamber crew are infrequent but verge on Ellingtonian dissonance. However, there are no quarter notes here to puzzle European-American ears. Athanas offers spoonfuls of polite klezmer too and the result is a formal-wear fusion. To some this would be jazzy, as it might have been back in Weimar Germany in the late 1920s.

The Belgium-based Hijaz is a well-rounded band of improvisational Arabic music. The percussion could have been recorded louder on their two CDs (*Dunes*, 2008; *Chemsi*, 2010) but they infuse their music with jazz sensibilities. The oud, piano and nay make for, as jazzers would say, an excellent 'front line'. *Ila Sadiqi* is a suite that piles on the pensiveness until it spreads its wings, when you can imagine Django Reinhardt and Stephanne Grappelli swinging to it. They played superbly at a 2011 London concert and one suspects they'll be even better in the future.

So while The Sachal Studio Orchestra is certainly a ground-breaking band, there is nothing 'new' about jazz in the Muslim world. Indeed, Muslim musicians have given us some of the real greats of Jazz, and the most exciting and innovative jazz now comes from Muslim regions. Their records have encouraged newer players to reject the more rigid *Down Beat* and music degree stereotypes. Of course, there will always be bands in Cairo and Beirut who sound as if they've just got off a flight from New York City. But look a bit deeper and you will be pleasantly surprised.

The West is so ignorant of the vast musical landscape of the Muslim world that even traditional styles seeming old-school in Istanbul could strike wild applause in Köln and Chicago. But there is more to jazz than New York and New Orleans. Not that the purists will approve of the eastward trend. All my life, older aficionados have derided the occasional innovation of mainly American artists, by saying, 'That's not jazz!'. Perhaps not as we have known it. But it's definitely getting a bit stuffy in here. Can we open the door, please?

ART AND LETTERS

}

ERBIL DIARY

Robin Yassin-Kassab

5 May

It was an annoying journey out: a thirty-mile lift to the train station, then a train, a bus, a plane, a transit zone, a plane; unfitting and refitting my belt, tired and prickle-skinned among the glassy hustling public, and the jarring mesh of duty-free odours, and the funneling tunneling lights. My night in Vienna, old Austro-Hungaria, was spent in a very contemporary airport hotel. The windows were sealed by regulation. I lay on the bed and watched TV – all I ever do in anonymous, upmarket hotels – on pillows too bulky, sheets too sterile. I watched too much Arabic Jazeera, slow eyes chasing the script on the news bar, about the killing in Syria, in Homs and in Dara'a. I slid to sleep to the hiss of air conditioning.

It was inevitable that I'd experience this transit day – from somewhere to nowhere, not yet to somewhere else – as an annoyance. My life at home was being disrupted, my comfortable routines, my standard small measures of time. The amount of experience allowed in a usual day's burst is regrettably small, not counting occasional epiphanies. But visits to places like Iraq, to meet writers who've lived through the worst, expand the amount. For this reason my account is labelled day by day.

6 May

Inaam Kachachi is a Paris-based novelist and journalist. Her most recent novel, available in English too, is *The American Granddaughter*, which concerns a young Iraqi-American woman who 'returns' to Iraq as a translator with the American military.

169

When Inaam returns home these days she finds that Baghdad, the cradle of her early life, has become a foreign city. Last time she was there an American soldier assumed she was the foreigner because she was dressed only in T-shirt and trousers, revealing her light skin, startling orange hair and (by her own description) her plumpness. 'When he passed by me he said "Hi Ma'am!" I replied in English,' (she puts on a parodic American growl) – '"Fuck you, I'm Iraqi!"'

Once she mentions her plumpness I notice it. She's elegant and swish with it too. Her size seems to be an outward manifestation of powerful inner warmth, as if her raging humour requires great space to rush about in. We'd met before, half a year earlier in Berlin, and we wave to each other as she comes through the Vienna airport gate.

So: eastern Europe, the Balkans, Turkey. And south over snowflaked mountains towards the flatlands of Iraqi Kurdistan. I think I glimpse the glistening Tigris from my port hole. On the other side of the river is Mosul, where Inaam's family originates (and, so rumour has it – much more distantly – mine too), and near Mosul are the ruins of Nineveh, where Ashurbanipal's library was buried and dug up, and with it the Epic of Gilgamesh, the earliest versions of the flood myth, the omens and divinations of the ancient world. I experience a frisson of firm location: my first time in Iraq, which is the homeland of all writers, the birthplace of literature, the Babel of stories. This is where human beings first discovered writing.

The airport is contemporary, spacious and airy. Our group of writers is processed through passport control and into a minibus, green fields and long grass on either side; after a kilometre we stop at a lonely concrete hut where our bags are scanned again. We change buses here, for security's sake.

And into the city. It's called Hawler in Kurdish, Erbil in Arabic, Arbaa-ilu (Four Gods) in Akkadian, and Urbilum (The Upper City) in Sumerian. It's the fourth largest city in Iraq, the largest in Iraqi Kurdistan, and the seat of the Kurdish Regional Government (KRG). Its population is well over a million, but it doesn't feel like that. It's spacious like the airport, low rise, and most of it is in very good shape.

Our hotel compound is surrounded by blast walls. The public side of the walls is painted with murals – prisoners breaking through bars, the pepsi logo, mountains and flowers. Our bags are searched and scanned at the entrance to the compound and again in the foyer of the hotel.

Once that's done I hurry to greet Ahmad Saadawi, the novelist, poet, painter and journalist, who I spy smoking in the lounge. I know his face from his Facebook profile and his voice from his unfinished novel *Frankenstein in Baghdad* (an extract of which is one of the very best contributions to the recent *Beirut 39* anthology). In the story a man finds work clearing debris and body parts from the Baghdad streets, and keeps the parts, and constructs a body which soon stands up and walks. Through such tragicomedy Ahmad remembers the dismembered, writes life from death, sews reality back into one surreal fabric.

We gather: the 'international' group, the Baghdad Seven poets' group, the Kurdish writers, the British Council staff. The British Council has organised this first Erbil Literature Festival to encourage the reforming of links sundered by decades of dictatorship, sanctions, occupation and war — this kind of thing is the very best of their work — and now Zaid Badri of the BC's Baghdad office tells us the local rules. Leave a note before you leave the hotel to say where you're going. Carry your fully-charged mobile phone at all times. Don't accept lifts. Only use the recommended taxi service.

We eat a meal. I sit with Ahmad, and the poets Samarqand al-Jabri and Soheil Najm, and I listen to their Baghdad lives. Stories of blood told through laughter and silence.

Rice and meat, salad and fruit, plenty to drink, the crackle of language. Laughter surpasses silence, and soon we swoop as one group up through the elevators to the bar on the ninth floor. The point of being here is the terrace's view of the citadel, or rather the walled tell, mountainous remnant of 8,000 years' litter. But after only five minutes of gazing, Zaid, whose mournful countenance is reinforced by his heavily joined-up brow, ushers us inside, for security reasons.

Some retire; some sit and talk. Zaid tells the foreigners that after a while dead bodies in the street no longer scare you. They only make you sad.

7 May

Into town to find breakfast. About half the men wear Western smart casual, about half wear the Kurdish variety — baggy *sirwal* trousers and a *kuffiyah* used as a cummerbund. One or two visible Arabs wear *dishdashas*. The ladies wear bright colours. People sit smoking and talking between the fountains on the plaza beneath the high citadel. KRG soldiers unobtrusively police the streets.

Kurdish is the overwhelmingly dominant language, and no Arabic newspapers are on sale, but everyone I speak to can speak some Arabic too. Several of the shopkeepers have returned from exile in Hackney, Manchester, Gothenburg. The atmosphere is pleasant, relaxed and friendly – which is just as well, since my phone has run out of battery. A banner draped across the entrance to the souq reads 'A Muslim Must Be Honest and Reliable with the People'. The sky is clouded and heavy with dust.

I buy a couple of hand-made goats for my children. The same shop specialises in illustrated rugs. Those hung on display include Chinese-fantasy rural idylls, the Imam Ali in green turban, a Virgin and Christ, the Prophet's mosque at Madina... and Massoud Barzani, president of the KRG and head of the Kurdish Democratic Party. Erbil is Barzani territory.

Both Kurds and Arabs are victims of the imperialist map. Neither won their unitary state from the conspiring of Mr. Sykes and M. Picot. But (excepting the Palestinians) the Arabs have had it somewhat better. The Kurds formed minorities wherever they lived, and in Ba'athist Iraq they met state Arabism's most fascistic formulation. In addition to regime assaults, and to the tendency of regional powers to instrumentalise the Kurds in their own conflicts, the Kurds have been plagued by tribal and factional division. The rival parties in Iraqi Kurdistan – the Barzanis and the Talabanis – have at times called on Iranian or even Ba'athist support against the other. (Rifts are currently in a state of abeyance. High officials have formally reconciled, but on the popular level resentment still thrives.)

It's lunchtime when I eat breakfast. It consists of a meat sandwich and soup which I recognise as Middle Eastern beside a deliciously spicy chutney I would have assumed was subcontinental.

Sated, I stagger to the hotel, and thence by minibus to a writers' round-table discussion. The Kurdish Writers Union, the Iraqi Writers Union and the Syriac Writers Union are represented. Plus the Anglophones. Rachel Holmes, the biographer, arts organiser and activist, deftly manages the four languages and the many loquacious writers speaking them. Simultaneous translation helps a great deal.

Speakers offer introductions to contemporary Iraqi Arab, Kurdish and Assyrian writing. Rachel talks about contemporary trends in English-lan-

guage publishing. Then over to the floor. For my turn, I say that this is potentially a time of opportunity for writers of Iraqi, Arab and Muslim
background; the West is translating more work than before; there's a genuine
popular interest in this part of the world. Then I praise two writers who I
believe are deserving of praise: Ahmad Saadawi and the great Hassan Blasim.

Saadawi and Blasim, in their different ways, emerge from the more fluid
pole of Arabic culture which over the centuries has challenged political, religious and poetic orthodoxy through esotericism, Sufism and symbolism. They
offer a textual poetry of sharp bright images, and of logical dislocation. It's a
writing which approaches dreaming, always visionary, often nightmarish.

Blasim, shortlisted for the Independent's Foreign Fiction prize, has published a collection in English translation called *The Madman of Freedom
Square*. The book contains stories on Iraq's bloody chaos, and migration,
and both at once; it mixes horror, comedy and the surreal; it slips between
persons, tenses and perspectives with remarkable accuracy and ease. It's
certainly some of the very best writing I've read in recent years. I gave a
copy to Booker-listed writer Mohammad Hanif, and Hanif agreed with
me: Blasim is shockingly good.

I had no idea that he was such a controversial figure in his own country.
I learnt afterwards that the British Council chose not to invite him to
Erbil, at least not in the literary festival's first year, so as not to attract
unwelcome publicity. It's true Blasim writes about sensitive subjects —
about blasphemy, self-hatred, sadism, sex, madness. It's true that his
dreams unsettle and provoke. But isn't that what a writer is for?

Several writers are eager to disabuse me of the notion that Blasim is
worth reading. The Iraqi prose writers of note in the conference hall —
Ahmad and Inaam — I'm happy to say, speak in his defense. But many are
embittered that Blasim has met European success. Do I detect a note of
jealousy? I do; but there's more to it than that. 'Art is beautiful,' says a
poet, 'but Blasim's work is dirty. Art should be spiritual.' — As if the spirit
were a Christmas tree fairy, pink and pretty, with useless wings.

'Tell it to James Joyce,' I say (or words to that effect), 'who wrote about
the stink of people sitting on the toilet. People thought he was dirty too.'

'If you took away the swear words,' puts in another, 'there would be
nothing left.' My breath is taken by that one. I cannot answer. The discussion drifts to other topics. At some point someone says that Iraq has suf-

fered a calamity 'beyond imagination'. I agree, thinking particularly of the couple of years which followed the attack on Samarra's Askari shrine, the destruction of the country's ancient social fabric in a manner more comprehensive than ever before, the ethnic cleansing of Baghdad, the mass flight of educated Iraqis, the filth of it all, the mass human failure, Western and Arab, Sunni and Shia.

After the terrible events of September 11, after one day of explosions, certain chatterers rather pompously asked how fiction could ever be relevant again. The question was asked more meaningfully after Auschwitz, and now must be asked again after Iraq. After this horror, does art have anything useful to say?

I think Blasim answers the question in the resounding positive. He shows us how to write after the collapse. He offers so much more than dirt. Yet (apart from online, at www.iraqstory.com) he hasn't yet been published in Arabic. This is a symptom of an Arab cultural tragedy which extends far beyond Iraq.

Inaam Kachachi describes how writers must pay Arab publishers to publish their work. Hassan Blasim refuses to pay, and so remains unpublished. Another writer explains that many distribute photocopies of their stories and poems for precisely this reason, just as they used to do under Ba'athist censorship. Surprisingly, not everyone complains about the exploitation. One man says the publishers demanded a mere five hundred dollars to publish his book, not the two thousand figure that Inaam quoted. But how many Iraqis have five hundred dollars to spare?

Dr Saad Iskander, director of the National Library in Baghdad, talks about the lack of a readership, about the illiteracy and semi-literacy which grips the country after educational collapse, about the lack of a national identity, or at least a consensual notion of national identity, despite or because of the decades in which (Ba'athist) nationalist discourse was ubiquitous.

It's a busy schedule. In the evening there's a poetry reading event in the Chaikhana Muchko, a traditional tea house built into the citadel wall. Ahmad Saadawi reads through the smoke. Then Soheil Najm, a gentle man of considered movements. His collections have intriguing titles – *Breaking the Phrase*, *Your Carpenter O Light*, *No Window Outside the Window* – and the images he puffs out like smoke rings hang intriguingly in the air. Soheil edits the *Iraq Literary Review*, which showcases English-language translations of previously untranslated Iraqi writers. And he's translated Saramago and Kazantzakis into Arabic. (Most of these writers are bridges).

Next, Nazand Begikhani, and most memorably (though I don't speak Kurdish) her poem on Saddam Hussain's campaign against the Kurds in the late 80s, when 100,000 were killed and 182,000 'disappeared'. She reads it with haunting emphasis on the long second syllable of the title and refrain: 'Anfaal, Anfaal'. (It was one of the dictator's peculiarities to name his genocides with Quranic or early Islamic names, 'Anfal' for the Kurds and 'Qadissiyyeh' for the attack on Iran.) Later on I read Nazand's collection *Bells of Speech*, which confirms my first impression; it's very fine poetry, clear, quiet and stark. Nazand's own character is similar: underlying her calm poise there's a rawness, an intensity. Her father and three brothers were murdered by the old regime. She's spent a life on the run, sometimes literally and always figuratively. She writes about exile, the persecution of her people and gender, about the uselessness of prayer and the pointlessness of declaring God dead. She's translated Baudelaire and TS Eliot into Kurdish, and is a member of Kurdish Women Action Against Honour Killing.

Once the visitors have had their say, local poets rush to take the mic. This, and the level of café engagement with the poems, the warm applause and the ears straining above clinking glasses and scraping chairs, attests to a powerful thirst for poetry in Erbil. The atmosphere echoes the literary cafés of Baghdad's famed Mutanabi street in the days before occupation, before sanctions, when Iraq boasted the Arab world's most accomplished readership. There's an old saying, 'Egypt writes the books, Lebanon sells them, Iraq reads them,' – which is perhaps a little unfair, as it forgets the books written in Iraq by such pivotal figures as Mahdi Issa Saqr, Saadi Youssef and Abdul Wahhab al-Bayati.

We spill out onto the street talking in our many tongues. Before long we've all been rounded into the minibus, and we're heading – flagging now – to the Syriac Writers Union in Ainkawa, a suburb home to Christian refugees from the south as well as to local Assyrians.

Again there is no translation, which is not a bad thing. Listening to poetry in a language which is unknown but which nevertheless belongs to a familiar family is something like reading Joyce's *Finnegans Wake*: you are conscious first of the music, and then of the rustling connotations arising from half-recognised words.

One poem is read in English, for the benefit of the British visitors. It's a very poor poem intended to thank the West for removing Saddam – 'When the tyrant's statue fell, birds sang, children smiled, the sun laughed' – that sort of thing. In the post-reading huddle on the steps outside, a man insists on distancing himself. 'This poem doesn't represent me. We don't agree with it. Yes, Saddam was a monster, but who brought him in the first place? And what happened after he fell?'

The Assyrian community treat us to another hearty meal. We sing Iraqi songs in the minibus afterwards.

During the night the sky's oppression finally breaks into a clanking, shrieking thunder storm. I watch it from my room's tall windows – snakes of lightening and lashing rain.

8 May

It's the Prose Fiction event at the KRG's Ministry of Culture and Youth. The Anglo session is ably hosted by Rachel Holmes, and includes Tahmima Anam, author of *A Golden Age* and *The Good Muslim*, and winner of the Commonwealth Writers' Prize; Bee Rowlatt, author with May Witwit of the epistolary *Talking About Jane Austen in Baghdad*; and me. Tahmima makes an excellent case (amid these cultures which value poetry foremost) for the necessity of the novel – 'for only through the novel can you see through someone else's eyes.' And Bee tells a very successful joke about an Iraqi in New York saving a child from a dog.

In the afternoon I buy a *sirwal* and jacket. I just have to. Next I buy a rucksack from a shop which sells American handguns beside Iraqi and Kurdish flags. After that I climb the steps to what's called the citadel, the enwalled *tell* thirty metres high. A large Kurdish flag flies from the highest point, a sun blazing out from red, white and green.

A photograph of Erbil in the 1920s hangs in the hotel lobby. Erbil then was the citadel alone, surrounded by brown ploughed fields. Across the millenia the citadel has been the seat of those 'four gods', and of a Syriac bishop, and Assyrian, Persian, Parthian, Roman and Greek governors. Once it was the centre of a Turkmen state. It declined after the Mongol depredations, like everywhere in Mesopotamia. Then in 2007 the citadel's inhabitants were evicted in the name of restoration. At this stage it looks like a questionable decision; a few big houses are being done up, and some excavation is going on, but most of the homes are already crumbling. (The restorers aim eventually to rehouse fifty families).

We go exploring. The straw-wattle rooms are cool and light, stairways climb over the roofs, each home has a garden and the figs still grow. Anita Sethi (the journalist) finds a slipper. I find a school book. It puts you in mind of Halabja, but nobody says so.

Dusk settles. In this incongruous setting a quartet plays European classical music. Then the highly-regarded poet Sarkawt Rasul reads. By now my ear is tuning in to Kurdish somewhat. (I think I'm listening to the Kurmanji dialect.) I pick out words I know from Arabic and Farsi. Sometimes I even believe I've picked up a poem's theme. I may be wrong.

Nazand reads. Soheil reads in Arabic.

There's enough time for members of the Baghdad Seven to read a brief poem each. One poet feels slighted. 'When we come here we are guests. We should be treated as guests, and given time to read like the local poets.' Sarkawt Rasul responds with icy politeness: 'On the contrary, Erbil and its people are known for their hospitable treatment of guests.' Does this dispute concern the reading schedule only or is it indicative of deeper Kurd-Arab tension? 'The latter,' an Iraqi tells me, rolling his eyes.

9 May

Tahmima Anam, Bee Rowlatt and I are reading to a packed hall of students and teachers at Salahuddeen University. Amongst the Kurdish students are a few refugees from further south. A girl fom Baghdad tells me she isn't forced to wear hijab in Erbil, and her parents, not having to fear abduction here, allow her to go out with her friends.

After tea (the same strong stuff served in waisted glasses in Turkey and all over Iraq) Bee and I host a workshop on journalism and blogging. Bee makes the thing work. She's a BBC World Service journalist, and a very good teacher. Of course, the students – engaged, eager, good-natured – contribute most of all.

In the evening we return to the Culture Ministry for the formal final event. Ministers and diplomats make formal speeches. Then the tone rises. There's wonderful music, and all the writers read.

Including Samarqand al-Jabri. She reads so beautifully, letting the words escape her lips one by one, with tender care, as if she fears for their fragility, that they might break. In her own life a great deal has broken: her father was a prize-winning chemist, also a Communist interrogated and tortured several times; he was executed in 2000. Samarqand has won prizes herself, an Emirati prize for her short story collection *Two Small Bears* and the Gold Prize in Baghdad for her poetry. She's currently finishing her third book of poems.

Back to the hotel, and then to a restaurant for our final dinner – the most epic yet.

While sampling the mezzeh I talk to Dr. Saad Iskander. By now the group has him codenamed Doctor Love. (Because when he came back from exile to manage the National Library he employed people who subsequently fell in love with each other, including a woman he fell in love with, who became his wife.) Saad is a Feyli Kurd. 'We're the old Baghdad Kurds, and we suffered enormously. We were Communists. We opposed the Ba'ath when it came first. Even my mother was arrested.'

The *masgoof* is brought to the table, a fish grilled beside an open fire. I know Baghdad is famous for its riverside *masgoof* restaurants, so here's another of those so-near-and-yet-so-far moments when I can nearly sniff the capital. Haroun ar-Rasheed, the Dar al-Hikma, al-Hallaj and al-Ghazali … the Mongols and the Americans, Saddam Hussain…

During the fish course I talk to Taman Shakir, head of communications at the KRG's Ministry of Culture, who tells me about being imprisoned as a young woman. She doesn't say exactly what happened to her, but she tells me she was ill until she was cured by counselling in Germany a decade later. Between prison and Germany she lived in the mountains, with the peshmerga. Then she says, 'Come back one day. You have to see Sulaymaniyah. You haven't seen the villages. You haven't even seen the mountains.'

And then sweets and fruit, during which I talk to Brendan McSharry, the hardworking but unruffled British Council director in Baghdad. He's flying out of Erbil in an hour, not direct to Baghdad on the domestic service because Iraqi Airlines may in an emergency land in a city – Mosul for example – in which security can't be guaranteed. So Brendan will fly to Amman, then on to Baghdad in the morning. He'll be met by an armoured convoy. He'll be taken to the Green Zone, where he lives in a mortar-proof pod. He isn't permitted to visit Iraqis who live beyond the Zone.

One writer I would have liked to talk to but can't is Choman Hardi. Now UK-based, the poet chose not to attend the Erbil festival. She felt her participation would be tantamount to normalisation with a regime which fails to recognise basic human rights. In April, while Arabs were demonstrating from Morocco to Bahrain, Kurds in Sulaymaniyah also protested against the corruption of the Kurdish region's two dominant parties. The KRG's security forces, in response, attacked protestors and journalists and imposed severe restrictions on the media.

10 May

Tonight I'll sleep in Vienna's airport hotel. Tomorrow I'll be in Scotland. Therefore at breakfast I eat as much hummus as I possibly can.

We gather in the lobby for a last time. Cheeks are kissed; emails are exchanged. The writers from Baghdad express their appreciation of Erbil. It's so clean and peaceful, whereas you can't walk down the street in Baghdad without meeting a checkpoint. Socialising is a tense and difficult affair. Bodies still show up in the street.

But they hope the situation will improve. Grimly they insist that it must improve soon. Among them there are Sunnis and Shia, and no sign of communal tension. That's normal, of course; before the invasion a third of Iraqi marriages crossed sectarian boundaries. And these writers are mainly leftists. 'The people realise now it was a mistake to vote for the religious parties. Saddam, the occupation, Iran – they all tried to divide us through religion.'

The Anglophones head for the airport. Long grass sways on either side. I'm heading back, via tunneling lights and duty-free stink, to the Vienna airport hotel and more al-Jazeera. The killing continues in Syria, in Dara'a and Homs and Banyas. I think of Damascus and Baghdad, of Soheil and Samarqand and Ahmad now back at home, and I remember the Syrian poet Adonis's lament for 'the different forms of obstruction that the Arab creator faces…in the form of politics and religion. He lives and writes in a state of siege, inspired by a mystery, from which he begins to weave a hope, which will open up a horizon, that will destroy the siege.'

WORK FROM IRAQ

A Child's Beginning by Hassan Blasim

We would wait at the side of the main road for the coffins to arrive. Bassim and I were eight. The war with Iran had entered its fourth year. The coffins were tightly wrapped in the flag and hoisted on top of the cars which had come from the front. We wanted to become adults because the adults stood in solemn sadness at the passing of the coffins, raising their palms to the sky. And we greeted the dead as they did.

And if a death car turned into our neighbourhood we ran through our muddy alleyways after it, and the driver slowed lest the coffin fall. Then the car chose the door of a sleeping house to stop in front of, and the women came out of the house screaming and crying, throwing themselves in the pools of mud and smearing their hair. And my friend and I would rush, each one to his mother, to tell her at whose door the death car had stopped. My mother would reply: 'Go wash your face,' or, 'Go to our neighbour Um Ali and ask if she has any spices.' And in the evening she slapped her face and wailed with the neighbourhood women in the slain person's house.

One day Bassim and I sat awaiting a coffin. We were eating sunflower seeds. We waited a long time, until we'd almost lost hope and turned home disappointed, when a death car appeared, approaching from the horizon. We ran behind it like happy dogs, competing to see who could overtake it. It eventually stopped at Bassim's door, from which his mother emerged, screaming wildly and tearing her dress in the mud pool. Bassim froze beside me, staring in amazement. His big brother noticed him and pulled him into the house. And me – I ran to my mother's lap sobbing hot tears. I said, 'Mother, my friend Bassim's father is dead.'

She said, 'Wash your face. Go to the shop. Bring us a half kilo of onions.'

(translated by Rana Zaitoon)

A Child's Country by Hassan Blasim

I was born in a country where everyone demands revenge on the present. From the rostrums they screamed, 'God's book and the Shariah, God's book and the Shariah'. From the newspapers poets and artists called, 'the Heritage, the Heritage'. And whenever I touched God and the heritage my heart would ulcerate and my fingers would rot.

These people were wounded. They were dreaming of healing their pain with the ancestors' bones and the incense of the tribe. While I was thinking of the soul, of music, of dreams, of bodies colliding with bodies, and of this universe whose mystery and wildness increase whenever we pluck from it a flower.

They screamed in my face, 'the Roots, the Roots' – but I was suspended in the air; my roots were nightmares. I was born in a mass grave. At night. Conceived by two corpses. The illusion and the past. And the sky was the colour of blood.

(translated by Rana Zaitoon)

Wings Designed to Fly by Ahmad Saadawi

Damn this desire to fly.
Damn these wings.
.....
This isn't a role in a play so I can take the wings off when the curtain comes down.
They aren't wings of wax which will melt in the morning on my way to work.
Neither are they invisible wings whose existence requires long discussion to prove.
They are neither useful for statues, nor for the metallic icons on top of car hoods.
They are wings designed to fly.

Clothes can't hide them nor can darkness ease their existence.
It won't clear your conscience to flutter them for a short while in the
morning in front of the bathroom mirror.
They can't be used to pick something up nor to cast greetings on the days
passing by.

They are here, tensing between the shoulders, torturing you for
eternity:
You, the freak fed on reptiles and mammals' blood.
They are wings to torture you, unless you use them to fly now, at this
moment
Without luggage
Or return tickets
On your long journey that never ends.

(translated by Rana Zaitoon)

God Is Not Dead For My Mother by Nazand Begikhani

'Truth is an illusion'
said Nietzsche

For my mother who has never been to school
truth is standing up calmly
after a deluge
planting a garden
with serene hands
speaking the language of trees
and understanding the alphabet of rain

For my mother truth is
reading the silence of my brothers' faces
as they lie in stone
and seeing in the blueness of the sky
a plume of light tracing a path

which stretches deep
beyond the cloud and the stars

When you can trace the white wings of your dead children
flying over the path of light in the azure of the sky
you don't need God to die

from Bells of Speech by Nazand Begikhani, published by Ambit Books

The Blue Shawl by Samarqand al-Jabri

My father knew he had a daughter of a different nature. It wasn't by chance that we were a family who knew a lot about telepathy. Since my innocent childhood mornings shone I had touched people's belongings and immediately seen their faces and known what they were thinking of. Sadness calling from their chests would pain me, yet sometimes I would be admitted to the worlds of their happiness. Whenever a little child went missing it was enough to bring me his shirt, dewed by his childhood scent. I would tuck my confident fingers in its fabric and close my eyes. The corners of my mind would take me to wherever the child was and, as if I were the mirror of the gods, I would determine his circumstances. Years have passed in which my only concern was those who went missing, or who were lost, or whose breaths were forfeited to waste.

It was a cold day when a stranger came, his features like the death that blows over the north's cities. He was wearing the uniform of plagued affiliations and parties. He spilt his tarry existence on the walls of my room and looked at me with worry:

'Are you Sarah?'

'How can I help you?'

'She's the wife of a very important man. Of course you can have all that you dream of if you find her.'

And he tossed me a blue shawl made of silk and embroidered with roses similar to those in my childhood dreams. He looked at my son Ibrahim with an examining eye and said he would return in two days for an answer.

An evening of tiredness, with dreams on the other side. I saw a woman with a white complexion; sadness had cut into her youthful face. The shawl was his present. He loved her but thanks to fate's mysterious interventions she married a man prominent in the state. She was not happy. She decided to buy another world without him. She left him, leaving everything behind her, on a day whose shining sun was feigned.

Here I am listening to the noise of gulls flapping happily. She is near the abandoned port. In my dream she looked into my face and said she would wait for me. The pleading of her voice took away my heart's negligence.

I didn't go. Confusion blended with the hours of my long day. The man returned and saw that for the first time I didn't have an answer for a man to whom nobody says no. They took my son Ibrahim in the hope that my empty lap would activate my desire to tell of the woman's whereabouts.

I left before the sun, and started the day pacing the winding roads leading to her place. The closer I came, the more prophetic warmth swept my frozen limbs.

I saw a house of dilapidated tin. Birds were sleeping in quietness as if beside a blessed shrine. I entered and saw her face, calmer than it had seemed in my dreams. She gestured for me to sit and she gazed at the sea opposite her.

'Certainly you will tell him, one way or another. He is so good at getting people to confess, especially simple souls like us.'

'He has taken my only child.'

'He has taken the love of my life. I accepted marriage hoping to save my darling but the prison bars were the beginning and the hidden grave was the end. Or rather, I decided what the end would be. I left him. Tell him where I am. My fear will not defeat me anymore. Take your child back while you're still able to salvage his life.'

I spent some of my day with her, accompanying another pain and another flood. Reluctantly I agreed to tell him her whereabouts.

Next day they returned Ibrahim to me, and I travelled with them in the armored car as it headed to the port. We approached the house. The birds never left their inner peace. As we came closer we heard her loud laughter. We entered hurriedly to find that she had tied her blue shawl next to the window, and that she had turned into a white gull. She looked at our blue faces, and she flew east.

(translated by Rana Zaitoon)

FOUR POEMS

Mimi Khalvati

Earthshine

Under a giant plane beside the gate where we said goodbyes,
under the plane's bare trunk where squirrels flatten themselves

on bark, next to the smothered plane whose ivy outraces branch,
under the two great planes where we stood vaguely looking round

for it was a clear night, the street empty and we, small gaggle,
newly intimate but standing apart, keeping our voices low

though they carried bright as bells as we counted the evening out,
gesturing towards the cars, deciding who would go with who

and gradually splitting off, under the planes with the squirrel dreys
hidden in all that ivy, but far off, behind and above the station,

there, where we looked pointing, like an Oriental illustration
of Arabian Nights, lay the old moon in the new moon's arms:

earthshine on the moon's night side, on the moon's dark limb,
earthlight, our light, our gift to the moon reflected back to us.

And the duty we owe our parents as the Romans owed their Gods
(for who will cradle us when we grow old?) spoke in the moon's pietà.

New Year's Eve

Night is a rush of noise, an Indian hilltown train
steaming up a mountain through Himalayan tunnels,

morning the destination, quiet as a mountain-top
after the snow has melted, the celebrants have left.

The first morning of the year, a Shimla of the mind,
its local aspirations – work, money, kinship, health;

a time to think things over, let them settle
in the recesses of imagination. They'll raise their heads

of their own accord, lean out of carriages to wave.
For now is the time of watering the splendid platform displays,

of gathering at The Ridge, the Scandal Point in the mall,
gossiping, fingering the oak and rosewood souvenirs.

In Shimla, mashkis will be carrying goatskin bags of water,
sluicing down the tarmac while I, at the last

hill station of the year, will bring the silence in,
fold it like a three-flower Kullu shawl on my table.

The Blanket

Cold, yes, under a sodium sky at three o'clock in the morning.
But there's this shawl to wear and tea with Manuka honey.

And across the only gap in the border, a thousand refugees an hour
pouring through Ras al-Jedir. An hour? By morning, my morning,

another five thousand, by lunchtime, another five and how many have even a striped hemp blanket? Fifteen thousand blankets!

Imagine one. The way it folds stiffly as a tent around the head
bent back, the shoulders jutting, knees drawn up, wrists free,

the lone triangular edifice. Feel the weave. Hairy, ridged.
Smell it. Determine the sightlines either side of the hollowed cheeks.

Imagine the scene in silence, not as it would be. The blanket
as a block, a wood carving. The tools: straight gouge, spoon gouge,

back bent, dog leg, fishtail chisels, V-tools, punches, vices;
hook knives, drawknives, rasps and rifflers, mallets, saws, abrasives;

slip waterstones – how quiet they sound – and strops for sharpening.
Figure in a blanket. In acacia, sycamore or, most likely, olive.

The Soul Travels on Horseback

and the road is beset with obstacles and thorns.
But let it take its time for I have hours and hours to wait

here, snowbound in Lisbon, glad of this sunlit café
outside Departures, for an evening flight to Heathrow.

Being my soul's steed, I should like to know its name
and breed – a Marwari of India, Barb of North Africa,

the Akhal-Teke of Western Asia or a Turkoman,
now extinct? Is it the burnt chestnut colour of the ant

or grey as a Bedouin wind, the four winds that made it?
O Drinker of the Wind, I travel by air, sea, land

and wherever I am, there you are behind my back

pounding the cloud streets, trailing banners of cirrus

or as Platero once did, from fear or chill, hoofing a stream,
breaking the moon into a swarm of clear, crystal roses.

No, no matter your thirst, ride swiftly, mare, stallion,
mother, father, for without you, I feel forever homesick.

LOST PAVILIONS

Said Adrus

Of Indian origin, Said Adrus was born and grew up in Kampala, 'British East Africa'. In 1972, his family moved and settled in Switzerland. Said's own personal migration would take him eventually to London where he studied visual arts. He gained prominence as an artist participating in numerous group shows in the 1980s and early 1990s on the theme of identity and race.

This movement from one society to another convinced Adrus that culture is neither pure nor static. His work plays with the concept of hybridity and often illustrates the in-betweenness and exile that have characterised his formative experiences. Transiency and the phenomenon of traditionalism combined with technology have also informed his artistic output.

Adrus has exhibited widely. His more recent projects include *Fama_ Fame*, Berne, Switzerland 2010; *Wohnen*, Künstlerhaus Solothurn, Switzerland, June 2009; and *60x60 Secs*, a Motiroti travelling exhibition that visited London, Delhi, Karachi and New York, 2008/09. His films and installations have been shown at Tate Britain, Kunsthalle Bern, and The Bronx Museum Of Art, New York. He is currently a Visiting Fellow at University of East London.

In *Far Pavilion*, Adrus plays with memory, history and location using photographs, video installation and abstract watercolours. It focuses on the emergence of mosques in Britain, and the lingering memory of Indian soldiers in Britain, who fought in World War I, and ended up convalescing in the Royal Pavilion, Brighton.

Shah Jehan Mosque, Woking

Mosques inspire me. Culture and faith are negotiated within the walls of institutions. The very first mosques, such as the Shah Jehan Mosque in Woking, built in 1889, changed the topography of towns and cities way before museums and art galleries became fashionable architecture features. Whether you liked their architecture or not they were visually radical and aesthetically interesting.

The cityscape of urban areas at the heart of the inner city is often the scene of establishment of new mosques. The Pavilion project came to fruition because of my interest in what is happening in these spaces and as a result of them. The buildings in this series of images display exquisite arches. Not only do the arches have an aesthetic and structural role, but they also symbolise the building of bridges and the creation of dialogue.

A mosque must negotiate its way culturally in relation to its environment. Once it has been built it implies permanency: the Muslim community it serves is here to stay.

East London Mosque

The notion of permanency that the mosque illustrates is often what scares countries unfamiliar with these structures. We see this in Switzerland's ban on minarets. It is ironic that this fear sits simultaneously with the rich historical concept of the mosque in Europe, for example in Cordoba, Granada and other cities in Andalusia.

The influence of the East can be found in the architecture of mainland Europe. We see this in the windows of Venice. These are spaces of faith and architecture that have had direct impact on the environment in Europe. I am drawn to the story of the Royal Pavilion in Brighton, which was constructed by Dr Gottlieb Wilhelm on the orders of the Royal Family in 1889 as a seaside holiday destination. It housed an array of exotic artefacts and was built in the Indo-Saracenic style, imported from colonial India. This ornamental architectural triumph, so contrary to the prevalent style of its setting, was closely tied to the Raj. It was later deemed fitting that the Royal Pavilion be used as a hospital dedicated to treating soldiers from the Indian subcontinent injured during World War I. It was their presence that led to the building of the first military cemetery dedicated to Indian Muslim Soldiers.

Brookwood Cemetry, Woking — the Military cemetery that forms part of the Commonwealth Graves. These tombstones are from the reburial that took place in the late 1960's from Horsell Common Muslim Burial Ground, after the graves had been vandalised.

The Muslim Burial Ground in Horsell Common in Woking was created because of its proximity to the first purpose-built mosque (The Shah Jehan) indicating the fate of many Indian soldiers brought to the building for treatment. The need for a mosque and a burial ground was the consequence of the Brighton Pavilion being used as a hospital.

MOSLEM CEMETERY

THIS ENCLOSURE WAS BUILT IN
1915 AS A BURIAL GROUND FOR
INDIAN SOLDIERS WHO LOST
THEIR LIVES IN SERVICE TO
THIS COUNTRY DURING THE
GREAT WAR. THE GRAVES HAVE
BEEN REMOVED BUT THE WALLS
REMAIN AS A REMINDER OF THAT
SACRIFICE AND ITS ASSOCIATION
WITH THE EASTERN WORLD.

THE HORSELL COMMON
PRESERVATION SOCIETY
HOPE TO RAISE FUNDS FOR
THE COMPLETE RESTORATION
OF THIS HISTORIC RELIC.

Please do not destroy it

*The Secretary
Horsell Common Preservation Society*

STATUTORY LISTED HISTORIC BUILDING

As a result of frequent vandalism in the 1960s, the bodies in The Muslim Burial Ground in Horsell Common were transferred to the Military Cemetery at Brookwood in 1968.

From the very first mosque in Woking to the newer ones in East London and Regent's Park — all have negotiated a new space enabling the evolution of Muslim culture in Britain. The transformation of the surrounding area and the building of a sacred space herald this process.

Using montage I have transposed archive film of the First World War with contemporary images of Brookwood cemetery, in an effort to convey the interconnectedness of these moments in time.

One strand which informs my work is the concept of architecture. The other is more personal and pays homage to my late father who fought in the First World War. I use exhibition shots which capture the projection of my film *Lost Pavilion IV*. Using montage to reinterpret images, I transpose archival movies with contemporary images of the site. The Muslim burial ground in Woking evokes a stillness that is solitary and eerie, yet tranquil and calming.

THE MAN FROM BENI MORA

Aamer Hussein

Desert, white sand rippling, reddish sky. A figure, on a white horse, head wrapped in a scarf and covered in a hat, wearing an assortment of Western clothes: boots, jodhpurs, a short jacket. As it comes closer we see it's probably a very young man or a boy.

Then, from the distance, a number of horses, ridden by men in long robes. The first figure pulls out a gun and shoots. There's a round of gunfire, one of the horsemen falls, and the first figure's horse is wounded.

Another figure approaches, also in a robe, and shoots in the air: his shots might sound a code, as the other riders disperse. We see him: he's tall, beardless, frowning.

He gets off his horse, goes to the first figure who's lying in the sand, unconscious, wounded perhaps. He takes a flask from his hip, splashes water on the recumbent boy's face, then lifts the boy's head and shoulders in his arms. We see the boy's features; not a boy after all, but a pretty young woman in her twenties, with narrow long eyes and an upturned nose.

- Ruby?

He's shaking her.

She wakes up, in a big white bed, switches the lamp on.

- What time is it? she asks.

- Six. You should be going soon. You seemed restless in your sleep. You called out my name.

- I dreamed we were in Beni Mora again. They were chasing me. And then you came....

We follow her to her car, as she drives through city streets, to a hospital we recognise on the edges of Belgravia. As the titles come up on screen, she enters the hospital. We follow her to her office, see her name on the door. Dr Rubina Hasan. *Umair recognises the actress, Alina Murad: she's also credited as the producer. She's known for her versatility, plays traditional roles as well as transgressive parts. She's said to have been a belly dancer somewhere in the Gulf before she came to acting.*

The serial is titled GHAZALI.

- *Professor Umair Omar?*

- *Yes.*

- *The London Library. We're holding two of the books you asked for. Margaret Smith's biography of Algazzaly, and the Montgomery Watt study.*

- *I'll be there to pick them up this afternoon by five.*

- *Late hours today. We're open till half past seven.*

Episode 3

The interior of a tent. She's sitting up in bed, reading. He comes in. Tall, broad shoulders, slight stoop; in his mid- to late thirties, perhaps. He has reddish hair and hazel eyes.

- Why are you keeping me here? Why did you kidnap me? When are we going back to Beni Mora?

- You're not well enough to travel yet. And I didn't kidnap you, I rescued you. What were you doing riding in the wilderness alone after sunset?

- That's hardly your business. Can I have another book? I've finished the one you brought me.

She hands it to him. We see the pale yellow cover, the bold red letters of its title: *The Rise and Fall of Islamic Thought*, by Ahmed Naseem Ghazali.

He sits down on a chair near the entrance of the tent.

- I have the book he wrote about travelling with the Touareg, he says. It was his doctoral dissertation.

- He's an excellent writer. Travelogues, philosophy, history....

- He's not bad. Tends to superficiality.

- I wouldn't say you were the best judge. But when are you getting me out of here?

- The doctor says you're still in shock. I'm going to Beni Mora today, when I come back in three days I'll take you there.

Why Beni Mora? Umair thinks. Is it even a real place? He does a search on his mobile and remembers where he's seen it before: in that old orientalist chestnut, The Garden of Allah, *starring Marlene Dietrich. He remembers the film was taken from a novel. What are they doing here, the producer, the scriptwriter, reproducing an orientalist chestnut? The titles say this film is 'inspired by the novel of the same name', but he's never heard of an Urdu novel called* Ghazali, *nor of the writer, a woman. He turns to his book, but leaves the television on. There's a long scene he's aware of, with the young woman leaving her bed, stealing a horse, riding across the desert. He wonders if the film crew really went to North Africa, or whether they shot the film in Sindh or Balochistan. The exteriors are impressive; the whites and reds, the sky, sand and date palms of the opening have given way now to rock, scrub, barren pathways. The silent scene ends in a hill town that looks authentic: white buildings, winding lanes. Digital technology, he thinks. To recreate the past. Must be set in the fifties.*

Episode 4

Now she's in a hotel ballroom, in a long white gown. She's with a girl who looks European. The people around her are speaking French.

- We're going to meet Dr Ghazali, Ruby. The hotel manager said he was here and asked if we would join him for dinner. I said we'd be delighted if instead he'd join us.

- I don't know if it's a good idea to meet a writer you've read; he's probably very old and a bore.

- Oh, I hear he's a fascinating man. The French authorities don't like him. He spreads subversion among the natives, rebellion…

He approaches, in a dinner jacket, joins them at their table. That man we know from the desert.

- Oh, Miss Warburton. I know Miss Hasan. We've met. I rescued her from the desert bandits on the outskirts of Beni Mora. (He sneers.)

- Dr Rubina Hasan. She's a surgeon, the European girl says. I told her not to ride alone but she's a headstrong girl.

- I didn't know who he was, though. Why didn't you tell me?

- I didn't want to spoil your pleasure in reading...

The period atmosphere of the film is effective because it's created impressionistically. You, the viewer, are in the past, which could be the 40s or the 50s, even has touches of the 60s; but it's also timeless. Umair recognises the actor playing Ghazali. Babur Awan. One of the best known in Karachi. Earlier he was confused by the dyed hair, the greenish lenses.

- Why did you run away? Ghazali asks.

- You were keeping me against my will....I knew I could get back alone to Beni Mora.

- You didn't get back alone. You were being followed by my men. It wasn't safe for you to ride alone.

Umair has noticed now that they deliver their lines in a mannered way that moves from the naturalistic mode of television drama to something measured, almost staccato, akin to declamation or chanting. He thinks the lines have been written in blank verse, to scan.

- Do you spend much time in England, Dr Ghazali?

- I have a house there in Surrey. That's where I'm planning to write my book about Beni Mora. My grandfather left it to me. My mother was English.

Umair wakes up on the sofa; he's been trying to write the first chapter of his memoir, which is meant to be a recollection of a happy youth; he was reading a rather turgid translation of The Alchemy of Happiness *online. The serial's on again, he remembers. It's on every night of the week, from 2-3, often too late for him to watch, but he's become addicted. He wonders why the hero has been named after Ghazali; we know he's a polymath, but nothing else seems to link him to a theologian and a mystic. Let's see, he thinks, and switches on to watch:*

Episode 7

In the recap that flashes on the screen, we see Rubina and Ghazali, both in Western wedding dress, outside a building that announces its function with a big sign: THE ISLAMIC CENTRE.

Then they're in an English country garden, in winter clothes. In the backdrop there's a big house, the kind of mansion that heritage TV and Bollywood delight in. The grounds are covered with snow; the lake is icy.

Ghazali is talking:

- I first went there when I was very young. I studied Arabic in Oxford. In Beni Mora I set up schools and taught children to read. One day someone asked me to lead a congregation in prayer because they think all educated men are religious scholars and though I'd learned it all as a boy, I found to my shame I'd forgotten. It was then that I first became close to my maker whom I'd always taken for granted and began to pray as often as I could, sometimes more than five times a day. I came back and did my doctorate in Islamic Studies, travelled to Cairo...

- Yes, I loved Beni Mora, Rubina is saying. You know my father sent me here to England when I was very young, barely fourteen, and I haven't been back to Lahore since. I have memories of home but Beni Mora was nothing like what I remember, I had never seen the desert before, but yet some part of me felt as if I had come to a place that I knew, where I may even once have belonged. I loved the simplicity of the people and even more I loved the boundlessness of sand and sky. Sometimes in those absences I felt I was alone in the presence of something greater than I was, though I don't believe in anything but absence...

- Do you know they say reason never leads you to faith? Your heart does. It comes like a light that enters you. Look around you, Rubina: look at these gardens that are frozen over, the leaves gone from the trees, the birds flown South....they'll be back, and then they'll be gone again. Can this happen without an order in our world, and someone who creates that order so that nothing varies, even change is changeless... You know they say that God is the greatest artist? The world is beautiful, Rubina, and that beauty comes from Him.

Ghazali's monologue continues, lyrical, hypnotic. Umair feels he's heard the words before, and thinks, at first, that they might be paraphrased from the Quran. He reflects on the beauty of Urdu, of its sounds, which like its letters reach his eyes, reach something in his inner ear that the other languages he knows don't reach. Indian syntax, Persian images, Arabic alphabet, terms he doesn't always understand. He remembers how a teacher once told him that Persian was tactile and descriptive but Arabic excelled in abstract contextual terms. If Persian praises God's beauty (jamal), he thinks, then Arabic evoked His splendour (jalal). The thought of beauty reminds him of Ghazali's namesake and he wonders whether these words are borrowed from the original Ghazali's. ('Ghazali', Margaret Smith wrote, 'thinks of plants and flowers not only as things of beauty and a source of keen delight to every lover of nature, but also as displaying the wisdom and loving kindness of God, Who has given the fruit its rind so that it may be protected from the birds.') And as Ghazali's onscreen namesake intones his enconium, the seasons around him change: leaves appear on the trees, pear blossoms. We are in an English spring garden. Swans glide on the pale surface of the still lake. The foliage of summer. Then the leaves fall, red, olive and burnt gold. Colours explode on film like fireworks, nearly artificial, but recognisably those of the world around us. Once again Umair suspects the use of digital technology. Ghazali and Rubina walk through these changing landscapes of a virtual world, their clothes changing with the seasons. They're holding hands, laughing. Umair thinks that the changes indicate the passing of time in the film, but he's wrong: the changing seasons were Ghazali's fantasy, and suddenly we're back to winter, to Rubina's point of view.

- That's the way of nature, Rubina says. I'm a doctor, I believe in my work and in saving lives and serving my kind that way, that's my only mission; I don't believe in faith, or in a Creator. My father was an unbeliever and he brought me up that way. I'm amazed that an intellectual like you can believe in a first cause. I think it's just accidental collisions and a fusion of particles. You know what my dream is? To go back to the country I left behind and set up a hospital there. I'm going to do that, Ghazali, very soon...

- And us? What about us?

- Won't you come back with me? Can't you help? As you did in Beni Mora?

Umair wants to keep on watching, but his mind is sleepily wandering. It's unusual to see a woman speaking of atheism so directly in a commercial teleplay. He's noticed that Pakistani drama serials often seem to be about religion. He's seen one in which a rich boy discovers religion to come close to the poor teacher's daughter he loves, but loses her anyway to close conflict and death. He's seen one in which a Hindu refugee is drawn to Islam by the simple faith of her benefactor. He's seen one in which two headscarved women, visiting from the States, have to fight the prejudices of their chic Karachi hostesses who neither fast nor pray. Most often, the religious win, but they aren't what you'd call fundamentalists. You also see bigots, both men and women, in these plays, and they're comic when they aren't downright evil. There's a battle on going and it's difficult to draw the lines between the devout and the bigoted, male and female. The atheists, of course, are in their own enclosed world. But what's unusual is to find the heroine speaking the lines of devil's advocacy, without villainy or parody, just in normal, if scathing, tones. Alina Murad's mildly scandalous reputation makes her even more convincing in her portrayal. Is that why she chose to produce the film? To give an atheist a voice?

When his attention returns to the play, Ghazali and Rubina in their night clothes are fighting wordlessly in their bedroom: he isn't sure whether he's switched the sound off, but he's too lazy to reach for the control which is lying on the floor. He looks at the subtitles instead.

- You said you wouldn't go back to work for six weeks. We've been married a fortnight. What about our plans to return to Beni Mora?

- You knew who I was when you married me. You knew you were marrying a doctor.

Ghazali flings some clothes into a suitcase, walks to the hall where he pulls on an overcoat which he retrieves from a coat-rack, puts on shoes and goes out into the night. Then we see a vintage car driving through foggy streets. It draws up at the Savoy Hotel. We watch Ghazali descend. *Umair had thought there'd be an accident. That Rubina would rush to wounded Ghazali's bedside and there'd be a reconciliation.*

Episode 9

A montage of still and moving images, in colour and in sepia.

    Ghazali, in Beni Mora, teaching children.

    Rubina, giving birth. (That's a long, silent scene).

Ghazali in the jungle, on safari. (He has a gun, but remember the story is set in pre-conservation times, when even a good man's allowed to hunt; or maybe he's culling.)

Rubina in Karachi, building a hospital in a village.

Ghazali, in Zulu territories, teaching adults, writing English letters on a blackboard.

Documentary footage in black and white (is it genuine?) of a hospital being inaugurated by a ribbon-cutting dignitary in a long coat and a tall woolly hat.

Rubina, with her son, walking by the sea, playing ball.

Ghazali, writing. A series of books on travel, history and time. Their phantom covers flash on the screen and we wonder at his rate of production.

Ghazali's voice over the virtual images of book covers. Oddly enough, in English.

- Dearest love - you may wonder that I still call you that, but the pain you caused me made me understand that there's more to life than beauty, and I'm back to doing what I do best. I feel you found your way to what you believed in. I hear you are a dedicated doctor and your hospital is thriving. You achieved what I never could; I'm just a scribe, and do what little I can, but that's the road I know, travelling, teaching and writing about what I see and the history of the places I visit. Then I travel on. Each one of us on the path we found that suited us best, you with your science and me with my wandering search. I'm back in Beni Mora. I don't know how long I'll stay. I want to go to Andalusia next; it's so long since I wrote my book about it. But I'm tired and a little ill and for now Beni Mora is where I'll rest.

Rubina, on a balcony in an old villa overlooking the sea in Karachi's Clifton, feeding pigeons. She sits down, takes the letter from a silver tray, reads it; she's about to tear it up, then changes her mind.

Umair goes away for two weeks, travels in Italy, Scotland, and Yorkshire. He's been thinking about the serial; he ordered the book the film derived from, but when it arrived from Pakistan he saw they'd sent the wrong book, and anyway the scriptwriters in Pakistan tend to adapt quite freely from the novels they dramatise so they'll

have changed it all, particularly the sequence of events. But he wants to know what
happens to Rubina, to Ghazali, though he knows that like life the endings of Paki-
stani serials can be inconclusive, even abrupt.

It's not showing late at night any more, and he can't trace a change of time on the
Sky menu. But he knows that the last one he saw can't have been the final episode.

Then one night he decides to try on YouTube. Nothing. He finds two episodes on a
TV website, both of which say 'final', but he doesn't know whether that means the
serial has ended, or just that the episode online is the last one shown. He downloads
the first one.

Final episode 1

- Headache, Headache.

The child was wailing all night.

He's in a hospital bed now, in a private room.

Meningitis. He might not survive.

Help.

He's all I have.

- Only prayer will help, the nurses say.

Delirium.

She's sitting beside the boy's bed.

His breathing is ragged.

Ghazali has sent her his latest book, *Prayer in Islam: Selected Translations*.

Almost as a reflex action, she brought it with her. She opens it.

- You win, Ghazali. I'm asking for help. You could say I'm praying. For my
son who is also yours.

She hears his echoing voice as she reads:

God is the light of the skies and of the earth.
The semblance of His light is that of a niche
in which is a lamp, the lamp within a glass,
the glass is a glittering star as it were, lit with the oil
of a blessed tree, the olive, neither of the east
nor of the west, whose oil appears to light up
even though fire touches it not, - light upon light
God guides to His light whom he will.

- I don't know who You are, she says, or if You or Your light exist, but tonight I'm prepared to pray to You to save my child.

She covers her head with her shawl and repeats the words that might bring back the light.

Final Episode 2

You are in Beni Mora, where you almost always seem to find yourself after dark. The sand, dotted with distant date palms, stretches away from you, towards the horizon, seeming to slip away, from under your feet. You're calling. You know your child was sleeping safely beside you when you last opened your eyes. But now he isn't there. You're barefoot and the sand burns the soles of your feet. You're calling, in the dark. Then, in the distance, the man in white. You know you've been there before, in your dreams, but you can't wake yourself up this time. The child is beside the man, holding his hand. Who are you, she calls, do I know your name, tell me your name…He stretches out his hand to you.

- Ghazali?

You wake up. The child's breathing is even now. You go to the window: you can see the faint first shimmer of light on the water and you know the night is almost over.

REVIEWS

MARYAM AND THE MAULANA

Ehsan Masood

It is a scene that still carries fond memories: the sight of the postman standing outside the front door of my grandfather's Karachi house laden with a cardboard box marked with the Royal Mail's trademark red livery. The box would contain books from England, carefully packed by my father who was working in London while my mother, sisters and I spent some years in 'the Land of the Pure'. During the late 1970s, the 'Islamic republic of Pakistan' provided thin pickings when it came to affordable English language reading material, something that my father understood well. So he became what was in effect a one-man book club for his three children: asking us what we would like him to send, adding in his own recommendations, and dispatching the contents 5,000 miles away. Even now, thirty years later, I can still feel the excitement as we peeled back the layers of tape and cut through the string when the boxes would arrive.

The contents were rarely, if ever, predictable. Shakespeare one month, the novels of Ian Fleming and Orwell another. Textbooks on physics or mathematics; books on English grammar and lots and lots of pulp fiction. However, one author was a perennial. Over the five years from 1979 to 1984 when I lived in Karachi, I got to read just about everything produced by Maryam Jameelah Jameelah, a New Yorker who had converted to Islam from Judaism. During the early 1960s she journeyed by ship to Lahore to begin a new life as the adopted daughter of Maulana Abul Ala Mawdudi, founder of the Jamat Islami.

All of Maryam Jameelah's books began and ended with the same text. The foreword would introduce the author by recalling her story of how a super-intelligent, bibliophile American found solace and truth in Islam, how she abandoned the bright lights of New York city for Lahore. The back cover of most titles would carry the headline 'Muslims awake', and in it she would remind her readers of the central message of each of her titles: 'The evils of atheism and materialism, supported by all the forces of modern technology are working day and night to destroy us . . . we foolishly choose to tread the path of an alien civilisation.'

So you can imagine the excitement with which I turned to Deborah Baker's enchanting biography of Maryam Jameelah Jameelah. All my childhood memories came flooding back. The genius of *The Convert* is that those of us who thought we knew Maryam Jameelah Jameelah from her writings all those years ago didn't really know her at all – and I would include among them Maulana Mawdudi himself, the man who invited Maryam Jameelah to emigrate to Pakistan and in whose house she would eventually come to live.

One of the first questions that Deborah Baker's biography answers is one that I least expected: none of Maryam Jameelah's readers had any idea what she looked like. That's because, while most of her books include a 'photograph' of the author; the photo in question is of someone in full-length

---

Books mentioned in this review

The Convert: A Tale of Exile and Extremism by Deborah Baker,
Minnesota: Graywolf Press, 2011
Mawlana Mawdudi and Political Islam by Roy Jackson, London:
Routledge, 2010

---

black burqa, with just her hands and feet visible. It is a disturbing, almost haunting image and begs the question: why would anyone reproduce a photo of themselves without showing their face? What Baker discovers among the letters and manuscripts that she found in the Maryam Jameelah Jameelah archive at the New York Public Library are real photographs: yes photographs of herself and her family in Pakistan (they are reproduced on Deborah Baker's website). So Maryam Jameelah did want us to know what she looked like after all.

Leaving aside the ambiguity over her public image, who is Maryam Jameelah? Baker confirms the basic story printed in the hundreds of thousands of copies of Maryam Jameelah's books: that she was born Margaret Marcus in 1934 to middle class Jewish parents assimilated into American life and firmly pro-Israel. Baker reveals that the young Margaret had a deep awareness of the broader politics shaping world affairs after the war. It is likely that this was common for children of her background and generation as many if not most of America's Jews would have had family in Europe, and their fate would have been everyday conversation in dining and living rooms across New York. But Margaret's sympathies lay as much with the plight of the Arabic-speaking peoples, and especially the Palestinians, as it did with those of the Jews. And in childhood the history of the Arabs would become her passion: she would read tales of Arab heroes; play-act famous battles, immerse herself in the music of Umm Kulthoom and, most unusually for a child of her age, marvel at how the Arabs held out against modernity.

In *The Convert* we also learn that she was not one to keep her opinions to herself and would challenge her parents to justify theirs. Why was it, she would ask them, that a homeland for one people meant homelessness for another; how was it, she would say, that her own people who had experienced torture could stand by while injustice was being visited on others. Aged 11 she promised herself that she would one day go and live in Palestine or Egypt, 'not to convert them, but to make sure they stay just as they are'.

Clearly she was no ordinary pre-teen, but Margaret was different in other ways too. Her mother records that she didn't speak until the age of four, and when she did it was not the speech of a toddler, more like that of a young adult as she spoke in complete sentences. Growing up she found relationships difficult; both with boys and also with adults whom she was continually, angrily challenging. Anyone who crossed Margaret on the topic of the politics of the Middle East appears to have been caught in a hurricane of contrary facts and opinion. She spared no one, not parents, teachers, friends, or colleagues. Baker also tells us that Maryam Jameelah had a long history of mental illness, with a tendency towards violent behaviour – though how violent is not made clear. Regular visits to psychiatrists yielded little and she spent much of the 1950s in and out of mental institutions. The picture that emerges is that of a bright child, mentally unwell and terminally misunderstood by elders and peers, who increasingly found it difficult to fit into the society and the culture into which she was born.

By the time she was in her late 20s, Margaret Marcus had become Maryam Jameelah. At the same time she had also been expelled from two universities and was unable to find paid employment. Worse still, she was by now facing an ultimatum from parents who had decided that they would take no financial responsibility for her into adulthood, and just wanted to get on with their own lives. The ultimatum was thus: either get a job or head back to the psychiatric hospital. In some desperation she searched for a Muslim country to emigrate to and struck up correspondence with a variety of Islamic luminaries of which Mawdudi was one. Pakistan was not her first choice destination, but by the early 1960s, faced with the prospect of life on the street, or another spell in a psychiatric hospital, she took up the Maulana on his offer of a new life with his family and set sail for Lahore.

Once in Lahore matters did not improve for the young convert. There was a new country and language to get used to; new social norms and customs to absorb, and then there was the peculiar situation of a strong-minded and assertive Western woman who had come to live in the house of an Islamic political leader whose views on women would have been regarded as Victorian even by the Victorians. The women of the Mawdudi household — no shrinking violets either — were horrified at the ease with which she could strike up conversations with the male members of the family; her tendency to lecture and her penchant to discuss her personal problems with strangers. Maryam Jameelah in Lahore turned out to be little different to Maryam Jameelah in New York: dogmatic, argumentative, temperamental and prone to occasional fits of violence. The Mawdudis arranged for her to live with a different family, but this didn't work out. They finally sent her to live in Lahore's infamous Pagal Khana, literally, madhouse, before she was rescued by a man called Muhammad Yusuf Khan, a businessman who would later become her publisher. Maryam Jameelah in turn became his second wife and together they had five children.

Maryam Jameelah's troubled inner life stands in diametric contrast to her outward success as a polemicist, champion of tradition and propagandist for the Jamat Islami. Here was a Jewish American ready at every opportunity to dish the dirt on the West, and proclaim the superiority of the East. It couldn't have got any better and for a long, long time the Jamat revelled in their catch. Maryam Jameelah was never in the party's A-list. She never attained any high office, indeed never held any position. No woman ever could as the party's hierarchy was reserved for men and only for men. But she was for a time possibly the most influential woman that the Jamat would ever tolerate. She had direct access to Mawdudi and, through her pen and her prodigious output of books, articles and pamphlets she had access to a mass audience including restless teenagers like me.

The intended audience for Maryam Jameelah's books were Pakistan's middle classes. Those of us who attended English-language schools, who read gossipy magazines, watched American sitcoms and dreamed of fast food – way too expensive even for middle class pockets in those days. Her message to my generation was that our lives were worthless unless we changed our ways; and that the West, which we looked to escape to, was the last place on Earth we needed, or wanted to be. The only way to find meaning and save ourselves was to accept Islam as interpreted through Maryam Jameelah's pen.

The Islamic world's printing presses of the 1970s were white hot with Westo-phobic literature, mostly written in bad English. Maryam Jameelah's books felt different though at the time I wouldn't have been able to say why. Looking at them now there is no mistaking that she read widely, and had a lawyer's ability to analyse an issue and quickly come to a conclusion, without really thinking if it might ever be wrong. Virtually all her output consisted of strings of quotations from western books, sandwiched with her own pungent comments. There is also no mistaking the tiresome, hectoring, shrill voice. She writes like an angry mother, or a bullying older sister. Her writing also completely lacks any curiosity, or sense of doubt. Maryam Jameelah's world was a black-and-white space. This was a polemicist who clearly knew what she wanted for herself; but more than that she knew what she wanted for the rest of us too.

Here she is in *Islam and Modernism*, a collection of essays published in 1968, arguing for the Islamic state and the return of the Caliphate:

> Because the idea of an Islamic state is an anathema in a world dominated by opportunism, these modern educated leaders tell us that we must accept the abolition of the Khalifate as permanent and dismiss any possibility of its revival in the future. Politics and government based on religion is branded as 'medieval'. Therefore in order to take their place in the modern world, Muslims must reconcile themselves to secular rule. To expound this argument books have been written in certain Muslim countries blaming the Khalifate for all the evils afflicting us throughout history. It is claimed that Khalifate is not really part of Islam because the Holy Prophet's mission was limited to preaching. He never wished to rule. Only expediency forced him to do so. Intellectual dishonesty could scarcely sink

to more abysmal depth. Islam cannot live without a community. And the Islamic community cannot survive without organised leaders.

This particular essay is entitled: 'Can Islam be Reconciled with the Spirit of the Twentieth Century'. In an essay of less than 3,000 words, she attacks western clothing, demands that Shariah be established, and argues that Muslim women not seek employment outside the home. 'Thus we have demonstrated why it is not possible to reconcile Islam with the "spirit of the twentieth century". The more we Muslims try to "reform" Islam to make it "compatible" with modern life, the weaker we shall become. We Muslims shall grow in strength and vigour not by "moving along with the trends of the time" but by fighting against it'.

For Maryam Jameelah no such thing as change or compromise ever existed. And even when she was patently wrong, in her mind she was definitely right. In the title of the book for example, where she confuses modernism, a movement in art, with modernity – she was definitely right. For Maryam Jameelah, true Islamic culture was a puritan culture. She wrote that music and entertainment were at best frivolous; at worst, they took humans away from God and were therefore sinful: 'The devout Muslim's attitude towards life is serious and sober and the teachings of Islam place their emphasis upon the faithful discharge of one's duties to God and to one's fellow man rather than the right to leisure', she wrote in another book.

Maryam Jameelah's notion of the nature of her adopted faith and its role in human life and society was at odds with Pakistan in the early 1960s. This was a country characterised by optimism and innovation at all levels of society, as well as much goodwill to and from the wider world. There's a famous cover from *Life* magazine of crowds flocking to greet President Eisenhower's motorcade as it drove through Karachi during his visit in 1953. Pakistan wasn't just attractive to American presidents; it was also a magnet for many a celebrity Muslim convert, and not just Maryam Jameelah.

The country in its first few decades was a living laboratory for a post-imperial independent Muslim state and not surprisingly attracted idealistic new Muslims who believed they could help shape its future. Among them was the Austrian writer and diplomat Muhammad Asad, whose *Road to Mecca* helped inspire Maryam Jameelah's own conversion in the following decade. Asad was an early convert to the idea of *Pakistaniat* as the coexistence of piety and power. He befriended the famous poet and visionary, Sir Muhammad Iqbal in India, and settled in newly independent Pakistan, joining the civil service initially as a senior official in the foreign office and later as the head of the department for religious reconstruction, representing Pakistan at the United Nations in New York. For Pakistan's founders Asad was much more than a diplomat and thinker: he was a trophy Westerner, someone whom they were proud to parade at meetings of the UN, watched perhaps enviously by the representatives of India and those from more established Islamic societies.

The Maulana would have seen Maryam Jameelah in a somewhat similar light. But there was far more to their relationship and to how they came to a meeting of minds. In *Mawlana Mawdudi and Political Islam*, the British academic Roy Jackson tells us that the young Mawdudi was a precocious child, taken to writing from an early age, certain of his opinions and no friend to authority figures. The Maulana too was fond of lecturing and also found it hard to maintain friendships and working relationships with people who were his intellectual or political equals. He comes across in Jackson's book as not unlike Maryam Jameelah except that he was much more practised and skilful a political operator than Maryam Jameelah, and over time manoeuvred and moved to sideline those who could challenge his authority or his leadership of the party.

In his correspondence with Maryam Jameelah, it is evident that he admires the way in which she arrives at Islam through a reductive process, because that, in essence, reflected his own credo, and that which he enforced on his party's members and affiliates. The Jamat's great attraction across college and university campuses in the 1960s was its claim to a kind of faux rationality, which went something like this: Islam was the most perfect way of life because it represented everything that the West was not. It followed that real Muslims had to avoid the trappings of Westernisation, such as gender equality, minority rights, secularism, unfettered capitalism and Communism (a big issue for Islamists back then). But what they absolutely needed was Western science and technology, without which no Islamic revival would be possible.

Still, in inviting Maryam Jameelah to live with his family, Mawdudi would have taken an almighty gamble. Membership of the Jamat was not merely a matter of filling in a form and turning up to meetings, or stuffing envelopes at election time. Members were selected after many months of attending classes and lectures and would have had to pass rigorous tests of religiosity and demonstrate an ability to memorise and regurgitate the Maulana's expanding religious canon. Yet such was his confidence in his new disciple that Maryam Jameelah was allowed to skip the homework and piety tests and sailed straight into the Mawdudi family home.

I left behind my Maryam Jameelah collection in Karachi when I returned to London in the mid 1980s, but one book has stayed with me throughout that time. It's a slim volume, 59 pages of text with a purple cover and the title, as always, written in capital letters, with the familiar 'Muslims Awake' on the back cover. Perhaps more than her other pamphlets *Modern Technology and the Dehumanization of Man* illustrates the depth of its author's distancing from one idea that Mawdudi and the Jamat were very determined followers of—that Islamic salvation lay in getting ahead in technology.

Re-reading it now *Modern Technology* is on so many levels a confusing cacophony of ideas sometimes held together by not much more than her own cement of certainty. She romanticises pre-industrial science. She decries what she sees as the Godlessness, amorality and hyper-specialisation of the modern scientist and she celebrates indigenous peoples, whether in America, or Arabia, repeating the belief, long since questioned, that they lived in harmony with their fellow humans and nature. Where she is on more solid ground is in the book's core idea that industrial-era technology is no friend to the environment; and she is sound in her lament for the polymath, the multi-talented scholar, thinker, poet, politician, long extinct in the modern academy.

She makes her intent clear at the outset: 'Many modern educated Muslims will tell their more traditionally minded brethren that we can become just as modern and up-to-date and still preserve a pure Islamic way of life. The purpose of this essay is to demonstrate the fallacy of this almost universally accepted delusion'. She continues: 'Nature was and still is viewed by scientists as an enemy to be conquered, dominated, exploited and manipulated to serve human ends. Modern science is guided by no moral values but naked materialism and arrogance'.

Modern science for Maryam Jameelah begins with Copernicus and Darwin and she cites both as examples of scientists whose discoveries were used to justify an understanding of nature in which God had no role to play.

None of this is new, unusual or surprising. *Modern Technology* is after all a book of its time: a time in which Muslim communities, long surpassed by the West in advanced learning, looked for comfort in the memory of past greatness. But Maryam Jameelah's purpose in writing *Modern Technology* is not to glorify the old. She had a more subversive agenda.

In 1962 when Maryam Jameelah arrived to become a member of Mawdudi's Lahore household, her mentor was a national figure on the Pakistani political stage and his party was built around a core of educated technocrats. He encouraged his younger lieutenants to study science and engineering subjects knowing full well that political and military power is also a function of dominance in science. In that sense Mawdudi's understanding and appreciation of modern science was entirely instrumentalist. Scientific knowledge for Mawdudi was a means to an end, and was not an end in itself, as that would imply it had value and would therefore contravene his belief and teachings that all useful knowledge started and ended in the Qur'an.

In 1976 when she published *Modern Technology* she had been in Pakistan 14 years. The big break with her mentor had happened more than a decade ago when he had sent her to live in Lahore's mental hospital, the Pagal Khana. Reading the book again, what struck me was the fact that Mawdudi is entirely absent from the list of sources. She was still being published by the Jamat and would have known full well its leader's views on science but *Modern Technology* contains not a single reference to a Mawdudi speech, pamphlet or book.

She does quote extensively from Islamic sources, except that one of the names she quotes would have been regarded then by the Jamat as not very Islamic, indeed, bordering on the heretical. Clearly, no one at Jamat was checking her work prior to publication otherwise they would have spotted and deleted the generous references to the work of American-Iranian perennialist philosopher Seyyed Hossein Nasr. Nasr gets star treatment in her book, as does the Turkish thinker Badiuzzaman Said Nursi.

She quotes from Nasr's *Man and Nature* to denounce the followers of Darwin and Copernicus and to argue that man and nature are connected, not only to each other but possibly also to God. Ironically, Darwinian thinking and especially the Tree of Life is an endorsement of the idea that man and nature share more than a connection, something Maryam

Jameelah may want to reflect on today. But be that as it may, linking man, nature and God sails close to the Sufi concept of *Wahdat alWujood* (Unity of Being), which is anathema to arguably the majority of Sunni Muslims. Equally it implies that man has no special role on Earth, and by extension deserves no special privileges.

If this is what Maryam Jameelah meant to say, if this is what she believed in the mid 1970s, it suggests a parting of the ways from her mentor long ago. And it suggests that Maryam Jameelah was not-so-secretly urging her adoptive country's youth to rebel against the prevailing climate of scientism and ask deep and searching questions about the nature of technology. America of the 1960s and 70s was where environmental economics and bioethics began to be discussed. Reading one of Maryam Jameelah's books was often a very tiring activity because of her habit of interrupting her narrative with large chunks from other peoples' books. But in *Modern Technology* this had possibly the effect that Maryam Jameelah intended: it introduced me and other teenagers in Pakistan to the ideas of some of the most exciting thinkers of the 1960s and 70s. People such as Dennis and Donatella Meadows, who co-wrote *The Limits to Growth* and whose ideas on greening economics have never been as influential as they are today. Maryam Jameelah also quotes from Alvin Toffler's *Future Shock* and includes one sentence from the book that will surely resonate with anyone grappling with the regulation of biomedical or communications technologies: 'Laws cannot remain law if they must change every day'.

Maryam Jameelah's *Modern Technology* helped its readers to see science in a different context, and her canon overall provides insight into the arguments of someone who has resolved to rebel against modernity. Her books, like those of the French-born surgeon Maurice Bucaille also provide readers with a small window into the minds of some of those who convert out of one religion and adopt another. Many of the books by both these authors constitute a kind of accounting ledger in which the 'Islam' column always shows a healthy profit when compared with Christianity or Judaism. In arguing the case for her chosen faith Maryam Jameelah was quite possibly enacting for a public audience her own internal arguments for crossing the Judaism/Islam divide.

But my view of the impact of her works is not shared by all English-speaking commentators. Among the perception of Maryam Jameelah's

THE AUTHOR

Thus do I, an American-born convert, speak through this picture to my Muslim-born brothers and sisters misled by an education hostile to all that Islam stands for and blinded with its false standards and ideals.

Maryam Jameelah in a picture that appeared in most of her books and as she projected herself to her devoted readers. The photograph hid much more than simply the author's face.

impact is that her books have helped to radicalise Muslims all over the world. Furthermore, this perception has gathered momentum especially in the years after 9/11. For those who believe in linear cause-effect relationships Maryam Jameelah joins the list of authors, alongside Mawdudi, Banna and Qutb who must share some of the blame for post-9/11 violent extremism. And before them, Ibn Abdul Wahhab and Ibn Taimiyyah, too.

Did Maryam Jameelah — indeed did any of these names — inspire martyrdom operations? It's a question that continues to tax many, including intelligence agencies, university academics, novelists, newspaper columnists and think-tank staff all over the world. Such is the idea's appeal that it has its own term: it is known as 'the conveyor-belt hypothesis'. Though she doesn't refer to it in quite the same way, the conveyor-belt hypothesis also troubles Deborah Baker, and it occupies the latter part of *The Convert*.

The book's finale is Baker's trip to Pakistan in 2007 in which she interviews Maryam Jameelah in her Lahore apartment, determined to establish her position on violence. Islam is no stranger to the experience of violence between its elites and among its many traditions. We have much regicide and fracticide in our history. The question that troubled Deborah Baker as she scraped deeper and deeper into Maryam Jameelah's history was whether she, even in a small way, bore fractional responsibility for the violence experienced by twentieth-century Islam.

'For nearly a year,' Baker writes. 'I had shifted from fascination to mistrust of this woman, a woman whose core beliefs struck deeply at my own and yet whose critique of the West was both familiar and unerring. Her letters moved and perplexed me. Her books unsettled me, stirred me into another way of looking at the complacent assumptions of my world.' In a final encounter with her subject, Baker quotes passages of Maryam Jameelah's books back at her. She reads out passages about hatred of the West; she recites passages that glorify jihad; and she asks Maryam Jameelah whether she feels any responsibility for the radicalisation of young Muslims. Maryam Jameelah becomes defensive. She seems to lose the rapid-fire confidence of her earlier encounters with Baker, and points to examples of her later journalism denouncing violence. Baker's face-to-face interviews with Maryam Jameelah are among the book's most gripping passages, but her final question sits uneasily in a book that is otherwise so carefully researched. The conveyor-belt hypothesis is the wrong answer to a difficult problem. Indeed, it is almost child-like in the simplicity of its thinking.

Over the past four decades, hundreds of thousands, if not millions have read Maryam Jameelah's works. Among them will be readers from all walks of life, readers from many countries and cultures, readers holding to a pot pourri of opinions. Collectively, they will have read millions of other books, and consumed many other forms of media. If for argument's sake, one in every million turned to violent extremism it is impossible to say which book, which film, or which TV programme directly resulted in a reader, or a viewer taking up arms.

There is no evidence that Maryam Jameelah herself ever committed acts of terror. But one American writer who did, and who also shared some of her views is Theodore Kaczynski. Kaczynski is otherwise known as the 'Unabomber' and wrote *The Industrial Society and Its Future*, a 35,000-word essay claiming that technology destroys nature and decimates communities. In this essay he proclaimed openly that acts of violence are the only way to return societies to a pre-modern age, and boasted that he would carry out such acts. Kaczynski was jailed in 1998 for killing three people during a 20-year campaign of terror that began in 1975 – his legal team succeeded in persuading the judge to commute the sentence to life imprisonment on the grounds that he was mentally unwell. When Kaczynski was arrested, his collection of books included Machiavelli's *The Prince*, and it turned out that he was a Harvard University alumnus.

So if we do accept that reading Maryam Jameelah induces extremist behaviour, then by extension, Maryam Jameelah's own influences ought to have contributed to some extent to her own extremism. As we know, in her books she cites (voluminously) the works of other writers. Initially, Mawdudi dominates. But by the 1970s, her circle of references widens to include authors such as Dennis Meadows and Seyyed Hossein Nasr.

Which of these should we blame (even in a small way) for the moulding of Maryam Jameelah?

PAKISTAN: RECKONING AND REDEMPTION

Iftikhar Malik

It is almost a cliché to say that Pakistan is in crisis. The mantra has been repeated since its inception as an idea and its evolution as a state. Pakistan is undoubtedly one of the most studied post-colonial polities, and never ceases to attract scholarly and journalistic attention. An enormity of academic studies, personal reportages and hasty comments – including those by the present reviewer – abound in libraries and Internet sites. Almost all these studies and reports repeat the familiar litany that Islam is the main rationale as well as predicament of Pakistan, that the military and mullahs are its nemesis, and that obliging and often corrupt politicians operate as 'the enemy within'. We are systematically led towards a doomsday scenario. Pakistan has been described as a 'tinderbox' by the Indian journalist M J Akbar, and as sliding towards oblivion by a string of western academics and writers. Somehow Allah, Army and America have all conspired to create a declining security state. Yet, Pakistan is still there!

Pakistani expatriate scholars often fall into the same trap. Pakistan's problems are essentialised and seen as a product of its 'caesarean' separation from Mother India, its failure in establishing an enduring democratic system despite all the efforts and public demands, and its continuous travails with India and the West. A few whirlwind visits to a city or two and conversations with some retired generals or parleys with a few select individuals often held in private living rooms or at the Western embassies are what counts as field work in this hugely complex, immensely populous and highly politicised country. Visits to madrassas or *mohallas* (neighbourhoods) remain non-existent; empirical work at schools and colleges across the land does not take place, and fieldwork among human right activists across the regions does not matter at all to such specialists. The tribal regions, the Federally-

Administered Tribal Areas (FATA), and the interiors of Balochistan and Sindh are routinely characterised as no-go areas or badlands where the future of 180 million people is being tarnished through one million ongoing mutinies. No wonder that, despite being over-researched, Pakistan as a society remains illusory! The three books under discussion here mark a refreshing departure and merit some added attention, though they offer mutually divergent pictures of Pakistan.

Farzana Shaikh, who is currently an associate fellow at Chatham House, begins by suggesting that just as there have been multiple forms of Islam, there are numerous perceptions of Pakistan. While this is correct, it is hardly surprising. We are, after all, talking about a populous and immensely plural part of the world. And why should this be a problem? Even countries like the United Kingdom, Belgium, Italy and Spain may have similar challenges though, of course, with several substantial differences. Collective identity is always a fluid and evolving entity and in a mere sixty years of existence may not be enough time for a more permanent national identity to evolve. Israel, mentioned frequently by Shaikh, has serious ideological problems not just with its Arab population and neighbours but also amongst its own Jewish Zionist hard core who differ over the nature and direction of the state's very Jewishness. Yes, India has done better. But perhaps that has something to do with the fact that it inherited the mainstream institutional framework from the Raj, is advantageously located away from the restive frontier regions, and has been fortunate to have a long list of founding fathers who, unlike their mostly flamboyant Pakistani counterparts, built up enduring institutions. However, even the Indian identity is comparatively young and still evolving, though claims by Jawaharlal Nehru and others of its historicity are no less trivial.

Shaikh is particularly angry about political Islam. The post-9/11 multi-dimensional spotlight on Islam has caused, among others, two kinds of attitudes amongst Muslims: defensively aggressive and apologetically defensive. Shaikh is firmly in the aggressive category. But can we blame all of Pakistan's ills on political Islam? And is it a phenomenon unique to Muslims? Is it all that different from Hindutva, Zionism and Christian Zionism, which like political Islam have been with us since the early nineteenth century? The recent volatility is not solely an intra-Muslim problem; it is equally linked to the acute imbalances within international systems which have often

helped literalists gain primacy over other strands of scriptural interpretations. Political Islam with all its variations is a rallying cry for change and for
the displacement of corrupt and humiliating systems, yet like other literalist
ideologies it lacks systemic alternatives. While fighting hegemonies several
of its trajectories have a strong tendency to become hegemonic themselves.
Corruption, despotism and foreign intervention in Pakistan's affairs have
only increased the mystique of political Islam given its powerful components
such as resistance, sacrifice, bravado, utopianism, shared brotherhood and
austerity. Following the dissolution of the communist regimes it has asserted
its own space, and here its various manifestations are surely located beyond
the orbit of simplistic and monolithic definitions.

Books discussed in this review

Making Sense of Pakistan by Farzana Shaikh, London: Hurst & Company, 2009, pp. ix+274.

Pakistan: Beyond the 'Crisis State' edited by Maleeha Lodhi, London:
Hurst & Company, 2011, pp. xxv+391.

Pakistan: A Hard Country by Anatol Lieven, London: Allen Lane, 2011,
pp.xv+560

Like most modernist Pakistanis, Shaikh has internalised a simplistic and
overtly negative explanation of political Islam, which is then projected as
the bane of Pakistani existence. Historically, Muslim modernists in India
had aggregated several regional and ecclesiastic groups to form a loose
alliance to obtain a territorial identity but then their successors failed to
deliver on the problems of political and economic disempowerment, and
here the Islamists began to offer themselves as an alternative. Political Islam
is not just about violence, it is also, as in the case of Pakistan, about religious parties working through the ballot, harnessing the media, cultivating
their own constituencies, and frequently working with ruling parties in
government. Putting these Islamists on a par with the militant elements is
not only incorrect but rather naïve. The spectre of Talibanisation does not
mean that the entire heritage of political Islam in Pakistan is in shambles
and hopelessly arcane.

Despite her interviews with a vast array of generals, Shaikh seems to follow the usual critique of the military as an exploitative institution. The army roped in Jihadis, especially in 1971 and then again during the 1980s and 1990s, to wage civil and regional wars, as if the Jihadis had no autonomous agency of their own. The military is definitely the strongest pressure group in the country where, like Indonesia, Venezuela, Argentina, Nigeria, Myanmar and other places it views itself as the guardian of a state surrounded by hostile forces. One can also think of contemporary Iran under the Guardian-Clerics sharing a similar perception of domestic and external challenges. Irrespective of what Generals Ayub Khan, Yahya Khan, Zia-ul-Haq and Pervez Musharraf did to civic institutions, Pakistanis, since 2008, have found in their army an institution which is much more than simply a scheming secret service and a collection of capricious generals. Its operations in Swat, FATA and elsewhere have cost it large-scale casualties, and its stand against a belligerent India has the support of most Pakistanis. Of course, it would be ideal if the generals stayed aloof and let the politicians establish constitutional politics but let us not forget the general-presidents have been either brought in by their external backers or were provided full protection as surrogates. Both the United States and the United Kingdom tried to shore up the isolated and unpopular General Musharraf right until his last day — at the expense of the country's democratic and judicial prerogatives. Even now, following the midnight operation against Osama bin Laden on 2 May 2011, and despite unanimous parliamentary resolutions rebuking US drone attacks, the Pentagon, CIA and the State Department continue to cultivate and confide in the Pakistani generals. The US is unwilling or uninterested in taking Pakistani public opinion seriously. So we can't blame everything on the army.

Shaikh lists all the contentious ideological and structural problems including the ambiguous idea of a Muslim versus Islamic state, the predominance of the military and the mullahs in Pakistan's politics, and the numerous failures at reform. Her book is definitely not a history of Pakistan and perhaps that is why she keeps traversing the decades and personalities, even at the risk of repeating herself. Despite her fascination with M. A. Jinnah, the founder of Pakistan, and the Sufi poet Muhammad Iqbal, who first came up with the vision of Pakistan, Shaikh does not hide her disappointment with the country's post-1947 leaders. The Pakistani elite constantly ignored the quest for a consensual identity and that became Pakistan's major malaise. While her prefatory remarks and the major section of the book are interspersed with an unflinching critique of how Pakistan was imagined, created and has been mismanaged, her epilogue quite briefly surmises the dynamism of its media and civil society but only as a passing reference. She seems to have lost all hope in the makers and elites of Pakistan. However, a vast majority of Pakistan's people – the inheritors of the Indus lands – are surely its stake holders as well and not just mute bystanders confronted with gigantic challenges. Do they not matter?

In sharp contrast to Shaikh, the journalist and former ambassador Maleeha Lodhi is overly optimistic. Her anthology is a collection of upbeat articles and it is decidedly a mixed bag. Contributions vary in terms of originality, research potentials or new analysis. Articles by Ayesha Jalal, Ahmed Rashid, and Shuja Nawaz in fact summarise their already familiar writings on the evolution of Pakistan, the Taliban resurgence and the military's systemic ascendancy. Saeed Shafqat goes beyond the usual configurative analysis of the Pakistani elite and detects shifting ideological positions even among the religious cadres along with the entry of the lower middle classes into military and political arenas, though some political patterns remain unchanged. Meekal Ahmed and Ishrat Hussain – 'the insider-outsiders' – dwell on the familiar macro-economic situation offering some genuine prescriptive analysis, but one wonders about their own incapacity to implement a reform agenda when they ran the roost! It is the younger contributors such as Moeed Yusuf, Ziad Alahdad and Muddassar Malik who, by trawling rigorously through data, offer systemic alternatives to the current malaise in sectors like the economy, energy and education. Lodhi offers a considered piece, highlighting three significant developments under General Musharraf: the July 2007 military assault on Lal Masjid in Islamabad, which was under siege by a group of militant students, ending in the death of 154 people; the dismissal of Justice of the Supreme Court of Pakistan, Iftikhar Mohammed Chaudhry, in March 2007, which produced the lawyers' movement and led to an uprising; and the assassination of Benazir Bhutto in December of the same year that brought the Peoples' Party to power. These events not only hastened Musharraf's exit but also left their enduring impact on the country. As a consequence, the country became more vulnerable to internal fissures.

However, the best contribution comes from Mohsin Hamid, the novelist. He enumerates the country's diverse potentials, dynamic human resource-fulness and its innate cultural vitality, and argues passionately that if har-nessed properly, they can be used to usher in a new beginning. He emphatically urges Pakistanis to rely on themselves, broaden the country's tax base, minimise dependence on external assistance, and enhance the country's versatility and creative genius. 'A brighter future awaits us if we, as Pakistani citizens, are willing to pay for it', he declares. Beyond the reck-oning, there is hope.

Some hope can also be gleaned from Anatol Lieven's book. He offers us a more comprehensive and closer-to-the-grassroots analysis than Shaikh and Lodhi, who somehow shy away from getting closer to the rigours and com-plexities of Pakistani life. That Lieven has a family connection to South Asia is obvious from his dedication. His grandfather was involved in a military operation in the tribal regions towards the end of the Raj in the 1930s. A professor at King's College, Lieven began as a journalist for *The Times*: in 1988, he reported on Mujahideen defiance in Afghanistan, during the 1990s he covered the turmoil in Chechnya before moving on to Washington D.C. on a fellowship. In between, he turned into an academic; and *Pakistan: A Hard Country* combines serious scholarship with reportage to offer a detailed, insightful and sympathetic analysis of 'what is wrong with Pakistan'. Lieven gives us a first-hand experience of grassroots realities in Pakistan, while displaying a broader perspective on regional and international geo-politics. He neither predicts doom nor loses sight of the harrowing challenges faced by Pakistan. One of his strongest points lies in his encounter with Pakistan's societal realities based on kinship and localism where honour, redress and a strong sense of religious identification – often criss-crossed by ethnic, tribal and sectarian divisions – play a vital role and might even keep this otherwise highly populous and plural country together.

While writing this book, Lieven tells us, he was tempted to turn it into a requiem given 'the pressures on Pakistan from without and within'. But his exhaustive findings did not let him take that route. The increased mili-tancy not just in the FATA but all across the country and especially in the idyllic valleys of Swat, Dir and Buner, has certainly been unnerving for those who had felt all along that the troubled country, like its past, would somehow be able to pull through successfully. Its creation amidst the greatest migration in human history, its partition in 1971, its long ordeals under military regimes, a growing population, the post-1979 influx of millions of Afghan refugees, the post-9/11whirlwind of war theatres in its western border regions, and then the horrendous Earthquake of 2005 had all tested the morale, patience and resourcefulness of the Indus country as its neighbours and the world at large appeared apathetic to this predominantly Muslim state. Moreover, the floods of 2010 – hypothetically equivalent to two earthquakes and two tsunamis – further depleted Pakistan of its meagre resources. With foreign assistance in short supply, the 20 million or so displaced people had to rely on their own inner strength and the charitable nature of their fellow citizens to survive. Maybe this binary continuum of turbulence and resilience kept Anatol Lieven hopeful.

Lieven sees in Pakistan a multi-layered society where forces of tradition and modernity compete and persist without reaching any finale. While most of the rural and tribal population follows agrarian and kinship based lifestyles, the urban areas and even the hinterlands may also surprisingly retain 'islands of successful modernity and of excellent administration', which may allow for some optimism in harsher times. The biradari-based loyalties anchor Pakistan and Diaspora Pakistanis on a myriad of smaller but vital clusters, which somehow keep delivering where otherwise the state institutions may remain inadequate. In a way, these 'small republics' allow some local redress and even if the state may be inefficient or non-existent, they keep the boat afloat.

The early chapters of the book, interspersed with personal interviews and experiences in the hinterlands, try to summarise the movement for Muslim nationhood in British India. It was a diverse movement with divergent pathways among the Indian Muslims, assuming Deobandi/purist and Barelvi/sufist dispensations. Since the 1980s, the latter schisms have become even more acute given momentous national and regional developments. Jinnah's modernist followers might have espoused a progressive outlook yet, in a clear sense, they would never demur from the Muslim credentials of their people and that is where the Muslim League, in the 1940s, turned to slogans like 'Islam is in danger'.

The second part of the volume is an in-depth analysis of 'what makes Pakistan'. Lieven leads us through a detailed discussion on religion, justice, military and politics. And he comes into his own when he describes the social structures of Pakistani societies. Pakistan, it seems, is working informally whether one visits the *hujra* of a khan/malik, the tribal leader, or a *haveli* of a *wadero*, the feudal landlord. The sardars in Balochistan and their counterparts in Sindh are the bastions of power and authority at the local level where an unquestioned loyalty is exchanged for full protection. The khans and sardars are like *mai-bap* (father-mother) for most of the tenants or *haris*. In rural Punjab — itself quite diverse with three or four main political economies — local clan leaders resort to a kind of consultative or *panchayati* system offering rudimentary justice which, as in the case of Mukhtaran Mai who was gang raped as a form of honour revenge, may be quite abrasive. Unlike Balochistan, both Sindh and Punjab have local but no less powerful hierarchies, which are land-based but could also proffer spiritual status due to their family linkages with some Sufi shrines. Such *pirs* or spiritual leaders are often powerful landlords whose influence reaches all the way to Karachi and Islamabad, and even if they happen to be ordinary landholding people, their spiritual prestige and pretensions allow them pre-eminence within the socio-political echelons.

In the province of Khyber-Pakhtunkhwa, where a strong sense of equality prevails as stipulated by the Pushtun code called *Pushtunwali*, the clerics play a very decisive role. Here the Jihad tradition may certainly be linked with this particular aspect, which has become quite pronounced since British times. The khans and maliks, especially within the FATA, may seek to work with Islamabad on the basis of mutual interdependence and convenience, but the mullahs often try to establish their own independent power basis. Central Punjab, like Karachi, is largely urban, literate and entrepreneurial, yet political patterns here are again based on a traditional system of patronage, especially when the police and other administrative units are found wanting in delivering justice. In his discussion on various forms of Islamists and Islamic parties, such as Jamaat-e-Islami, Jamiat-i-Ulama-i-Islam and the evolution of the Pakistani Taliban, Lieven reveals first hand information on shifting boundaries between these regular parties and their Jihadi counterparts. Many leaders of the violent militant groups such as Jaysh-i-Muhammad, Lashkar-i-Jhangvi and Anjuman-i-Sipah-i-Sahaba Pakistan were former members of Jamiat-i-Ulama-i-Islam, while Jamaat-e-Islami furnished the ultra-violent Lashkar-e-Tayyaba and Tehreek-i-Nifaz-i-Shariat in Swat with their members. Both Jamaat-e-Islami and Jamiat-i-Ulama-i-Islam follow Deobandi traditions and benefited from Islamisation under General Zia-ul-Haq and from the partisan politicking by General Musharraf.

Lieven does not refute the primacy enjoyed by the Army within the Pakistani political spectrum and acknowledges the fact that its preoccupation with India has played a crucial role in creating a specific mindset and corresponding policies across the various official echelons. Other than Kashmir, the generals and security agencies including the ISI (Inter-Services Intelligence) are worried about India in Afghanistan, where it is assumed that its major role is to encircle Pakistan, between Afghanistan and the unstable and mutinous region of Baluchistan. The generals bank on predominantly Pushtun Taliban in Afghanistan as their major allies in neutralising India's influence on their western flanks.

There is a great deal of praise and admiration for Pakistani media in Lieven's book. The media has enhanced its position over the last decade and has assumed a flagship position in informing and influencing public opinion. Lievin notes: 'In the twenty years between my stay in Pakistan in the late 1980s and the writing of this book, by far the most important change on the Pakistani political scene (other than the rebellion of the Pakistani Taliban) has been the proliferation of television and radio stations during Musharraf's period in power.' However, as in many other sections of society, he finds that anti-American sentiments are pervasive amongst broadcast and print journalists. Indeed, the US is the first port of call for any and all blame. It took years before Pakistanis accepted that it was not the US but their own Taliban who were committing terrorist attacks. Even the academics at the University of Peshawar, a city where suicide bombings are a weekly if not a daily occurrence, refused to incriminate their fellow Pakistanis for causing extensive fatalities and grievous injuries to countless innocent civilians. However, the events in Swat following a steady increase in the expansion of the local Taliban and their feared march towards Islamabad brought the PPP regime, the army and other important political parties together behind a major military operation.

His earlier contacts with Pakistani leaders and generals help Lieven provide an accurate portrait of the current state of affairs in Pakistan. He goes back to the history of the Raj and its relations with Kabul through the past two centuries, which featured frequent warfare, periods of watchful calm and occasional surrogacy, and subsequently resulted in the demarcation of borders and the evolution of administering tribal agencies through an indirect system. Lieven travels to Swat to meet local functionaries and notables such as Afzal Khan Lala, who refused to vacate his village even at the worst times of the Taliban insurgency. Here in the scenic valley he feels a strong nostalgia for early princely rule.

Like many Western journalists travelling in the developing world, Lieven had convenient access to prime ministers, generals, journalists and local chieftains – something that is not available to home scholars – yet his study does not suffer from any lack of exposure to the lives of the vast majority of Pakistanis. He met the Soomros tribe in Sindh; went boar hunting with a self-conscious Mumtaz Ali Bhutto; shared long sessions with a fast-talking Mustafa Kamal, the former mayor of Karachi and a devoted supporter of Altaf Hussain of the Muttahida Qaumi Movement (MQM); and noted a litany of praise for Benazir Bhutto from Javed Jabbar, the minister for information in Benazir's first administration. He met students, Jamaat-e-Islami activists, women lawyers, journalists, activists of various parties and a string of pirs and tribal leaders from Multan and Sindh. These interviews and extracts from conversations means his book reads more like a personal journey than a scholarly inquiry. But his analysis is always cool-headed, balanced and well informed.

'Pakistan is quite simply far more important to the region, the West and the world than is Afghanistan: a statement which is a matter not of sentiment but of mathematics', Lieven declares. No doubt prophesies of its imminent demise will continue. But as Lieven notes, the country does have a future. It will somehow 'muddle through'.

BEING AMERICAN

Hassan Mahamdallie

When Balbir Singh Sodhi, a Sikh living in the US, was murdered in supposed revenge for 9/11, his killer told police 'I stand for America all the way'. Cynthia Weber, academic and film maker, reports that advertising executives, fearing an anti-Muslim and wider racist backlash, dreamed up a 30- second Public Service Announcement (PSA) TV advertisement entitled 'I am an American'. It was made up of a number of Americans from diverse ethnic backgrounds (although none recognisably Muslim by appearance or dress) saying to the camera 'I am an American'.

The commissioners were so pleased with the resulting positive reception that they drew the conclusion that the advertisement 'made a measurable difference in our society' and 'helped the country to unite in the wake of the terrorist attacks'. However the advertisement did not prevent a backlash against Muslims and other minorities living in America. Bush's declaration, as he geared up the American military machine and government instruments of internal repression, that you were either 'with us or against us' exposed and widened fault lines both between US citizens and non-US citizens and between those who laid claim to the US nationality.

Weber decided to make a series of films in response to the PSA advertisement that demonstrated 'that the simple declaration "I am an American" is fraught with complications and paradoxes, particularly when it is meant to express citizenship, identity, tolerance, nationalism, patriotism and justice'. It should also be pointed out that she was a bit upset at a fellow British academic who told her, in the aftermath of 9/11, that 'America got what it deserved'. A shocked and angry Weber thought 'I want to ask her – What America? Which Americans?' The result is an intellectual, photographic and filmic journey, as Weber seeks out people in the US that represent 'the fear of difference', chronicled in this fascinating book.

236

Weber encounters numerous stories of lives that expose the many para-
doxes and contradictions papered over by the phrase 'I am an American'.
Take, for example, Guadalupe 'Lupe' Denogean, a retired marine who
Weber tells us became the latest Iraq war's first 'fast-tracked' US citizen.
Denogean, the son of Mexican migrant labourers, became one of the first
US casualties of the war. While stationed in Basra he was blown up in a
grenade attack that left him with severe head injuries, burst eardrums and
shrapnel wounds. Upon his arrival at the hospital, Denogean filled out a
questionnaire that asked if he had any special requests. Yes, he wrote: He
wished to become a US citizen. A week later George and Laura Bush visited
his hospital bed and granted him his wish. Thereafter George Bush could
not resist the temptation to use the story of the grateful Denogean in his
speeches.

> 'I Am An American': Filming the Fear of Difference by Cynthia Weber,
> Bristol/Chicago: Intellect, 2011

Weber puts Denogean's story next to that of Jesus Suarez del Solar from
Tijuana. He was told by a US army recruiter that if he joined the Marines he
could transfer after two years into the US Drug Enforcement Agency (DEA).
That was a lie. Jesus was sent to Iraq where he was blown up and killed after
stepping on an unexploded US cluster bomb. The US government told
Jesus's father Fernando that his dead son could be made a 'posthumous US
citizen'. Unlike Denogean, Fernando came to national prominence after he
uttered the word : 'No'. 'At the funeral', Weber writes, 'Jesus's coffin was
draped with the US flag. Before burying Jesus, Fernando replaced the flag
with the Mexican flag. With his hand over his heart, Fernando stood next to
his dead son and his grieving wife and sang the Mexican National Anthem".
When Weber visits Fernando Suarez del Solar in a trailer in California she
sees that his car is adorned with stickers that announce his political views:
'Support our troops, Bring them home NOW!', 'Bush Lies, Who Dies?' and
'I support Iraq Veterans Against The War'.

Weber's subjects are arranged into three categories; Soldiers, Civilians
and Collateral Damage. The first category is self-explanatory, the second
category documents those involved in America's 'other war' that is taking

place on the US Mexican border, and the last chronicles individuals caught up in the sweep net of the US's internal war on terror apparatus, including a couple made into internal 'refugees' post-Katrina.

All the individuals that Weber seeks out have stories to tell that slowly and cumulatively begin to tear the American flag apart at the seams. Indeed Weber has all her subjects photographed holding the flag. Significantly nearly all of them, in different ways, approach the flag as a physical object in a tentative and sometimes subversive manner. Put plainly, most of them refuse to be uncomplicated patriotic flag-wavers. They variously want to juxtapose images against the flag, or superimpose images such as the peace symbol over it or wish to hold it in unconventional ways, including upside-down. It seems that many were beyond the point of wishing to 'seize back' the flag.

The second part of Weber's book is made up of brief academic commentaries on the project. I wearily acknowledge that the make-believe world of visual-arts academia forces one to seek legitimacy in post-modern linguistic torture, so one should not be surprised that the commentaries add little to the sum total of the book.

But '*I am an American*' did get me thinking, although it has to be admitted that my conclusions are not that profound. But what did strike me was the sterility of having a debate about humanness and our connections with one another within a nationalistic framework. At this point I have to admit a bias. I unconditionally support the struggle of excluded individuals and groups to gain full citizenship rights through being recognised as 'belonging' to a particular nation. I do not care much for governments that refuse people rights of nationality and ration it out to groups such as migrant workers and asylum seekers. I believe that 'belonging' is ultimately rooted not in nationality or ethnicity but in solidarity. I have never described myself as 'English' and I never will to my dying day. The notion of 'Britishness' means absolutely nothing to me – I happen to have been born on this particular rock off the coast of mainland Europe and that's it. Patriotism and national pride is a total anathema to me. I regard legitimisation of hybrid labels including 'British Muslim' as absurd and meaningless pursuits. I am forced to carry a British passport to travel across national borders but I have no particular attachment to said piece of card, paper and biometric data. Having said all this I am not unaware that maybe I am in a position to say these things precisely because 'I am British'.

The problem as I see it is that by 'buying' into the idea that nationhood, American or other, is always going to be a compromise. As Weber chronicles in the case of Jesus Suarez del Solar, and as his father Fernando recognised, 'dying to be an American' is a cruel absurdity too far.

In an article in *The New York Review of Books* Mark Danner described post 9/11 America as being in the grip of a 'state of exception', a state that is on a never-ending loop. 'In the name of security', he notes, 'some of our accustomed rights and freedoms are circumscribed or set aside, the years during which we live in a different time. This different time of ours has now extended ten years – the longest by far in American history – with little sense of an ending. Indeed, the very endlessness of this state of exception – a quality emphasised even as it was imposed – and the broad acceptance of that endlessness, the state's exception's increasing normalisation, are among its distinguishing marks'.

I am reminded of all those still languishing, victims of Obama's broken promise, on that strip of America known as Guantanamo Bay. If Danner is right and the exception is now the norm, what are the repercussions for those who strive towards a more pluralistic definition of what it means to say 'I Am An American'?

THE ARABIC MAIMONIDES

Jerry Ravetz

Like any great thinker, Moses Maimonides (1135-1204) presents paradoxes to the inquirer. In his case, the paradoxes are patent, and deeply unsettling or enlightening, depending on your point of view. In this book by a distinguished Israeli academic, Maimonides is presented in the context of his own time, and with her deep scholarship worn very lightly, she displays him as something other than what generations of pious admiration have assumed.

We start with the history, that Maimonides is universally accepted as the greatest of Jewish thinkers. He contributed two epochal books: the *Mishneh Torah*, where Jewish law was codified; and *The Guide for the Perplexed*, a synthesis of faith and reason that strongly influenced all subsequent pre-modern philosophers. Besides those, he wrote extensively on religion and medicine, some very illuminating letters survive, and a fair amount is known about his life.

Maimonides in His World: Portrait of a Mediterranean Thinker by Sarah Stroumsa, Princeton: Princeton University Press, 2009

The first paradox is a major clue to the whole story. In what language was his unique guide written? The natural answer: Hebrew. But it is wrong. He wrote in Arabic! It was what they call Judeo-Arabic, analogous to the Yiddish of the Ashkenazi Jews in a German-language milieu. But it was not the vernacular of the time, as the Sephardi Jews spoke (and the survivors still do) 'Ladino', related to the Spanish language of the time. However, Arabic was the language of the philosophers, and (as the analysis makes clear) it was with the philosophers, who were largely Muslim, that Maimonides was in dialogue. All those Hebrew-Israeli enthusiasts who are so confident of the essential inferiority of Arabic-Muslim culture would find this a most unsettling paradox: their greatest intellectual hero thought in Arabic!

There is an incidental paradox, in that the rabbis in the south of France denounced the guide and indeed turned it over to the inquisition for burning. But that is hardly a paradox; he was doing his thing and they were doing theirs. But there is another paradox in the text. The book itself is not a particularly transparent guide for the perplexed; the editor of the great English translation (Shlomo Pines) confessed that there seems to be some hidden message in the strange ordering of the sections.

Stroumsa's thesis is that Maimonides was essentially a 'Mediterranean' thinker. This does not indicate a single uniform culture, but rather families of coexisting cultures, related in various ways through space, time, religion and rulership. And certainly, Andalus, with its mixing of Muslim, Christian and Jewish streams of thought, was truly Mediterranean. When forced by circumstances to leave, Maimonides got a job at the other end of the Mediterranean, in Egypt.

The culture of medieval Spain has been somewhat romantically described as 'the world of the three rings'. This derives from one version (of Friedrich Heer, not of Lessing) of the tale of Nathan the Wise, who was asked by the (wise) King Alfonso X, which is the best religion. The answer came in the form of a mathematical puzzle of three connected rings, which is familiar to Americans as the logo of Ballantynes beer. The three are inseparable, but if you remove one the other two fall apart. Certainly the three religions coexisted in Spain, even after the gains of the earlier Reconquest, as nowhere else in the West. But by the time of Maimonides, that culture had passed its peak, and therein we find even more paradoxes.

It is known that early in the lifetime of Maimonides, Andalus was conquered by tribesmen from North Africa, the Almohades, who brought with them, it is thought, a primitive and puritanical version of Islam. Rather unusually among Muslim sects, they actually believed in those forced conversions which non-Muslims have assumed to have been the norm. The records are not conclusive, but there seems to be a consensus that Maimonides and his family actually converted (outwardly), and that he went to Morocco for his studies. We should recall that it was easier for Jews to 'pass' in Muslim cultures, since their special dietary laws, being the same as those of their hosts, would not betray them as they did in Christian cultures.

Contrary to popular assumptions, we learn from this book that the Almohades were not total barbarians. They had their own well-formed ideas about religious doctrine and (common to Muslim and Jewish cultures) the problems of articulation of religious law. And therein lies the most striking of the paradoxes. For it seems that the Muslim culture generally had the same sort of learning, of commentaries-piled-upon-commentaries, as the Jews. For ultra-Orthodox Jews, the elaboration of commentaries, and the resolution of differences between versions, is still at the core of religious practice itself. Every now and then, there appears a great scholar who tries to make a summary of this vast and untidy corpus, so that ordinary people can know how to interpret the hundreds of injunctions for the religious life. Maimonides' *Mishneh Torah* was one of these, and was actually the most ruthless in the author's determination to hack away all the undergrowth and reveal the simple truths. Indeed, it appears from the text and also from letters, that he did not find such elaborated discussions particularly useful or interesting, nor did he have much respect for those who practiced this arcane discipline. At this point Stroumsa permits herself a speculation. Could there have been a source, outside of the Jewish tradition, where Maimonides received the idea of drastic simplification? It is there, in the codifications of the Muslim tradition that he would have learned from the Almohades, particularly when studying as a Muslim in Morocco.

This is truly paradoxical indeed. Could it be that the greatest of Jewish thinkers not only thought in Arabic when doing philosophy, but absorbed a Muslim tradition when articulating Jewish religious doctrine? But then, why not? As Strousma reminds us, Maimonides was heir to a 'Mediterranean' culture, in which the Jews were an important and respected presence. We should not let our perspective on the age of Maimonides be distorted by the later half-millennium of exclusion and oppression in Christian Europe. In modern times, we have seen how many fields of secular thought have been influenced by Jews (either religious or not), and now this is accepted as quite natural. Why should Jewish thought not have been influenced by outside influences – Islam – in that earlier age, when the religion was accepted as one of the 'three rings'? Only those who believe in some Divine dispensation granting uniqueness to the Jews, not merely as a people but also as thinkers, would on reflection find this unacceptable.

The relevance of this story to the present is not at all paradoxical. In the twentieth-century Jewish settlement in Palestine, there were important Jewish thinkers who advocated an appreciation of the Muslim and Arabic cultures, acknowledging their richness and their historic contribution to Jewish life. They were only a minority at the time, and they were effectively forgotten in Israel, as it was conceived around an Ashkenazi ascendancy with Hebrew grafted on. Now, in these perilous times, there are ever more Israelis who know that mutual respect and reconciliation with Palestine are necessary, not merely for the security of Israel, but for its long-term survival. This book, by a professor at the Hebrew University, makes a very important contribution to that cause.

THE CATALYST FOR KNOWLEDGEABLE GENERATION

SELANGOR FOUNDATION

For further details, kindly contact us at :

Corporate Affairs Unit
Menara Yayasan Selangor, No 18A, Jalan Persiaran Barat
46000 Petaling Jaya,
Selangor Darul Ehsan,
Malaysia.
Tel : +603 - 7955 1212
Fax : +603 - 7954 1790
Email : Info@yayasanselangor.org.my
www.yayasanselangor.org.my

ET CETERA

ASSESSMENT

EDWARD SAID

Vinay Lal

Several years after his death in the autumn of 2003, Edward Said, who had attained the rank of 'University Professor' at Columbia University, continues to elicit an equal measure of adulation and vitriolic criticism. Though university professors are a dime a dozen, the designation accorded to Said was unusual, reserved for about a dozen to twenty faculty who are deemed to have attained distinction without comparison; similarly, it is not often remembered that 'Columbia University in the City of New York' is the full title by which one of the most distinguished institutions of higher education in the United States wishes to be known. However controversial Said may have been, whether on account of his thesis on 'Orientalism', which is commonly believed to have given rise to both postcolonial studies and 'colonial discourse analysis', or as a consequence of his unflinching advocacy of the rights of Palestinians and his equally trenchant critique of the place of Zionism in American political and intellectual life, he was never anything less than Columbia University's star attraction. Said, on his part, could never tear himself away from the university, or the city of New York; though he accepted visiting professorships at universities such as Harvard, or Johns Hopkins, where as a freshman in 1978 I first heard of him in hushed whispers, it is at 'Columbia University in the City of New York' that he put down roots. An urban intellectual to the core, Said was drawn to the liberal cosmopolitanism of New York, a city immortalised by Woody Allen among others as the cultural if angst-ridden home of American Jews. It is here that a Palestinian would display the imagination and daring to think of himself as the last German Jewish intellectual in the world.

Orientalism

Before we move to the question of location in addressing Said's work, and the all-important consideration of to which extent the opposition (in his own words) of being both 'housed' and 'unhoused' ought to inform our understanding of his life and intellectual endeavours, it would be best to commence with an assessment of *Orientalism* (1978) and the politics of its reception. Those with a considerable familiarity with Said's oeuvre have sometimes argued that his books from around that period — *Beginnings: Intention and Method* (1975) and *The World, The Text, and the Critic* (1983) — are more substantial works of literary and cultural criticism, but there is no doubting the fact that *Orientalism* would come to acquire an unrivalled importance for humanistic scholarship as well as for launching Said's career as a public intellectual. His unflinching advocacy of the Palestinian cause is, in many respects, much less controversial than the arguments put forward in *Orientalism*; but I suspect that Said's forays into politics, to the point where he earned a seat on the Palestinian National Council, would have commanded less attention had he not first demonstrated a mastery over literary texts and unveiled the contours of a secular humanism that would become his intellectual trademark. Much like Noam Chomsky, who had established himself as the dominant figure in linguistics before he initiated his relentless critiques of American self-aggrandisement and empire-mongering, Said had the prudence to recognise that both the passion and authority of his literary criticism would bear salutary consequences for him in his political work.

The thesis of *Orientalism* is in actuality quite unexceptional, even if it continues to provoke some to fury and to rather predictable if absurd charges that Said was hypocritical, launching critiques of Western civilisation from his lofty position at an Ivy League institution in the supposed artistic and cultural capital of the world. Said is perhaps being confused here with Mohandas Gandhi: when asked what he thought of Western civilisation, the 'wily sage' — one of the many designations by which the Mahatma was brought into the orbit of instrumental reason — replied, 'I think it would be a very good idea.' If anything, as I shall argue later, Said was a bit too much enamoured of 'Western civilisation', and his thesis in Orientalism is rather modest, something like the equally plausible view put forward in recent years by John Mearsheimer and Stephen Walt that 'the Israel lobby' has not merely contaminated American foreign policy but seriously corroded the possibilities of genuine intellectual exchanges in the public sphere. Orientalism, Said argued, is a style of thought resting upon an epistemological and ontological divide between 'the Orient' and 'the Occident'. The body of work that Orientalists — scholars, administrators, travelers, missionaries, savants, public commentators, essayists — produced about the Orient tells us very little if anything about the Orient, but it does tell us a good deal about the intellectual presuppositions that shaped the worldview of Europeans. The Orientalists, moreover, were writing not only for reading publics in Europe (and later the United States), but also for Orientals themselves. The epitaph from Marx's *Eighteenth Brumaire* that graces *Orientalism* says it all: those who cannot represent themselves will be represented by others. The native perforce had to understand that his own history was better known to the European than it was to himself.

By the late eighteenth century Orientalism had come to acquire a decisive place in Western intellectual traditions, and it is of course no accident that Britain and France were amassing huge empires at that time. Throughout the eighteenth and nineteenth centuries, colonial territorial acquisitions continued to grow, and the British in India, to take one notable example, came to a gradual awareness of the epistemological imperatives that they were called upon to exercise. The native had to be known if he was to be governed effectively, his languages had to be mastered, and some understanding had to be gained of the revenue and administrative systems that the colonial state stood to inherit. The British would thus be furiously engaged in the work of translating works from Indian languages into English, creating grammars and dictionaries of Indian languages, mapping and measuring the land, counting the natives, enumerating the flora and fauna of the land, and myriad other tasks upon which the British brought to bear the insights, however dubious they were on many occasions, of cartography, anthropometry, craniometry, ethnography, photography, archaeology, and so on. One prominent scholar of British India, the late Bernard S. Cohn, has described the different modalities — topographical, surveillance, anthropological, travel, survey, historiographic, enumerative, among others — by means of which the British came to acquire a comprehensive knowledge of India. Orientalism is then to be understood also as the entire institutional apparatus which enabled European powers to know, define, and master their colonised subjects. This vast body of information created, it has been argued, an essentialised body of knowledge about the 'other', and the complexity of a civilisation, in the case of India, was reduced to a set of tropes, among them the ideas of an unchanging India, a despotic past, the effeminate Hindu, the fanatic Muslim, the conniving Brahmin, the preponderance of the collective over the individual, and the irreducible attachment of natives to their religion and caste.

Numerous criticisms of *Orientalism* would soon emerge, commencing with the argument that Said was wholly unappreciative of the good intentions of most Orientalist scholars, and that the prejudices of a few Europeans blinded Said to the fact that European scholars had created an unprecedented and immensely sound body of knowledge about non-European societies. A second and not entirely unrelated strand of criticism is insistent in its claim that Said had not really contributed anything substantively new on the question of European scholarship about the Other. Many of Said's ideas, his critics allege, are anticipated in the writings of the Egyptian philosopher Anouar Abdel-Malek, the Malaysian scholar Syed Hussein Alatas, and the Indian historian and diplomat K. M. Panikkar; indeed, the earliest of Cohn's essays, dating to the first half of the 1960s, appear to prefigure the notion that the discursive apparatus of colonialism was, if anything, more destructive of indigenous cultures than anything that might have been achieved by the force of arms or the economic transformation of the land under colonial rule. Moreover, the critics ask, what is so truly exceptional about Orientalism, considering that, to take two figures at random, the fifth century BCE historian Herodotus and, 1,600 years later, the great author of the *Divine Comedy* who had the temerity to consign Prophet Muhammad to hell, there is scarcely a European narrative of the Other that is free of prejudice or hostility?

Though Said would scarcely have contested the argument that most narratives of the Other are laced with prejudices, or that the history of European representations of non-European cultures is rife with instances of racism, it is critical to understand the relationship of colonialism to Orientalism. By the late eighteenth century, it was no longer a question of a representation here or there that was contaminated by this or that author's prejudices; rather, a systematic mode of representing the Other, emboldened by an institutional apparatus to which various sorts of experts lent their services, had come into place. Drawing upon the insights of Foucault,

Said was to delineate a specific relationship of power to knowledge that had
as its consequence the creation of a discursive episteme that was totalising
in its explanatory reach. This is what distinguishes Said's intellectual contributions from those of his predecessors, whose achievements were by no
means inconsequential. *Orientalism* is also at heart a book about the hazards
of representing a culture distinct from one's own. With what authority and
license, and with what consequences and effects, does one write about the
Other, and how does one do so without doing some injustice to those one
seeks to represent?

Identity: Politics and Aesthetics

A complete inventory of critical readings of *Orientalism*, which I shall not
attempt here, yields much that is predictable — and some surprises as well.
The more complex responses were, curiously, not unexpected. Some critics
alleged that Said had homogenised the Orientalists, failing to make distinc-
tions between travelers, armchair scholars, men who sought kinship with
the East and those who served the empire, those with command of one or
more non-European languages and those without, and so on. Said had, in
other words, stereotyped the Orientalists, much as the Orientalists were
supposed to have stereotyped the Orient. This is much less interesting than
the argument that Said appeared to posit an epistemological rupture in the
late eighteenth century that set off the pre-colonial word a bit too neatly
from the world under colonialism. If, as Said seemed to be arguing, European intellectual practices and knowledge systems had acquired an overwhelming dominance, how could one even speak of a pre-colonial world
except through the categories of knowledge inherited through colonialism?
Moreover, in Said's narrative, power remained the exclusive preserve of
European colonisers, and the colonised people, even in civilisations with
long and complex histories, seemed incapable of offering any intellectual or
cultural resistance to the profound encroachments upon their worldviews
and lifestyles. If, even in the most totalitarian systems, fissures and slippages
allow some amount of negotiation, howsoever miniscule, over the question
of power, how could Said possibly have allowed himself to believe that in
colonial encounters power lay almost entirely on one side? It is to address
this criticism that Said would, more than a decade later, seek to make

amends in *Culture and Imperialism* (1993), a book both engrossing and tiresome in parts. On the one hand, Said extended the analysis on offer in *Orientalism* to demonstrate, with consummate skill, how even canonical works of literature or music at seemingly great remove from politics betrayed the worldview of European colonisers; on the other hand, Said assumes a didactic and sometimes hectoring tone, offering almost rudimentary analyses of works of 'resistance', from Syed Hussein Alatas's *The Myth of the Lazy Native* (1977) to 'Subaltern Studies', which Said ordained as necessary works in a well read person's library.

But *Orientalism* elicited, as I have suggested, some more unusual readings. Some in the Arab world mistakenly began to view Said as an uncritical advocate of Arab nationalism, just as many in the United States, both among his admirers and detractors, supposed that Said was a champion of identity politics. On both counts, Said's position was unambiguously clear. Said himself never mistook his own condemnation of the representational regimes which had rendered the Arab into a caricature for an endorsement of Arab leaders, and he was never less than forthright in his utter disdain for Arab states which had succumbed to authoritarian political tendencies and obstructed the creation of a climate of opinion conducive to the free exchange of ideas and creative intellectual work. While he would have questioned the moral authority of the West to designate this or that country as a 'failed' or 'rogue' state, his own criticism of Arab states which appeared to emulate the Oriental Despotisms that Orientalist scholars had much fantasised about, grew more acerbic over the years. Said was alarmed not only by the human rights abuses and the difficulty of producing intellectual work in the Arab world, but also by the credence with which far too many Arabs received 'out-moded and discredited ideas', such as the notion that the Holocaust was a fiction perpetrated by the Elders of Zion.

It would be an understatement to suggest that Said refused to be drawn into the identity politics that has so energised, not always productively, American university campuses. Whatever his solidarity with ethnic, religious, or linguistic minorities in the US, or with people of the global South, he was not an unequivocal supporter of ethnic studies centers or the idea that works of literature were to be championed because they were authored by black women, Chicano gays, or Vietnamese Americans. There had been talk of 'dead white men' for a decade before Orientalism was published, but

Said did not anticipate the extent to which many aggrieved communities would look to *Orientalism* as the text that would galvanise them to seek their proper place in history books. As the canon wars intensified through the 1980s, many scholars and activists looked up to the author of *Orientalism* as someone who was calculated to support them in their endeavour to gain recognition for their histories and their literatures. Not unlike some of Said's detractors, his admirers also mistakenly read *Orientalism* as a general treatise on the evils of Western scholarship, overlooking the fact that Said was concerned principally with the conquest of knowledge wrought by colonialism and with the consequences of imposing an epistemological and ontological divide between an inert 'Orient' and a purposeful 'Occident'.

Said, then, had little tolerance for the idea that all Western texts are irretrievably contaminated, and he was similarly not prepared to abide by the view that texts exist in 'pure' and 'impure' forms. Had many of Orientalism's readers persisted with the book to the end, they would have encountered his warning about 'second-order Orientalism', or what transpires when the entire canvas of Orientalist thought or much of it begins to be replicated in the works of Indians, Africans, or Arabs, especially in the works of those who ironically adopt stridently nationalist views. Said would have rejected the argument that only Indians, Africans, or Arabs are entitled to interpret their own cultures or that traditions can be hermetically sealed. While Said was obviously sympathetic to calls made on behalf of intellectual traditions representing the work of non-western, indigenous, and women writers, he strenuously resisted demands to drop 'classics' from university syllabi, much as he saw no merit in sanctimoniously invoking living non-European non-males as necessarily more inspired, wise, learned or sensitive persons. Indeed, one of Said's most enduring legacies has been to show how works that reflect the prevailing consensus in a society constantly betray themselves, and he urged that these texts be read for their gaps, fissures, and dissonances. While he found justifications of imperialism abhorrent, Said rightly thought that only the narrowest conceptions of identity and nationalism informed the outlook of those who would entirely jettison Conrad, Kipling, T. E. Lawrence, or Rider Haggard in the name of political correctness.

There are, nevertheless, serious criticisms to be made of Said's intellectual stances as a reader of texts and interpreter of cultures. The field of postcolonial discourse with which Said's name is most closely identified has

sometimes been critiqued if not savaged for its insensitivity to considerations of political economy, and what is certainly striking is that the heyday
of postcolonial discourse and the attachment of a portion of the American
academy with what came to be called 'theory' — those who 'did' theory,
which meant among other things reading and even more importantly citing
one among several theorists such as Foucault, Derrida, Levinas, and
Deleuze, recognised each other as members of a guild, and consigned those
who didn't do theory to second-class membership — all transpired at a time
when the United States was on a virtual rampage in its quest for full spectrum dominance. While the poststructuralists and postcolonial theorists
imagined that they were altering the world with their narratives of alterity,
hybridity, and resistance, inequalities between the global South and global
North, and within each 'block', increased; labor unions were largely deci-
mated; barriers to global capitalism's aggressive expansionism were eroded;
walls came up where none had existed before; and the United States seemed
set to reign as the world's lone superpower. None of this appeared to make
an iota of difference to the theorists in the academy, many of whom, in any
case, had no engagement with wider publics. It is to Said's credit that, at a
time when the very idea of the public intellectual had become nearly obsolete and certainly discreditable in the academy, he always strove to engage
with a much wider swathe of the reading and thinking public than most of
his contemporaries.

There is a more profound irony at work: even as Said assumed the mantle
of a public intellectual, acquiring a profile as a staunch advocate of Palestinian self-determination, even perhaps betraying on occasion an inclination to
be seen as part of the intifada, the high culture of the West remained the
focus of nearly all of his intellectual and creative energies. Said never disguised his aesthetic preference for the canonical works of Western literature
and music. Even when he lauded the work of creative writers such as Faiz
Ahmed Faiz, Mahmud Darwish, and Naguib Mahfouz, he reserved his most
sustained analysis for Western texts. In *Culture and Imperialism*, Ranajit Guha,
Syed Hussein Alatas, and C. L. R. James receive a modicum of critical attention, but this is in relation to his assessment of the work of postcolonial
scholars whom he thought deserving of approbation and wider readership.
In a similar vein, while Said remained critical of representations of Muslims
and Arabs in scholarly works as much as in the popular media, there is noth-

ing to suggest that the wide world of Islamic learning had ever caught his attention. He seemed just as uninterested in Ibn Khaldun, the fourteenth century Arab historiographer and sociologist, as he was in nearly contemporary Islamic thinkers such as Said Nursi (1876-1960), whose work as a scholar and exegete of the Qur'an at a time when Turkey under Atatürk was on the road to militant secularisation might have given Said some cues on how to negotiate questions of cultural difference.

Said's critique of identity politics never seriously engaged a vast and immensely complex literature, which ranges from folklore to analytic philosophy in the Anglo-American tradition, on personal, political, and philosophical identity. That may not have been his intellectual brief, but his indifference to subaltern literatures and popular culture surely has some relation to the neglect of issues of class and justice in his work. Many will predictably point at once to his advocacy of the rights of Palestinians, but the matter is not so easily resolved. Consider, for example, the following: where the world over Martin Luther King Jr. is rightly celebrated for his heroic resistance to white supremacy in the American south, Said only refers to him — and with barely any evidence — as an example of the impossibility of finding an intellectual or major public figure in the United States who was not contaminated by the virus of Zionism. In 1994, the year of the Rwandan genocide, Said gave several interviews where he spoke about the violence being perpetrated upon Palestinians; and, yet, the massacre of the Tutsis seemed not to have registered sufficiently with him to make any reference to yet another holocaust. If the state of Israel is rigidly predisposed towards thinking of the Holocaust as the paradigmatic atrocity and evil of modern times, Said embraced the view, if not always explicitly, that Palestinians are the paradigmatic instantiation of victimhood at the present juncture of history. Said did not, it appears to me, give much thought to the consequences of abiding by this unfortunate reversal.

The 'Housed' and the 'Unhoused'

For a man who lived in exile and reveled in the idea of being an outcast, Said was also, as should be apparent by now, 'housed' in various ways — at Columbia University in the City of New York, in the high literature and opera of the West, and in well-defined aesthetic preferences. The 'unhoused and the housed': that distinction appears in Said's own writings, and in that opposition is writ large the tale of many principal narratives that have informed his life and work. It can be argued that the entire tapestry of Said's writings, the largest collection of which bears the title *Reflections on Exile* (2000), is woven around multiple ideas of exile. The Marxist critic Aijaz Ahmad alleged that postcolonial intellectuals such as Said, quite oblivious to their own positions of immense privilege, had fetishised the intellectual in exile. Ahmad viewed postcolonial theory as the handiwork of scholars who conveniently overlooked considerations of class and even made themselves out to be 'refugee' intellectuals. But Ahmad is scarcely the first critic to have pounced upon the fact that exile is a knotty subject. The poet Ovid, banished from Rome by Augustus in 8 AD, famously declared, '*Exilium mors est*'. Most likely any urbanite removed to a garrison town, rendered utterly bereft of the company of poets, aesthetes, and women, would have felt the same. Victor Hugo, by contrast, found exile rejuvenating. In fifteen years of exile on the island of Guernsey, Hugo penned some of his most famous works. He may well have said, '*exilium vita est*'. But what of Said: did he live somewhere in the space between banishment and belonging, construing some forms of banishment as akin to belonging, and some forms of being housed as much less desirable than being unhoused?

Said had a rather nomadic upbringing, one of many reasons why throughout his life he refused to be satisfied by any simple and nurturing conception of 'home'. He has often related how his life was a series of displacements and he felt himself to belong, if at all he belonged, between cultures. Though Said was born in Jerusalem in 1935, his parents were shuttling between Egypt and Palestine. His childhood summers were spent in Lebanon. In the predominantly Muslim Levant, where the Christians largely belonged to the Greek Orthodox church, Said's father — who had acquired American citizenship — was an Episcopalian while his mother was a Baptist. Asked to say something on his memoir *Out of Place*, Said described the title as meaning 'not being able to go back. It's really a strong feeling I have. I would describe my life as a series of departures and returns. But the departure is always anxious. The return always uncertain. Precarious.' One can speculate that Said must have found it apposite, alarmingly apposite, that his family home in Jerusalem had been taken over by a fundamentalist Christian organisation based in South Africa. Not only did Said view Israel as an apartheid state, but he also understood that fundamentalists gravitate towards each other just as rogues find rogues. Why should Christian fundamentalists not have found Israel hospitable, if not to their ambitions, at least to their idioms of totalitarianism? The house of humanism, Said saw for himself, had been built over by religious fundamentalists. Yet however much Said might have wanted to reclaim the house where he had been born, he remained uncertain about wanting to be 'completely at home'. 'I suppose it's sour grapes', Said told an interlocutor in 1996, 'that I now think it's maybe not worth the effort to find out' what it means to be at home.

Said saw modern Western culture as fundamentally a creation of exiles. Perhaps the experience of his own people, whom he described as largely 'dispersed exiles', led him to this conclusion. The ironies, Said would have been the first to recognise, were compounded in that the Palestinians had been rendered into exiles by another people of exile. Israel's 'War of Independence', Said was to write, 'was a catastrophe for Palestinians: two-thirds were driven out of their homes and country, many were killed, all their property was seized, and to all intents and purposes they ceased to exist as a people.' Pit exiles against exiles, and out comes a nation-state. And nation-states, as we know, are notoriously protective of boundaries, incorrigibly hostile to the nomadic modes of life. However much this may be the modern condition, and notwithstanding the fondness of a literary scholar for irony, Said had much more in mind in thinking of the inexorably exilic foundations of modernity. An essay from 1984 that would furnish the title to his collection *Reflections on Exile* reads thus: 'In the United States, academic, intellectual and aesthetic thought is what it is today because of refugees from fascism, communism, and other regimes given to the oppression and expulsion of dissidents.' Nearly all the figures that Said held in esteem — C. L. R. James and Joseph Conrad, Erich Auerbach and Theodor Adorno, Mahmoud Darwish and Faiz Ahmad Faiz — were émigrés and intellectual refugees, as were those, such as T. S. Eliot, with whose aesthetic and political views Said was in acute disagreement but whose centrality to the culture of the modern West was beyond question.

Throughout his life, Said retained a prolific interest in intellectuals and writers who had trafficked across borders, cutting across territorial and cultural boundaries. He was greatly moved by the idea of the noble life of the labouring intellectual in exile — an exile in which the labour was rendered more difficult, more poignant, marked by the 'sense of dissonance engendered by estrangement, distance, dispersion, years of lostness and disorientation', and thus requiring 'an almost excessive deliberation, effort, expenditure of intellectual energy at restoration, reiteration, and affirmation that are undercut by doubt and irony.' If Auerbach and Adorno remained for Said towering examples of the discerning intellect, one has to ask how far Said thought that their experience of exile had furnished them with insights not ordinarily available to others. Joseph Conrad, a Polish émigré to Britain who scarcely knew a word of English before he was 20 and went on to become one of the greatest novelists in the English language, was the subject of Said's doctoral dissertation, and he appears frequently in Said's writings as the supreme example of the exilic consciousness. Though Said remained unceasingly critical of Conrad's inability to see the non-West except through Western eyes, and scathingly characterised him as possessed of 'gringo eyes' that would not allow him to fathom 'other histories, other aspirations', he never begrudged Conrad his literary genius and, what is more germane, was quite certain that Conrad's writings bore the mark of the 'sensitive émigré's obsession with his own fate' and his ceaseless struggles to be securely moored in his new surroundings. The exile sees with sharpened eyes and ultimately gives birth to a new form of consciousness, the consciousness of those who are 'housed' by virtue of being 'unhoused'.

The idea of exile, then, must be read (in Said's language) contrapuntally, that is against the grain, in intersection and conversation with thoughts that might be construed as the very opposite. In doing so, one begins to approximate Said's own understanding of the notion of 'exile as a permanent state', a notion otherwise at odds with the conventional sense of exile as a transient stage, a country from which one returns to one's homeland. The exile bears within herself or himself a recollection of what has been left behind and plays this against the present experience. Said has described this as 'counterpoint' in music, and it is illustrative of his method that he should have, so effortlessly and with such panache, carried over an argument from music to a much wider domain. For Said, the notion of exile entails a different form of space-time compression as his essay, 'On Last Causes', originally delivered as one of the Tanner Lectures in Human Values, so elliptically suggests. In contrast to resigned capitulation, Said quotes Adorno, 'the uncompromisingly critical thinker, who neither superscribes his conscience nor permits himself to be terrorised into action, is in truth the one who does not give up. Furthermore, thinking is not the spiritual reproduction of that which exists. As long as thinking is not interrupted, it has a firm grasp upon possibility. Its insatiable quality, the resistance against petty satiety, rejects the foolish wisdom of resignation.' The exilic mind, Said is here arguing, refuses to habituate itself to academic pieties, to accepted readings of texts, to the satisfactions of power, and to the comforts of surrender to some transcendent force. Elsewhere calling to mind Adorno's *Minima Moralia* (*Reflections from a Mutilated Life*), Said says that 'language is jargon, objects are for sale. To refuse this stage of affairs is the exile's intellectual mission.' To be alert, vigilant, critical, contrarian — to be all this is to be always in exile. Only the exile has that awareness which comes with contrapuntal understanding.

Ample as has been the climate of feeling and thought engendered by the frequent occurrence of the trope of exile in Said's thought, the contrapuntal reading of Said necessarily entails at least a brief and critical reflection on the complete banishment of religion from Said's work. Said pushed religion into a fugitive existence. He was a steadfast and uncompromising secularist, and he frequently pointed out that it is from the Italian humanist Giambattista Vico that he learned that men make their own history. Said consistently argued for 'worldliness' — a sustained interest in the affairs of the world, an advocacy for the 'space of history' rather than the 'space of the sacred or divine', and an awareness of the fact, which Said brought out with great subtlety in *Culture and Imperialism*, that many forms of otherworldliness and detachment were disguised forms of engagement with the world. 'Worldliness, secularity, etc. are key terms for me,' Said remarked in 1993, and adds that alongside his 'critique of and discomfort with religion' he had become 'ill at ease with jargons and obfuscations', with 'special private languages of criticism and professionalism'. In this respect, at least, Said was to signal his departure from the work of some famous contemporary postcolonial theorists.

Said remained to the end of his life a staunch secularist. Late in life as he grappled more intensely with his illness, Said became interested in what he has called 'late style'. Many people in his position would have turned to the comforts of religion. Said denied himself this outcome: if men and women make their own history, he was not about to call upon his Maker as his life hung on a thread. Said's integrity, intellectual liveliness, and passion drove him at this juncture to a fuller exploration of some of the ideas which had crossed his mind over the years and were now fertilising into a new set of reflections on music, the subject of exile, and the relationship of the changing contours of thought to the proximity to death. His essay on *Freud and the Non-European*, appearing in the year of his death, suggests that Freud's *Moses and Monotheism* (1937), published a year before Freud escaped to London to live out the last few months of his life, was a product of 'late style'. Freud was to argue for the non-Jewish origins of monotheism; taking this argument further, Said proposes that 'quite differently from the spirit of Freud's deliberately provocative reminders that Judaism's founder was a non-Jew,... Israeli legislation countervenes, represses, and even cancels Freud's carefully maintained opening out of Jewish identity towards its non-Jewish background.' The arguments of Said's posthumously published essay, 'Thoughts on Late Style', form a fitting conclusion to this essay as they do to Said's own life. Here again is Adorno, another German Jew — he who had suggested, apropos the works belonging to Beethoven's third and final period (the last five piano sonatas, the Ninth Symphony, the last six string quartets, among others) that 'late style' might constitute a form of multiple estrangement. Beethoven abandoned all interest in ensuring some commensurability between his music and the social order; indeed, Adorno has argued, he displayed indifference to the question of continuities in his own work. It is characteristic of 'late style' that the artist, in Said's language, 'achieves a contradictory, alienated relationship' with the social ethos of the time. The 'late works' of the artist 'are a form of exile from his milieu.' The admixture of estrangement and worldliness with which Said approached his own life gives all the necessary cues that a politically aware reader of his works might require.

CITATIONS

Introduction: What's the Big Idea? by Ziauddin Sardar

There are numerous translations of Rumi's Masnavi. The best, rather old, are *Discourses of Rumi* (London: John Murry, 1961) by A J Arberry, and *Teachings of Rumi*, abridged and translated by E H Whinfield (London: Octagon Press, nd). I have used Peter Washington's *Rumi, an Everyman* edition (New York: Alfred Knopf, 2006), which selects the best from a combination of translations; although I have edited the stories.

On the 'Unthought' of Islam, see the brilliant *The Unthought in Contemporary Islamic Thought* by Mohammed Arkoun (London: Saqi Books, 2002); and his *Rethinking Islam: Common Questions, Uncommon Answers* (Boulder: Westview Press, 1994). There are numerous new editions of Muhammad Iqbal's *Reconstruction of Religious Thought in Islam*; but my own copy is a 1965 edition from Ashraf, Lahore; the quote is from page 134.

On western perceptions of Islam, see Ziauddin Sardar, *Orientalism* (Buckingham: Open University Press, 1999) and Peter Morey and Amina Yaqin, *Framing Muslims: Stereotyping and Representation After 9/11* (Cambridge: Harvard University Press, 2011). The fatwas of Sheikh Salih bin Fawzan are widely available on the net. An English translation of the Moroccan Moudawana is available from: **http://www.musliminstitute.org/upfront/front-featured/making-reform-real-moroccan-family-code**

Muslim Cosmopolitanism by Bruce Lawrence

For Bruce Lawrence's own and related essays on Muslim cosmopolitanism, see 'Competing Genealogies of Muslim Cosmopolitanism' in Carl W. Ernst and Richard C. Martin, *Rethinking Islamic Studies — From Orientalism to Cosmopolitanism* (University of South Carolina Press, 2010): 302-327; and also

'Muslim Cosmopolitanism in the Age of Globalisation' delivered at Michigan State University's Muslim Studies Program 5th annual conference, *Beyond Islamic Studies: De-Essentialising the Study of Muslim Societies*. On Marshall Hodgson and Ibn Khaldun as precursors of Muslim cosmopolitanism, see, 'Islam in Afro-Eurasia: A bridge civilisation' in Peter J. Katzenstein, ed. *Civilisations in World Politics: Plural and Pluralist Perspectives* (Routledge 2010). Chapter 7: 157-175.

There are many assessments of Istanbul predicting its future success as a cosmopolitan hub. See Perlin Dervis, Bulent Tanju, Ugur Tanyeli, *Becoming Istanbul – An Encyclopaedia*, (Garanti Gallery, 2008). For the best anthropological study of contemporary Istanbul as a cosmopolitan complex, see Öykü Potuoğlu-Cook, 'Beyond the Glitter: Belly Dance and Neoliberal Gentrification in Istanbul', *Cultural Anthropology* (2006:21/4): 633-660. There are also many sources on Istanbul's Jewish communities – their history, fortunes and prospects — in Ottoman and modern day Turkey. One of the most recent is also among the best: Laurent-Olivier Mallet, *La Turquie, les Turcs et les Juifs. Histoire, représentations, discours et stratégies*, (ISIS: Les Cahiers du Bosphore XLIX, 2008). For Jewish cosmopolitanism in Istanbul, no study rivals Marcy Brink-Danan, 'Dangerous Cosmopolitanism: Erasing Difference in Istanbul' in *Anthropological Quarterly* (April 2011).

Beyond the clamour of accusation or conspiracy theories, one can find a friendly, favourable assessment of both Nursi and Gulen as modern day Sufi scholar-activists in Bulent Aras and Omer Caha, 'Fethullah Gulen and His Liberal "Turkish Islam" Movement' in *Middle East Review of International Affairs* (4/4, December 2000): 30-42. Probably the fairest and most broad gauged assessment of the Gulen movement is Berna Turam, *Between Islam and the State: The Politics of Engagement*, (Stanford University Press, 2007).

On the complexities of Bukharan cosmopolitanism, see the recent conference at http://www.cambridge-centralasia.org/?page_id=10 and also on the migration of Bukharan Jews, a *TIME* magazine essay from this past summer:http://www.time.com/time/specials/packages/article/0,28804,2084273_2084272_2084262,00.html

Jihad, Anyone? by S Parvez Manzoor

For Carl Schmitt's thought, see his *The Concept of the Political* (Chicago: University of Chicago Press, 2007), *Political Theology: Four Chapters on the Concept of Sovereignty* (Chicago: Chicago University Press, 2006) and *Writings on War* (Oxford: Polity, 2011). For a more elaborate statement on Schmitt, download S Parvez Manzoor's, 'The sovereignty of the political: Carl Schmitt and the nemesis of liberalism', Athenaem Library of Philosophy (http://evans-experientialism.freewebspace.com/carlschmitte.htm).

Bruce Holsinger quotes is from page 9 of *Neomedievalism, Neoconservatism, and the War on Terror* (Chicago: Prickly Paradigm Press, 2007); and Michale Hardt and Antonio Negri quote is from page 12 of *Empire* (Harvard University Press, 2001). All quotes from Paul W Kahn are from pages 155 and 156 of *Political Theology: Four New Chapters on the Concept of Sovereignty* (New York: Columbia University Press, 2011). Other works cited: Herbamas et al, *The Power of Public Sphere in the Public Sphere* (New York: Columbia University Press, 2010); and W C Smith, *Faith and Belief* (Princeton University Press, 1979).

'The Race of Women' by Samia Rahman

The English translation of S Abul Ala Maududi's *Purdah and Status of Women in Islam*, originally in Urdu, was first published by Islamic Publications (Lahore, 1972) but has gone through numerous editions since then. There is some dispute whether al-Ghazali was the author of *Ghazali's Book of Counsel for Kings* (translated by F R C Bagley, New York: OUP, 1971), but the general consensus is that he was. Maulana Asharf Ali Thanawi's *Bihishti Zewar* (Jewels of Paradise) written in Urdu in the early 1900s, has been translated by Barbara Daly Metcalf as *Perfecting Women: Maulana Asharf Ali Thanawi's Bihishti Zewar* (Delhi: OUP, 1972). For everyday misogyny see Islam Channel.

Do You Believe? by Soha Al-Jurf

For the teachings of Thich Nhat Hanh, see his *Miracle of Mindfulness* (Rider, 2008), *Heart of Buddha's Teachings* (Rider, 1999), and *Peace Begins Here* (Parallax Press, 2004). The *Knowing Heart: A Sufi Path of Transformation* by Kabir Helminski is published by Shambhala (1999).

Heretics by Carool Kersten

The books mentioned in this essay, include: Claude Addas, *Quest for the Red Sulphur: The Life of Ibn 'Arabi* (Islamic Texts Society, Cambridge, 1993); Adonis (Ali Ahmad Said), *Sufism and Surrealism* (Saqi Books, London, 1992); Peter L. Berger, *The Heretical Imperative: Contemporary Possibilities of Religious Affirmation* (Collins, London, 1980); Leonard Binder, *Islamic Liberalism: A Critique of Development Ideoogies* (The University of Chicago Press, Chicago, 1988); Mary Louise Gude, *Louis Massignon: The Crucible of Compassion* (University of Notre Dame Press, Notre Dame and London, 1996); Robert D. Kaplan, *Monsoon: The Indian Ocean and the Future of American Power* (Random House, New York, 2011); Anouar Majid, *A Call for Heresy: Why Dissent is Vital to Islam and America* (University of Minnesota Press, Minneapolis, 2009); Louis Massignon, *La passion d'al-Hosayn-ibn-Mansour al-Hallaj : martyr mystique de l'Islam, exécuté à Bagdad le 26 mars 922 : étude d'histoire religieuse* (Paul Geuthner, Paris, 1922); Leo Strauss, *Persecution and the Art of Writing* (University of Chicago Press, Chicago, 1988); Sarah Stroumsa, *Freethinkers of Medieval Islam: Ibn al-Rawandi , Abu Bankr al-Razi and their Impact on Islamic Thought* (Brill, Leiden, Boston, Köln, 1999); Daniel Varisco, Review of Anouar Majid, *A Call for Heresy: Why Dissent is Vital to Islam and America,* (*Contemporary Islam* 4(2), 251-3)

Cousin Trouble by Ben Gidley

For examples of the 'roseate' account of Jewish-Muslim *convivienca* see Maria Rosa Menocal, *The Ornament of the World: How Muslims, Jews and Christians Created a Culture of Tolerance in Medieval Spain* (London: Little, Brown and Company 2002), Joann Sfar, *The Rabbi's Cat* (London: Random House,

2005), Violette Shamash, *Memories of Ede: A Journey Through Jewish Baghdad* (London: Forum Books, 2008), Nissim Rejwen, *The Last Jews of Baghdad: Remembering A Lost Homeland* (Austin: University of Texas Press, 2004), Rachel Shabi, *Not the Enemy: Israel's Jews from Arab Lands* (New Haven: Yale University Press, 2009 – although the quotation is from her *Guardian* article 'The problem with Israel's Jewish "refugee" initiative' 16 December 2010) and Sasson Somekh, *Baghdad, Yesterday: The Making of an Arab Jew* (Jerusalem: Ibis Editions, 2007 – Adam Schatz's review of this, quoted here, was published in the *London Review of Books* (Vol. 30 No. 21, 6 November 2008, pp. 23-25).

The term 'neo-lachrymose' is taken from Mark R Cohen, 'The Neo-Lachrymose Conception of Jewish-Arab History. Have present-day politics in the Middle East distorted our understanding of the Jewish-Arab past?' (*Tikkun Magazine* May / June 1991, pp. 55-60, later revised as the first chapter of *Under Crescent and Cross: The Jews in the Middle Ages* (Princeton: Princeton University Press, 1994). The term draws on Salo Baron, 'Ghetto and Emancipation: Shall We Revise the Traditional View?' *Menorah Journal* (June 1928). For Cohen, Bat Yeor exemplifies the neo-lachrymose; for an example of her work, see *The Dhimmi: Jews and Christians Under Islam* (Madison: Fairleigh Dickinson University Press, 1985). The quotation of James Renton is taken from the documentary '*The Grand Mufti', Nazi Collaborators*, Episode 8, Yesterday Channel, December 2010 and January 2011, drawing on his book *The Zionist Masquerade: the Birth of the Anglo-Zionist Alliance 1914-1918* (Basingstoke and New York: Palgrave Macmillan, 2007). The quotation from the Palestinian peace activist, Dina Jaber, is taken from Marcus Dysch, 'Promoting peace between Jewish students and Palestinian activists' *Jewish Chronicle*, November 19, 2009. The articles on Islamophobia as the new anti-semitism cited are Mya Guarnieri, 'Islamophobia: the new anti-semitism', *The Guardian*, August 26, 2010; Daniel Luban, 'The New Anti-Semitism: Recent attacks on Islam in the United , States echo old slurs against Jews', *Tablet Magazine*, August 19, 2010; Shlomo Sand, 'From Judaeophobia to Islamophobia' *Jewish Quarterly*, Summer 2010 and Matti Bunzl, 'Between Anti-Semitism and Islamophobia: Some Thoughts on the New Europe', *American Ethnologist* 32, no. 4 (November 1, 2005): 499-508 (expanded into the short book *Anti-Semitism and Islamophobia:*

Hatreds Old and New in Europe, Chicago: Prickly Paradigm Press, 2007). The quotes from Veronique Altglas and Christine Achinger are from unpublished articles forthcoming in the journal *European Societies*. Also quoted is 'A Mapping Report of Positive Contact Between British Muslims and British Jews', Alif-Aleph UK, 2005. The quotation that concludes the article is from Sasson Somekh, 'Maimonides, Rabbi Obadiah, and the neo-lachrymose concept of history' *Ha-aretz* 24 August 2001

The Tyranny of Profit by Stuart Sim

James Murdoch, 'The absence of trust', 2009 Edinburgh International Television Festival MacTaggart Lecture, 28 August 2009, can be downloaded from: http://www.guardian.co.uk/media/2009/aug/28/james-murdoch-bbc-mactaggart-edinburgh-tv-festival. 'Social Brain', the RSA's project, can be obtained from: http://www.thersa.org/projects/social-brain. Milton Friedman, 'The social responsibility of business is to increase its profits', is available from: http://www-rohan.sdsu.edu/faculty/dunnweb/rprnts.friedman.html; and Institute of Islamic Banking website http://www.islamic-banking.com/what_is_ibanking.aspx; provides their take on 'Islamic banking'.

Other texts cited in this essay, in order of appearance: Susan Strange, *Casino Capitalism* (Oxford: Blackwell, 1986); Slavoj Žižek, *The Sublime Object of Ideology* (London: Verso, 1989, p. 29); Slavoj Žižek, *Enjoy Your Symptom!: Jacques Lacan in Hollywood and Out*, (London: Routledge, 2008 p. x); David Cameron, 'Use the profit-motive to fight climate change', *The Observer*, 28 November 2010, p. 41; Zygmunt Bauman, *Intimations of Postmodernity* (London: Routledge, 2002, p. 175); Niall Ferguson, *Civilisation: The West and the Rest* (London: Allen Lane, 2011); Richard Wachman, 'Dutch bankers' bonuses axed by people power', *The Observer*, 27 March 2011, p. 46; Thomas Carlyle, 'Signs of the Times', in *A Carlyle Reader* (Cambridge: Cambridge University Press, 1984); Gethin Chamberlain, 'Inside the iSweat shops: Apple factories accused of exploiting Chinese workers', *The Observer*, 1 May 2011, p. 5; Dave Skarica, 'Addicted to Profits', http://addictedtoprofits.net.

All that Muslim Jazz! by Andy Simons

Here's a select discography of Muslim jazz. Get hold of some CDs, downloads a few tracks, and get grooving:

Ahmed Abdul-Malik — oud, Johnny Griffin — tenor sax
Jazz Saraha: Ahmed Abdul-Malik's Middle-Eastern Music (1958)
Riverside LP RLP 1121, Original Jazz Classics OJCCD 1820-2

Ahmed Abdul-Malik — oud
East Meets West (1960) RCA Victor LSP-2015
Jazz Sounds of Africa (1961-1962)
Prestige New jazz LPs 8266 and 8282, Prestige CD PRCD 24279-2

Stephan Athanas' Contemparabic Jazz Ensemble
Maluf, Malfuf & Groove — Live! (2001) MUSI CD 10003-2
Souk (2003) Musicora MUSI CD 10004-2

Hewar - clarinet, vocals, double bass, drums, percussion
(Syrian-Egyptian, but recorded in Lebanon)
Hewar 3806 1197 8906 [bar code graphic] (2004) Forward Music
Via: forwardmusic.net or via incognito.com.lb or incognito.net

Hijaz
Chemsi (2010) Zephyrus 012
Dunes (2008) belgiumwinewatchers.com

Yusef Lateef
Prayer to the East (1957) Savoy MG12117, SV-0210 CD
Eastern Sounds (New Jersey, 1961) Prestige PRCD 30012-2
Jazz Round the World (1963) Impulse A-56

Herbie Mann — flute
Impressions of the Middle East (1966) Atlantic 1475
The Wailing Dervishes (1967) Atlantic 1497

Masar: Hazim Shaheen-oud, Nawar Abbessi-piano, Miles Jay-double bass, Hani Bdeir-percussion
El 'Aysh Wel Melh (2006); Hazem Shaheen: Things That I Miss (2009) Incognito, incognito.com.lb or incognito.net

Aziza Mustafa Zadeh – piano / vocals
Aziza Mustafa Zadeh (1991) Columbia / Sony 468286-2
Jazziza (1996) Columbia / Sony COL 487897-2
Shamans (ca. 2003) Azerbaijani release – label unspecified
Aziza Mustafa Zadeh w / Bill Evans, Al Di Miola, Stanley Clark
Inspiration Limited Edition Azerbaijani release – label unspecified

Vagif Mustafa Zadeh – piano
Vagif Mustafa Zadeh [6-CD] UNOCAL / AICD 1401 www.azer.com
Jazz in Azerbaijan – Anthology [2-CD, var.] Sony / Jazz Ctr Azerbaijan

Salah Ragab and the Cairo Jazz Band
Egyptian Jazz (1968-1973) Art Yard LP 006 Via: dustygroove.com

Hossam Ramzy, Andy Sheppard & Guy Barker
Re-Orient (London, 1997) ARC Music EUCD 1982

Shusmo: Tareq Abboushi-bazouki, Lefteris Bournias-clarinet, etc.
One (ca. 2001) shusmo.com

The Sachal Studio Orchestra
Take Five Sachal Music (2011)
Official music video: hhtp / /youtube.com / watch?v=GLF46JKkCNg

Maryam and the Maulana by Ehsan Masood

Maryam Jameelah's books include Islam and Modernism, Islam Versus Ahl Al Kitab: Past and Present, Western Civilisation Condemned by Itself (two volumes), Islam and Orientalism, Islam Versus the West, Islam in Theory and Practice, A Manifesto of the Islamic Movement, and Correspondence Between Maulana Maudoodi *and Maryam Jameelah* – all published by her husband, Muhammad Yusuf Khan, Lahore, between 1960 and 1980.

Pakistan: Reckoning and Redemption by Iftikhar Malik

Books mentioned in this review include, Jaswant Singh, *Jinnah: India, Partition, Independence*, (New York: OUP, 2010); M. J. Akbar, *Tinderbox: The Past and Future of Pakistan* (Delhi: HarperCollins, 2011); Philip Oldenburg, *India, Pakistan and Democracy: Solving the Puzzle of Divergent Paths* (New York: Routledge, 2010); and Tariq Ali, *The Duel. Pakistan on the Flight Path of American Power* (London: Verso, 2008).

Being American by Hassan Mahamdallie

Mark Donner's *New York Review of Books* article, published on 13 October 2011, can be downloaded from: http://www.nybooks.com/articles/archives/2011/oct/13/after-september-11-our-state-exception/

Assessment: Edward Said by Vinay Lal

Edward Said wrote voluminously, and his shorter pieces on politics are archived on the net; but more critical to the arguments advanced in this essay are: *Orientalism* (1978; 25th anniversary edition from Penguin Books, 2003); *Culture and Imperialism* (1993; Vintage Paperbacks, 1994); *Out of Place: A Memoir* (Knopf, 1999); *Reflections on Exile and Other Essays* (Harvard University Press, 2000); *Power, Politics and Culture: Interviews with Edward W. Said*, edited with an introduction by Gauri Viswanathan (Pantheon Press, 2001); *Freud and the Non-European* (Verso, 2003); and 'Thoughts on Late Style', *London Review of Books* 26, no. 15 (5 August 2004): 3-7.

Said's comments on King are to be found in *Power, Politics and Culture*, pp. 209 and 327. His only essay on lowbrow culture, on the Tarzan movies of Johnny Weismuller, is rather uninteresting: see *Reflections on Exile*, pp. 327-36. In 'Israel-Palestine: a third way', *Le Monde Diplomatique* (September, 1998), Said critiqued Arabs for adhering to 'discredited ideas' about the supposed fictitiousness of the Jewish Holocaust. Among the essays in

Reflections in Exile which are cited in this essay, see 'On Lost Causes', 'Between Worlds', and 'Through Gringo Eyes: With Conrad in Latin America'.

The essays of Bernard S. Cohn on the British in India are collected together in *An Anthropologist among the Historians and Other Essays* (Delhi: Oxford University Press, 1987) and *Colonialism and Its Forms of Knowledge: The British in India* (Princeton University Press, 1996). Among those who are often mentioned as Said's predecessors, one might profitably read Syed Hussein Alatas, *The Myth of the Lazy Native* (London: F. Cass, 1977); K. M. Panikkar, *Asia and Western Dominance* (London: Allen & Unwin, 1953); and Anouar Abdel-Malek, 'Orientalism in Crisis', *Diogenes* 11 (December 1963): 103-40. *Edward Said: A Critical Reader*, ed. Michael Sprinker (Blackwell, 1993) is a good place to begin for assessments of Said's work, though this work is much less 'critical' than is suggested by the title; for trenchant critiques of Said, see Aijaz Ahmad, *In Theory: Nations, Classes, Literatures* (Verso, 1992) and Sumit Sarkar, 'Orientalism Revisited: Saidian Frameworks in the Writing of Modern Indian History', *Oxford Literary Review* 16, nos. 1-2 (1994): 205-24.

LAST WORD

9/11 AND ALL THAT

Merryl Wyn Davies

I like travelling by train.

The train connects me with the outside world. The train winds its way southward from the town centre near the head of the valley, snaking along the course of the river through villages that merge into a long strung out conurbation. It takes just as long in today's world of electric engines and automatic doors to reach the outside world as it did in the days of steam trains – the days when I was young and in awe of the old mausoleum of a railway station designed, as it happens, by none other than Isambard King-dom Brunel. There used to be four platforms and crates and crates of pigeons. Now the old station is the site of the local Tesco and across the car park one solitary rail track stands behind the small brick shed that is the ticket office.

This is my journey: one hour to cover twenty-five miles stopping at eleven stations to get from Merthyr Tydfil to Cardiff and connect with the world beyond the valley. This has always been the journey. I sit back and reminisce, and observe the effects of post industrialisation on a landscape created out of the first flush of the Industrial Revolution. But always I remember. After the second stop down the line, as we pull out of Treo-dyrhiw station wherever I am sitting, whichever way I am facing, I bow my head and remember. And pray God to grant mercy and peace of His Infi-nite Bounty.

De-industrialisation means trees are coming back to repossess the valley which now looks magnificent in all the hues of varying seasons and weather, of which we have a great deal. There was a time when I would muse about my favourite coal tip. It was perfectly conical, rising suddenly

271

from a patch of flat land on the valley floor. To the initiated it was obviously man-made, the detritus of coal mining not a naturally occurring outcrop of unnaturally perfect symmetry. Confusion might arise because this little mountain was copiously clad in grass with one vigorous sapling, a veritable tree, thriving half way up its steeply sloping side. They say it's the worms, something special about our worms, talented like no others at naturalising the bleak devastation of an industrial landscape.

I used to be amused by this particular vignette, this almost post modern signifier of the complex interrelationships of man, nature and industrial brutalism. It made me smile as, on every journey, I noted the progress of the sapling and contemplated the particular qualities of the grass worms conferred on industrial waste. Until the day I could no longer look.

A chug or chuff or two further down the valley there stood three as yet nude, rude and raw great tips, conical at their their tip tops but spreading wide skirts over the mountainside. These harsh black graceless piles of industrial realism were thrown up by the last working coalmine in the valley. They are gone now. Where they once stood an unnaturally green swathe of specially seeded grass is conspicuously spread over the gentle undulation of the mountainside.

So what exactly am I remembering? A bright, crisp October day that followed a week of rain. A perfect autumn day of blue sky and sparkling yellows, browns and rust colours of mountainside, bracken and trees. A day more than forty years ago. A day when all that passed as normal in my world of valley and mountain suddenly rebelled to disgorge death and devastation. I have never been able to forget the detail of that day. Though most of the time I forget to remember consciously. The scenes run continually inside my head. I have only to turn my mind's eye to catch sight of them. And in sight of those memories it all comes flooding back, tears well inside, I feel the old familiar sense of defeat, hollowed out by anguish and incalculable sadness.

The day of the Aberfan disaster is, has been, and I presume always will be alive in my mind. It is the day when one of those naked mountains of spoil turned liquid and rampaged down the mountainside to consume all the houses in its path and the village junior school just as everyone was settling into the first class of the morning.

What is man that coal should be so careless of him,
And what is coal that so much blood should be upon it?
(Idris Davies, *Gwalia Deserta*)

There is an answer to the poet's question. One hundred and sixteen children crushed and buried with their teachers, half a dozen houses and their
occupants gone in seconds, 144 souls in all consumed by the obscene tide
of slurry. An army of volunteers digging for days where there could be no
hope. Their only triumph the heart rending discovery of little broken bodies. No I never was privy to that part of the story – except that it was visible, reflected in the eyes of those who were. I saw them and their look will
haunt me all my days.

There were appeals, outpourings of redundant sympathy expressed
through genuine acts of compassion: they wanted wet weather gear for the
men digging through the dirt and people sent children's toys and children's
clothes to a town where an entire generation of children were lost to life.
There were reporters and cameras everywhere and visits by dignitaries,
royal and political. So, eventually, there had to be appeal funds and arguments about what to do as a memorial. It all came after. First, they took
the little bodies back halfway up the mountainside to the village cemetery.
There they made a garden of rest where parents and friends could come
and visit the lost generation of the village. You can see the enclave of white
marble arches surrounding closely packed graves. It's visible from the
train. So I bow my head and remember and pray, pray and remember every
time I go in or out of the valley. I never have to wonder what it is I am
remembering. The agony abides. That is the reality of disaster. That is its
true memorial.

I learnt a lot about memorials working on the local weekly newspaper,
my first job. We were a young crew just out of school or university, learning
our trade together, desperate to be Woodward and Bernstein or *Lou Grant*
– the American tv series we watched avidly intent on picking up pointers
about being 'real' reporters. Even in those more naive times, clearly we had
a lot to learn.

I remember the day when Steve came back to the office in tears. Allegedly two supposedly distinct and separate newspapers shared our office,
locally referred to as the *Merthyr Distress* (Express) and the *Rhymney Liar*

(Leader) – because ironically things were only true if printed in these news-papers of record. Anything else was mere noise written or said by people from 'off', in the interests and according to the sentiments of strangers. The Rhymney valley did not exactly generate sufficient news for a paper all its own. So Steve turned out as much as he could and for the rest: Rhymney got Merthyr's news. This, surely, was not enough to make a strong lad cry.

Steve had been to Senghenydd for the first time that day. On another October day in 1913, I don't know how crisp or bright, 439 men and boys from the village died when the firedamp down the pit ignited and the coal dust exploded. It caused a chain reaction of explosions resulting in the worst colliery disaster in British history. More than sixty years on and a junior reporter still had to tread carefully and listen to the agony that abides in the people who remain and came after in a place where the memorials are alive.

It was the same whenever we had to cover stories in Aberfan. There was the perennial challenge of the recurring 'vandals hit community centre' story. The community centre was built with disaster appeal money. It stood just across the road from the clutch of modern houses built to replace the ones swept away and re-house the survivors. Whatever questions one asked, they all led round to and back through the October day that defined this village, located it in time and preserved it in the aspic of other peoples' sensitivities and expectations. One was always talking about that day whether it was explicitly mentioned or not. Yet no one I ever spoke to in the village believed in memorials or anniversaries. Their houses groaned with gestures of remembrance provided by strangers as aid and comfort for their distress. Obviously, the survivors did not have the heart to throw such mementoes away, but there also seemed to be a peculiar ambivalence towards them. It was as if strangers wanted to direct these peoples' remem-brance in the ways deemed appropriate. Whereas people in the village where just getting on with their lives, the agony abiding and ever included.

So why am I telling you all this? As I write it is another bright and crisp October day and we have recently memorialised the tenth anniversary of 9/11. It seemed that for weeks wherever I turned on television, radio, the papers, magazines, the internet, everything – space itself – was devoted to every aspect and nuance of the trauma of that day. And I admit I avoided it all. No, a more accurate statement is that I turned away from it with conscious and deliberate calculation. The agony of that event abides within me. Like everyone else with access to a television screen, the events of 9/11 are stored in my neural network. They have coalesced with my personal benchmark of agony nearly experienced. Every time I think about 9/11, I end up thinking about Aberfan. The conjoint identification is the shared grief I offer to the horrific, devastating, overwhelming incomprehensibility of that abomination, that sacrifice of innocence in pursuit of patent evil.

And yet I cannot help wondering what it is I am being asked to remember? And conveniently forget?

What we are presented with is a superior grief, a suffering beyond all others. We are confronted by a very specific public truth insistently constructed from 9/11. The missing element in this memorial is common humanity, any possibility of shared experience of agony and loss. If the events of that one day in all their graphic detail and unimaginable terror are set upon a unique pedestal and made particular, then the response they evoke cannot be extended to all the other victims, the nameless and uncounted innocent dead heaped at the feet of the heroic dead of 9/11. In a world reduced to heroes and villains there is merely collateral damage in these other lives blown to oblivion, the oblivion that has no memorial, no remembrance. No agony can abide for us in things not nearly experienced because they were not of us, but separate and different.

The events of 9/11 have been made particular to the American soul and its national consciousness. They have been wrapped so tightly in the American flag that proper reflection is strangled. To me this is tragedy piled on agony. And it has its consequence in the most barbaric statement in contemporary politics: we fight them over there so that we do not have to fight them here at home. Keeping the streets of America — and Britain — safe vindicates untold, unconsidered and therefore unimaginable agony elsewhere. We are entitled to our security, quite simply they are not. Barbarism is placing personal exercise of power above justice and equity for each and every irreplaceable human being. And so Afghanistan and Iraq just happened. Time to move on, we are where we are. Except that we must all stop for the tenth anniversary of 9/11.

Our ability to feel, to empathise with the pain of others, is the great redeeming human and humanising capacity. It is what raises us to the consciousness that we are not lumbering robots, mere happenstances of random chance necessities. To rise to stand with angels, however, there can be no selective empathy, no equivocation about which agony is more worthy of our sympathy and attention. Suffering is made by politics, that most human, in the sense of error prone, undertaking. We cannot be politic or economical in recognising the human costs and consequences of political action. We are all responsible and answerable for the choices made in our name, with or without our informed consent, with or without democratic process.

It is a tragedy of immense importance that 9/11 has been constructed, manipulated and used to such devastating single minded nationalistic purpose. A day wrapped in memorial flags, symbolic, iconic and detached from consequences, exonerates empathy from anything but its own uniqueness. It diminishes our common humanity. And I fear makes no contribution to better mutual understanding. Justice is not done to innocent suffering when we are confused about who is innocent and who merely unfortunate.

I could not in all conscience be party to the memorialising of 9/11 because the agenda mobilising all the hours of television and the column inches overtly and tacitly underlined that the meaning of these memorials was political. Since 9/11 too little of politics has matured into thorough examination of consequences and culpability. When we place politics before shared agony, experienced equally in America as much as in Afghanistan, Iraq, Pakistan or anywhere that the tentacles of evil action and reactive response have reached, we are not intent on and committed to nurturing peace. We stand further apart ten years on because there are so many and so few memorials.

So what is it I am hoping we will remember? There is nothing in isolation. Evil arises in a context; it feeds on failings in individuals as well as communities and countries, it gorges on ignorance and negligence. Evil expresses itself through individuals but it is nevertheless a collective responsibility to understand how and in what ways it was permitted to arise and flourish. War is not justice, nor is it a surgical implement to open the pathway for justice. War compounds injustice, adds to the charge sheet of evil deeds and the body count of innocents slaughtered. We have as much responsibility to prosecute the evil done in the prosecution of war as in the perpetration of atrocity that was turned into a provocation for war. Unless we can arrive together at such points of equity we have learnt no lessons from 9/11. Not only will failure to find equitable understanding make a nonsense of such memorials as we permit, it will prevent us everywhere from fashioning reconciliation.

I like travelling by train. It gives me time to think. Next time I take the train I think I must bow my head for more than just the innocents of a day some 40 years ago. I must bow my head and pray for mercy and peace for all who have suffered: those of whose agony I am aware, and those whose suffering is a remote blur, a theoretical abstract probability. I need to bring the human cost of 9/11 and the events, the cycle of war, death, dearth and destruction that came in its wake, nearer and nearer to my conscious understanding until the agony of all the innocents becomes part of me, a living memorial. I owe the dead of 9/11 and all who died in the aftermath the old familiar sense of defeat, hollowed out by anguish and incalculable sadness.

And then I need to make politicians feel just the same.

I like travelling by train: its fills you with ambition as it carries you onward to new possibilities.

CONTRIBUTORS

Said Adrus is a British artist ● **Nazand Begikhani**, an acclaimed poet, is Senior Research Fellow at the University of Bristol and Editor-in-Chief of the Kurdish edition of *Le Monde Diplomatique* ● **Hassan Blasim** is a film maker and author of *The Madman of Freedom Square*, listed for the Independent Foreign Fiction Prize ● **Merryl Wyn Davies**, writer and Director of the Muslim Institute, likes to travel on trains because of her bad back ● **Ben Gidley**, senior researcher at the Centre on Migration, Policy and Society, University of Oxford, is co-author of *Turbulent Times: The British Jewish Community Today* ● **Aamer Hussein**, who was born in Karachi, is the author of five collections of short stories including, *Mirror to the Sun* (1993), a novella, *Another Gulmohar Tree* (2009), and a novel, *The Cloud Messenger* (2011) ● **Samarqand al-Jabri** is a prizewinning short story writer and poet from Baghdad ● **Soha Al-Jurf**, a Palestinian-American writer, speaks out in *Even My Voice Is Silence* ● **Robin Yassin-Kassab** is writing his second novel ● **Carool Kersten** is Lecturer in the Study of Islam and the Muslim World, Kings College, London ● **Michael Muhammad Knight** is an American Muslim novelist, journalist, performance artist and cultural provocateur. His books include *The Taqwacores*, *Impossible Man* and *Journey to the End of Islam* ● **Vinay Lal**, cultural critic and prodigious author, is Professor of History at UCLA ● **Bruce Lawrence**, whose love for Istanbul knows no limits, is Professor of Islamic Studies at Duke University ● **Hassan Mahamdallie**, editor of *Defending Multiculturalism*, works for the Arts Council England ● **Iftikhar Malik**, who is always gloriously optimistic about Pakistan, is Professor of History at Bath Spa University ● **S Parvez Manzoor** is allegedly an erudite critic based in Stockholm ● **Ehsan Masood**, a science journalist, is still recovering from reading too much Maryam Jameelah ● **Samia Rahman**, Deputy Director of the Muslim Institute, has given up her novel to write a book about Muslim misogyny ● **Jerry Ravetz**, a well-known philosopher of science, is rediscovering his Jewish Arabic roots ● **Ahmad Saadawi** is a Baghdad-based novelist, poet, painter and journalist ● **Ziauddin Sardar** is looking forward to finishing his book on Mecca ● **Stuart Sim** is Professor of Critical Theory at the University of Sunderland ● **Andy Simons**, former editor of the *IAJRC Journal* (the International Association of Jazz Record Collectors), can often be spotted playing the guitar with his band Swingtime Serenaders in colourful clubs.

CM
CRITICAL MUSLIM 03

FEAR AND LOATHING

July-September 2012 · Published by Muslim Institute · Hurst Publishers

In the next issue of
Critical Muslim

AbdelWahab El-Affendi on Islamophobia and Orientalism in the age of liberal paranoia, **Arun Kundnani** on the English Defence League and the rise of the far right in Europe, **Vina Lal** on Hindus who love Hitler, **Gordon Steffey** on Christian fundamentalism, **Fanar Haddad** on the sectarian schism in the Arab world, **Gary McFarlane** on the Tottenham Riots, **Farouk Peru** on self loathing Muslims, **Claire Chambers** on 'Four Lions', **Peter Clark** on Bernard Lewis and **Peter Mora** on Irshad Manji.

Plus a short story by **Suhel Ahmed**, six poems by **Stéphane Chaumet**, **Anita Sethi**'s dangerous bus ride through Iran, Ten Top Techs for Muslims and **Ziauddin Sardar** on his pet hate: the beards of Islam.